German Politics and the Jews

DÜSSELDORF AND NUREMBERG
1910–1933

Anthony Kauders

CLARENDON PRESS · OXFORD
1996

Oxford University Press, Walton Street. Oxford OX2 6DP
Oxford New York
Athens Auckland Bangkok Bogota Bombay
Buenos Aires Calcutta Cape Town Dar es Salaam Delhi
Florence Hong Kong Istanbul Karachi
Kuala Lumpur Madras Madrid Melbourne
Mexico City Nairobi Paris Singapore
Taipei Tokyo Toronto
and associated companies in
Berlin Ibadan

Oxford is a trade mark of Oxford University Press

Published in the United States
by Oxford University Press Inc., New York

British Library Cataloguing in Publication Data
Data available

Library of Congress Cataloging in Publication Data
Kauders, Anthony.
German politics and the Jews: Düsseldorf and Nuremberg, 1910–1933
/ Anthony Kauders.
p. cm. — (Oxford historical monographs)
Includes bibliographical references and index.
1. Antisemitism—Germany—Düsseldorf. 2. Antisemitism—Germany—
Nuremberg. 3. Germany—Ethnic relations. I. Title. II. Series.
DS146.G4K38 1996
305.892'4043324—dc20 96–12141

ISBN 0–19–820631–3

1 3 5 7 9 10 8 6 4 2

Typeset by Best-set Typesetter Ltd., Hong Kong
Printed in Great Britain on acid-free paper by
Bookcraft (Bath) Ltd., Midsomer Norton

CONTENTS

LIST OF TABLES

ABBREVIATIONS

BdL   Bund der Landwirte (Agrarian League)

BVP   Bayerische Volkspartei (Bavarian People's Party)

CV   Centralverein deutscher Staatsbürger jüdischen Glaubens (Central Association of German Citizens of the Jewish Faith)

DDP   Deutsche Demokratische Partei (German Democratic Party)

DHV   Deutschnationaler Handlungsgehilfenverband (German National Commercial Employees' Union)

DNVP   Deutschnationale Volkspartei (German National People's Party)

DVP   Deutsche Volkspartei (German People's Party)

KPD   Kommunistische Partei Deutschlands (German Communist Party)

LBIY   Leo Baeck Institute Year Book

NSDAP   Nationalsozialistische Deutsche Arbeiterpartei (National Socialist German Workers' Party)

SPD   Sozialdemokratische Partei Deutschlands (German Social Democratic Party)

USPD   Unabhängige Sozialdemokratische Partei Deutschlands (Independent German Social Democratic Party)

VfZ   Vierteljahreshefte für Zeitgeschichte

WP   Wirtschaftspartei (Business Party)

(Abbreviations for newspapers are listed in the bibliography.)

Introduction

> Rabelais . . . fancied that all sentences spoken or set down since the
> inception of man were 'frozen', were preserved intact in some inter-
> mediate sphere, from which the heat of recollection, of need, of
> anguish, could melt and recall them. Expelled from silence, language
> does its irreparable work.
>
> George Steiner, *Real Presences* (1989)

This study sets out to examine the nature and meaning of political anti-
Semitism in Düsseldorf and Nuremberg between 1910 and 1933. Most
treatments of anti-Semitism leave the reader wondering whether the
author has succeeded in identifying symptoms or providing explanations.
It will be no different in my case, and deliberately so. I take the study of
anti-Semitism to be not an 'experimental science in search of law but an
interpretive one in search of meaning'.[1] While I shall try to account for the
forces that may have had an effect on the 'Jewish question'—economics,
religion, individual agents—the topic under discussion is such that any
analysis remains 'intrinsically incomplete'.[2] I merely offer a further description, hoping that in the course of the book our understanding of Jew-
hatred in Germany between 1910 and 1933 will improve and the debate
centring on it will become more refined.

The subject of anti-Semitism also gives rise to questions concerning the
significance of Jewish–Gentile conflict in the 'greater order of things'.
Historians ask not only what role racism played in Hitler's thinking or
how important it was in attracting support for National Socialism; they
also wish to learn about its influence among those who did not vote for
Hitler or for whom National Socialism was never an alternative. Here
there are a number of points to consider.

First, the approach of this work is largely qualitative. This is so because
the insistence that quantitative research avoids the pitfalls of coincidence
and unrepresentativeness is convincing only if we distinguish between
different meanings. For instance, listing the number of times the word
'Jews' appears in newspapers is useless unless we know the context and
can appreciate that an editorial on the Rathenau murder is more important

[1] C. Geertz, *The Interpretation of Cultures. Selected Essays* (New York, 1973), 5.
[2] Geertz, *Interpretation*, 29.

than two lines announcing the performance of a Jewish theatre group.[3] I want to know what was said at crucial turning-points in German history, not how often something was mentioned in times of tranquillity, on topics of marginal interest.

Second, the 'Jewish question' was not of exclusive interest to the majority of Germans. Instead, they had several attachments and loyalties simultaneously, any of which may have been foremost in their minds, as occasion suggested.[4] By focusing on anti-Semitism, therefore, we are not judging *the* Germans, nor are we assessing the relative importance of Jew-hatred *vis-à-vis* other forms of collective identification.

Third, even if it will be difficult to convey a feeling for life in Germany by limiting our scope to the 'Jewish question', the study of anti-Semitism allows us to observe one aspect of society which often receives scant attention. In this connection it is worth quoting Clifford Geertz, whose *Notes on the Balinese Cockfight* display a similar impatience with calls to capture the great world in the little:

> The cockfight is not the master key to Balinese life, any more than bullfighting is to Spanish. What it says about that life is not unqualified nor even unchallenged by what other equally eloquent cultural statements say about it. But there is nothing more surprising in this than in the fact that Racine and Molière were contemporaries, or that the same people who arrange chrysanthemums cast swords.[5]

I have chosen Düsseldorf and Nuremberg because of their very different historical reputations.[6] The former, a predominantly Catholic city in the Rhineland, was characterized by relative peace between its Jews and Gentiles, while the latter, a Protestant enclave in Catholic Bavaria, was marked by open hostility between the two groups. At least this is what most secondary literature suggests, so that one purpose of this book is to discover whether these views of Düsseldorf and Nuremberg are in fact true. A further aim is to trace those factors which possibly accounted for the differences between the cities. In the language employed by the participants in the debate, can we detect religious, economic, or personal motives which explain why the Jews lived in relative comfort in one city whereas in the other they faced growing resentment?

[3] For the quantitative approach, see W. Hannot, *Die Judenfrage in der Katholischen Tagespresse Deutschlands und Österreichs 1923–1933* (Mainz, 1990), 12.

[4] E. J. Hobsbawm, *Nations and Nationalism since 1870. Programme, myth, reality* (Cambridge, 1990), 123.

[5] Geertz, *Interpretation*, 452.

[6] See Chapter 1 on how these 'reputations' came about.

This is, as far as I know, the first work on political anti-Semitism on a local level in this period. The advantages of such an examination are twofold: first, we can compare local agitation with national propaganda and thereby isolate the prejudices and peculiarities of individual towns and regions; and second, we can challenge the bias towards 'high' politics and intellectual history by offering a systematic approach to the issue rather than a collection of quotations from well-known personalities or 'influential' journals. For although we know much about the attitudes of prominent politicians, clerics, and philosophers on the 'Jewish question', few clues exist on how their ideas reverberated in the party correspondences, newspapers, and *Sonntagsblätter* of different communities throughout Germany.

Given this concern with local history, I shall treat each city ideal-typically; that is, neither national newspapers nor widely circulated journals will figure in my account; neither school books nor popular novels will be considered. I was forced, in short, to concentrate on documents confined or indigenous to the immediate environment of both cities, even if I remain fully aware of the fact that citizens in either town were affected by such works as *Soll und Haben*, *Licht und Leben*, and *Die Sünde wider das Blut*.[7]

The time period chosen reflects the growing concern among scholars to distinguish different phases in the history of German anti-Semitism.[8] While the late nineteenth century and the Third Reich have been examined in some detail, the crucial epoch marking the downfall of early political anti-Semitism and the beginning of a more vicious brand of Jew-hatred still needs its historians.[9] The tendency in recent work to treat the years of the Weimar Republic as an interlude between the racism of Wilhelm Marr and Hitler's *Mein Kampf* smacks of historical inevitability. Even those studies which emphasize the impact of World War I and the Revolution of 1918/19 on the development of racism do so without describing the process by which anti-Semitism gained influence among

---

[7] Nineteenth-century novel by Gustav Freytag; influential Protestant journal published in Elberfeld; racist tract by Artur Dinter. We need to remember that the early twentieth century no longer allowed for extreme regional varieties. Debates and affairs no longer ended at state borders and city gates, and mass literacy caused topics such as the 'Jewish question' to assume an abstract face, one often unrelated to developments which had made, say, Hamburg 'liberal' or Bavaria 'conservative'.

[8] S. Volkov, 'Kontinuität und Diskontinuität im deutschen Antisemitismus', *VfZ* 2 (1985), 225.

[9] There are, of course, important exceptions. These include the collections of essays edited by Werner Mosse and Arnold Paucker of the Leo Baeck Institute, as well as the works by Jochmann, Niewyk, and Lohalm, all listed in the bibliography.

'ordinary' people.[10] The following chapters attempt to redress this balance by concentrating on how the terms of the debate on the 'Jewish question' changed between 1910 and 1933.

A few notes on methodology are needed. Every work on this kind of subject faces the difficulty of trying to establish the nature and extent of anti-Semitism in society. One problem is the availability of sources. These are often scant, as is the case with information on clubs and associations, or they are rarely if ever recorded, as is true for sermons, family discussions, and arguments at the workplace. Sources can also be overrated or depreciated, depending on one's preferences and proclivities as a historian. Let us consider the following points.

First, police reports are of limited value because they tend to ignore charges of anti-Semitism and neglect meanings, trends, and subtle shifts in public opinion. Police agents, for example, seldom mentioned racism when they wrote on political parties or movements, and most reports focus on the possible 'revolutionary' or 'subversive' nature of different groups rather than on any anti-Jewish remarks by politicians or members of the audience that might have occurred.[11]

Second, personal papers and membership lists of social organizations present problems of another kind. Here we confront matters of interpretation that preclude clear-cut statements on the degree to which Jews were accepted or even integrated in society. For example, what do we make of Jewish membership in a local debating society? Was this a policy designed to further tolerance? Was it something no one cared to ponder over any longer? Or was it merely a formal and therefore artificial device which disguised the fact that the Jews remained an isolated group in the club?[12]

Third, motives, especially with regard to anti-Semitism, usually remain a matter of conjecture. Since we cannot ask the then Lord Mayor of

[10] George Mosse has repeatedly underlined that it was the war and its aftermath that transformed racism from theory into practice. Yet on the whole he refers to student fraternities, veterans' groups, anti-Semitic organizations, and right-wing parties, in effect the vanguard of radical racism, without suggesting how prejudice affected those less committed and less articulate. See, for example, G. L. Mosse, *Toward the Final Solution. A History of European Racism* (Madison, 1985), 17 ff.

[11] Anti-Semitism was either ignored because it was 'unimportant' or because it was taken for granted. See, for example, HStAD Regierung Düsseldorf 30653 d, No. 284 on an NSDAP meeting in Oberhausen in April 1930: 'Of course, as is the case with all Nazi speeches, the Jews were also attacked.' How many informants, one might ask, found it necessary to report such 'common knowledge'? Was it not more likely that most agents overlooked such comments when writing a three-page account of a three-hour meeting?

[12] As Werner Mosse has shown in the case of Paul Wallich, Jewish membership in exclusive associations did not automatically entail acceptance. See W. Mosse, *The German-Jewish Economic Elite 1820–1935. A Socio-cultural Profile* (Oxford, 1989), 153.

Nuremberg, Hermann Luppe, why he forbade his daughter to marry a Jew, or because we have no idea why a certain journalist stressed the racial side of the 'Jewish question' rather than the economic one, we need to exercise caution whenever questions of cause and effect arise. What is more, even if by some strange miracle we were allowed to interview a contemporary and discuss his or her motives, so as to identify particular sources implicated consciously or unconsciously in the formation of ideas, such 'references remain at most only probable, with the degree of probability related inversely to the novelty of the ideas and to the break between the past and the present. The most radical or "original" historical developments are by definition the least predictable.'[13]

In the main body of this work, I shall take a number of highly publicized news items which required comment, study the ensuing press coverage, and evaluate its content on the basis of previous material. Each newspaper was examined before, during, and after certain events. For elections this meant a period of thirty-one days prior to the actual poll, for scandals, affairs, and other sudden occurrences ten or fifteen days of coverage following the event. Each newspaper was examined over the same period of time, and both cities received equal attention. Only weeklies, and in particular the organs of the Protestant Church, were read from cover to cover. Finally, although newspapers are not always reliable indicators of social reality, they seem more dependable than many historians are willing to concede. Not only are they regular and constant and thus less arbitrary than the occasional document, because of their intimate ties with parties or churches, they also reflect what was read, believed, and called for at the time more closely than many other printed records we have at our disposal.

I would like to thank the following people for their help, advice, and goodwill: Lisa Hubler, Anna-Ruth Löwenbrück, Anthony Nicholls, Michael Parker, Peter Pulzer, and Jonathan Zatlin. I dedicate this study to my parents and to the memory of my grandmother, Irma Both (1905–1992).

[13] B. Lang, *Act and Idea in the Nazi Genocide* (Chicago, 1990), 200. See also W. Dilthey, *Selected Writings*. Vol. 1. *Introduction to the Human Sciences* (Princeton, 1989), 115: 'We typically find a transparent connection between character, motive, and action in the figures created by a poet, but not in the observation of real life.'

I
Reputations: The time before
World War I

He was forever being cheated by details that looked as though they
were significant if only he could find their setting. So he put everything down on the notion perhaps that if he (or a keener head) reread
the book twenty times, the countless facts would suddenly start to
move, to assemble, and to betray their secret.

Thornton Wilder, *The Bridge of San Luis Rey* (1927)

NUREMBERG

Religion and Class

A number of interpretations have been advanced to explain Nuremberg's
history of right-wing extremism in the Weimar Republic. Ian Kershaw,
for example, emphasizes the role of Bavarian Protestantism in the evolution of anti-democratic traditions:

The fervent attachment of the Bavarian Provincial Church to Orthodox
Lutherism, bolstered by a revivalist movement . . . and by evangelizing missions
from the turn of the century, promoted the extreme piety and intensity of faith
characteristic of Bavarian Protestantism. Despite many internal conflicts, the
'rational-liberal' wing of evangelical theology could make little ground in a Bavaria
dominated by highly conservative-orthodox Lutheran Protestantism.[1]

Other historians contend that Nuremberg was an industrial city which
retained a large number of small businesses, making it a centre of the 'old
Mittelstand', a group more likely to support the far Right after the war
than other sectors in society.[2] A more general reading of this trend refers

---

[1] I. Kershaw, *Popular Opinion and Political Dissent in the Third Reich. Bavaria 1933–
1945* (New York, 1983), 156. For a similar view, see H. Baier, 'Die Anfälligkeit des
fränkischen Protestantismus gegenüber dem Nationalsozialismus', *Tutzinger Studien* 2
(1979), 22.
[2] D. Showalter, *Little Man, what now? Der Stürmer in the Weimar Republic* (Hamden,
1982), 10; R. Lenman, *Julius Streicher and the Origins of National Socialism in Nuremberg
1918–1923*, unpublished B. Phil. thesis (Oxford, 1968), 30–1.

to the consequences of the First World War, which adversely affected Nuremberg's economy, as well as to the Bavarian Revolution, which saw a disproportionate number of Jews heading the councils and government. Whatever the arguments, however, a majority of specialists agree that Nuremberg and Franconia were 'prime anti-Semitic territory', and that Streicher was able to play on much existing resentment to create an atmosphere of hostility towards the Jews.[3]

Surprisingly, most evidence supporting this line of argument covers the period between 1918 and 1933. Thus little material exists on Franconian anti-Semitism before the war, leaving scholars heavily dependent on evidence from the Weimar and Nazi years. Indeed, nineteenth-century Franconia seemed no different from other areas in Bavaria in its approach to the 'Jewish question'.

Opposition to the proposed emancipation of the Jews in Bavaria in 1849/50, for example, was strongest in the oldest sections of the state, while the smallest number of petitions against the Emancipation Bill came from Upper and Middle Franconia.[4] Anti-Semitic parties, on the other hand, flourished in turn-of-the-century Munich rather than in Nuremberg.[5] Equally controversial is Kershaw's suggestion that Lutheranism was partly responsible for the emergence of a *völkisch* movement. In the first place, we need to recall that the 'rational-liberal' wing of the Protestant Church remained influential in such towns as Nuremberg.[6] More important, however, at least in regard to the Jews, is the fact that 'rational-liberal' theology never compelled Protestants to abandon their prejudices, and in many ways exacerbated them by insisting that Jews renounce their archaic practices in order to become enlightened citizens of a secular

[3] Kershaw, *Popular*, 235; E. C. Reiche, *The development of the SA in Nürnberg, 1922–1934* (Cambridge, 1986), 16; G. Pridham, *Hitler's Rise to Power. The Nazi Movement in Bavaria, 1923–1933* (London, 1973), 242–3; R. Hambrecht, *Der Aufstieg der NSDAP in Mittel-und Oberfranken (1925–1933)* (Nuremberg, 1976), 5–6; B. Z. Ophir and F. Wiesemann, *Die Jüdischen Gemeinden in Bayern 1918–1945. Geschichte und Zerstörung* (Munich, 1979), 204.

[4] J. F. Harris, 'Public Opinion and the Proposed Emancipation of the Jews in Bavaria in 1849–1850', *LBIY* (1989), 72 ff. See page 73: 'The president of Upper Franconia stated in his report that, "as in the other government districts", public opinion was against equality for Israelites, adding that there was no disagreement in this connection between Conservatives and Democrats and just as little between Catholics and Protestants.' See also E. Sterling, *Judenhaß. Die Anfänge des politischen Antisemitismus in Deutschland (1815–1850)* (Frankfurt, 1969), 160.

[5] E.-M. Tiedemann, 'Erscheinungsformen des Antisemitismus in Bayern am Beispiel der Bayerischen Antisemitischen Volkspartei und ihrer Nachfolgeorganisationen', in: M. Treml and J. Kirmeier, *Geschichte und Kultur der Juden in Bayern. Aufsätze* (Munich, 1988), 389.

[6] G. Hirschmann, 'Die evangelische Kirche seit 1800', in: M. Spindler (ed.), *Handbuch der Bayerischen Geschichte. Vierter Band. Das Neue Bayern 1800–1970* (Munich, 1975), 888, 892, 896.

state.[7] Similarly, liberalism and nationalism often went hand in hand, whereas 'extreme piety of faith' and 'strict obedience' cannot by themselves explain the rise of National Socialism. It was the 'dying middle', after all, made up of liberal parties such as the DDP and DVP, which contributed to the success of Hitler in the Weimar Republic. Finally, and this is especially important in our case, in the early twentieth century Nuremberg came under the influence of two religious figures who stood for tolerance and liberty in all areas of public life.[8]

As for Nuremberg's occupational structure, other villages and cities in Germany were equally marked by small-scale manufacturing, and there is no reason to believe that Nuremberg was uniquely disposed to the right-wing message because it was more 'middle-class' than, say, Berlin. In fact, Nuremberg was *the* industrial centre in Bavaria. In 1925, 72.9 per cent of the 179,176 persons working in all privately owned business establishments were employed in industry and 75.8 per cent of those were classified as workers, who thus represented 55.3 per cent of the entire workforce.[9] Whereas the total number of industrial firms employing ten people or less in 1925 was 10,057 (88.1 per cent), these firms accounted for only 19.1 per cent of the total industrial labour force. What is more, the proportional importance of small, medium, and large firms remained almost the same between 1907 and 1925, although the proportion of employees within each group shifted significantly in favour of the larger firms. This change occurred, however, not because larger businesses pushed out smaller ones, but because the growing labour force worked in fewer businesses of greater size.

If Table 1 reveals that the number of small companies remained stable, it also shows that an overwhelming majority of industrial workers was employed in firms not necessarily tied to *Mittelstand* interests. In 1907 and

[7] A number of books deal with this issue, including F. E. Manuel, *The Broken Staff. Judaism through Christian Eyes* (Cambridge, Mass., 1992) and D. Sorkin, *The Transformation of German Jewry 1780–1840* (Oxford, 1987).

[8] They were Christian Geyer of the St Sebald Church and Friedrich Rittelmeyer of the Holy Ghost Church. See G. Pfeiffer (ed.), *Nürnberg. Geschichte einer europäischen Stadt* (Munich, 1971), 422–3. For further pro- and anti-Jewish comments by Protestant figures in Nuremberg, see M. Eisenhauer, 'Die Nürnberger Synagoge von 1874. Zwischen Emanzipation und Assimilation', in: Treml and Kirmeier, *Geschichte*, 365 and A. Müller, *Geschichte der Juden in Nürnberg 1146–1945* (Nuremberg, 1968), 168. On the party political front, Nuremberg's liberals were if anything more democratic and less nationalistic than their counterparts elsewhere. See P. Müller, *Liberalismus in Nürnberg 1800 bis 1871: Eine Fallstudie zur Ideen- und Sozialgeschichte des Liberalismus in Deutschland im 19. Jahrhundert* (Nuremberg, 1990), 369–73.

[9] The following is based on M. Moore-Ziegler, *The Socio-Economic and Demographic Bases of Political Behavior in Nuremberg during the Weimar Republic, 1919–1933*, unpublished Ph.D. thesis (Virginia, 1976), 73 ff.

TABLE 1. Employment and size of the firms

Size of firm	% of all firms		% of all employed	
	1907	*1925*	*1907*	*1925*
Small (1–5 employees)	82.1	79.8	18.5	13.8
Medium (6–50 employees)	15.4	16.4	27.5	20.8
Large (over 50 employees)	2.5	3.1	54.0	65.3

Source: Moore-Ziegler, *Behavior*, 76.

1925, the most important industries in terms of the number of people employed were the metal-working industry; machine, precision tool, automotive and optical manufacture; wood-working; the textile industry; and trading companies. Altogether these industries comprised 63.5 per cent (1907) and 67.5 per cent (1925) of all those working in Nuremberg's industry.

Turning to the class structure of the employed population, we find that the proportion of industrial workers and artisans declined from 65.6 per cent in 1907 to 62.0 per cent in 1925, while the proportion of those working in commerce, trade, the household services, free professions, and the civil service rose from 32.9 per cent in 1907 to 36.5 per cent in 1925.[10] More important than these figures, however, is the fact that migration was seriously to alter the social composition of Nuremberg's population.

According to Martha Moore-Ziegler, immigration was 'so heavy throughout the nineteenth century that by 1900 immigrants comprised fifty-six per cent of the Nuremberg population. Of these, eighty-six per cent were born in Bavaria, eleven per cent in other German states and three per cent in foreign countries.' Whereas Nuremberg was overwhelmingly Protestant in 1818, less than a century later Catholics constituted almost one-third of the population: 'This large increase in the number of Catholics further pinpoints the major geographic source of nineteenth century immigration: the southern Catholic provinces of Bavaria rather than the immediate areas around Nuremberg which were predominantly Protestant.' During the Weimar Republic, Franconia again became the major source of immigration for Nuremberg.[11] This leaves us with a

[10] R. Gömmel, *Wachstum und Konjunktur der Nürnberger Wirtschaft (1815–1914)* (Nuremberg, 1978), 173.

[11] Moore-Ziegler, *Behavior*, 16–17, 71. By 1907 Nuremberg was becoming more homogeneous than other cities in Germany. Compared to Karlsruhe, Frankfurt, and Munich, the percentage of those born within the city and those moving to the city from the immediate

number of questions: Did the influx of south Bavarians modify the image of the Jew in the city? Was the impact of these immigrants greater in middle-class or working-class neighbourhoods? Was their definition of the 'Jewish question' related to their economic status before or after they arrived in the city, or was it independent of class and more closely connected to Catholic traditions in the south? Was immigration in the 1920s responsible for Streicher's success, or were Catholic citizens just as susceptible to the anti-Semitic message?

Let us briefly look at a number of issues raised by the above discussion. First, the relatively high percentage of workers corresponded to impressive SPD gains at the polls. In the 1903 Reichstag elections, Social Democrats received 56.9 per cent of the vote, compared to 31.7 per cent in Germany as a whole. In 1912 the figures were 60.4 and 34.8 per cent respectively.[12] In other words, Nuremberg was heavily working-class (even if we acknowledge middle-class support for the SPD), and it seems far-fetched to allude to a dominant 'petty bourgeois' element in the city unless we want to concede that most areas in Germany were at least in part *bürgerlich*.[13]

Second, if Nuremberg was middle-class, it preferred left-liberalism to other parties and movements usually identified with the *Mittelstand*. In 1903 and 1912, the Progressive Party secured between 27.2 and 28.8 per cent of the vote, while both National Liberals and Conservatives had little success. (In 1903, for example, the former won 7.9 per cent and the latter 2.2 per cent, while in 1912 neither party was successful. 'Other' parties, which presumably included Conservatives and supporters of the *Mittelstandspartei*, received 5.3 per cent in 1912.)

Third, Catholics, who made up about 30 per cent of the population, supported the Centre Party only half-heartedly. Nationally at 16.4 per cent of the vote (1912), the Centre had to suffice with 5.5 per cent in Nuremberg. Many of the city's Catholics, who were first or second generation rural immigrants and who were employed primarily in working-class occupations, turned to the SPD, given the Centre's 'preoccupation

---

countryside was on average higher. Yet compared to Bremen, Krefeld, and Aachen, Nuremberg had a greater intake of immigrants from areas outside its provincial borders. See W. Köllmann, *Bevölkerung in der industriellen Revolution. Studien zur Bevölkerungsgeschichte Deutschlands* (Göttingen, 1974), 118–19 and Gömmel, *Wachstum*, 34.

[12] Moore-Ziegler, *Behavior*, 305–6.

[13] For the 'petty bourgeois' nature of Nuremberg, see Lenman, *Streicher*, 31. Although the percentage of workers in Nuremberg's economy declined after 1900, it remained higher than that of Munich, where in 1907 48.9 per cent of the workforce was proletarian, a figure well below the 67.5 per cent found in Nuremberg. See K.-D. Schwarz, *Weltkrieg und Revolution in Nürnberg. Ein Beitrag zur Geschichte der deutschen Arbeiterbewegung* (Stuttgart, 1971), 20.

with the *Mittelstand* and . . . its failure to do more than slow down the polarization of both society and politics along class lines.'[14]

Fourth, ideology, religion, and class structure all affected how people in Nuremberg perceived the 'Jewish question', but it is impossible to determine which in the end was decisive. The SPD may have had a considerable ideological influence on the Catholic worker, but his upbringing in Oberammergau or Augsburg, or his socialization among Protestant colleagues and his (occasional) contact with the Church also influenced his specific response to anti-Semitism. A Protestant peasant, who had spent most of her life in rural agrarian communities, and whose image of the Jew was mainly confined to cattle-dealers, upon moving to the big city was suddenly confronted with the Eastern Jew, the Jewish merchant, dentist, and shopkeeper, as well as with a host of rumours and stories about Jewish bankers, journalists, and politicians. In short, religious traditions, class allegiances, or ideological persuasions alone cannot explain why a person liked or disliked Jews. None of these factors should be dismissed, of course, but neither ought we to accept them as sufficient answers, all the more so since in our case they all happened to prove erroneous.

The Jews

This book is not a history of the Jews in Düsseldorf and Nuremberg. While I agree with Hannah Arendt that an 'ideology which has to persuade and mobilize people cannot choose its victim arbitrarily',[15] I have my doubts as to whether *specific* intances of anti-Semitism can be explained by showing that Jews were concentrated in certain occupations or that some of them headed revolutionary parties. We all know that charges against the Jews would not be 'nearly as persuasive if they did not bear some relation to ascertainable fact and to a hard core of genuine evidence'.[16] We also know, however, that numbers and statistics are unable to explain anything unless we imbue them with meaning. Consider the following points.

First, even if I could demonstrate that a greater proportion of Jews wielded power in one city than in another, it would not explain the behaviour of anti-Semites. Jews virtually 'controlled' the press in Berlin, but this did not make the national capital any more anti-Semitic than other large towns in Germany. Or, to take a more recent example, American Jews today are influential in a number of areas, including the

---

[14] D. Blackbourn, *Class, Religion and Local Politics in Wilhelmine Germany. The Centre Party in Württemberg before 1914* (New Haven and London, 1980), 194–5.

[15] H. Arendt, *The Origins of Totalitarianism* (San Diego, New York, and London, 1979), 7.

[16] P. Pulzer, *The Rise of Political Anti-Semitism in Germany and Austria* (London, 1988), 14.

arts ('Hollywood'), the press (*The New York Times*), and politics ('the Jewish lobby.'), yet most people would concur that anti-Semitism is a much more potent force in Poland, where a Jewish minority of 4000 faces preposterous accusations from all quarters.

Second, there is the problem of detail. If it is true that Jews in prominent positions provoke anti-Jewish feelings, how many Jews do we need to make a causal connection seem plausible between their presence and the existence of anti-Semitism? Is one Jewish politician enough, or does it take hundreds of Jewish pawnbrokers to acknowledge a relationship between the 'objective' and 'subjective' side of Jew-hatred? More important in our case, how can we judge whether the Jew in Nuremberg or the Jew in Munich or even the Jew in Berlin was 'responsible' for anti-Semitism, given that so much was dependent on abstract theories which emanated from elsewhere and did not require local verification?

Third, in both Düsseldorf and Nuremberg anti-Semitism was seldom linked to particular Jews. In fact, one must look hard to detect any references indicating that anti-Semitism was somehow the result of who the Jews were or what they did in either city, and although this hardly proves the opposite, namely that it was immaterial whether Jews were visible or vocal for anti-Semites to hate them, we need to keep in mind that in both towns little evidence can be unearthed to suggest that the Jewish communities themselves served as pretexts for the anti-Semitic cause. The following passages further underline these observations.

Jews first settled in Nuremberg and its environs in the eleventh or twelfth century.[17] Here they experienced the same restrictions and persecutions as their brethren elsewhere. Like most Jews, they depended on the goodwill of the local rulers, who placed heavy taxes on them in return for a limited measure of security. As in other towns of Central Europe, violent assaults by the Gentile majority were frequent. In 1349, following a pogrom which cost over 500 lives, the Jews were expelled from Nuremberg for the first time. Rare signs of peaceful coexistence, as when a group of patricians 'danced at a Jewish wedding', as well as the more general fact that ritual murder cases never occurred in the city, did not prevent the Jews from being expelled a second time in 1498/9, only now they were to return after a much longer period of exile, namely in 1850.

In the ensuing years, Nuremberg's municipal council tried everything to prevent trade between its citizens and Jews from the surrounding villages. This practice was not uncommon at the time. In both Cologne

---

[17] The following is based on Müller, *Geschichte*, 27–33, 46–50, 108–11, 129–31, 139–43. On the Bavarian Edict of 1813, see S. Schwarz, *Die Juden in Bayern im Wandel der Zeiten* (Munich, 1963), 187.

TABLE 2. Jewish population in Nuremberg

	Number of Jews	% of total population
1852	87	0.16
1867	1254	1.61
1871	1831	2.20
1875	2453	2.69
1885	3738	3.25
1895	4737	2.92
1905	6681	2.34
1910	7815	2.35

Source: Müller, *Geschichte*, 158, 170.

and Augsburg, for example, where the Jews had also been driven away, the latter were allowed to enter the city only in the company of a local official and had to leave the town by dusk. As late as 1787 'soldiers and officers' were forbidden to borrow money from Jews, and throughout the eighteenth century enlightened ideas on the 'Jewish question' were seldom if ever heard in the city. All this was compounded by the Bavarian Edict of 1813, which stipulated that Jews could reside only in areas already inhabited by them, thus making Nuremberg the only large town in Bavaria without Jewish *citizens*.

This changed with the Revolution of 1848/9, when Josef Kohn became the first Jew in over three-and-a-half centuries to settle permanently in Nuremberg. Only fifteen years later 1254 Jews resided in the city.

Very rapidly Jews entered positions of prestige and influence in Nuremberg's social and political life. David Morgenstern represented the city as a Democrat in the Bavarian parliament until 1855, while his co-religionist Wolf Frankenburger acted as a Progressive MP from 1874 to 1889. Among prominent National Liberals we find Gustav Josephtal, who also headed the Jewish community. On the left of the political spectrum, Gabriel Löwenstein served Nuremberg's Social Democrats as a Bavarian MP until 1905, when he was succeeded by the laywer, Dr Max Süßheim. Jewish burghers were also active in the provincial government of Middle Franconia, among them Anton Kohn, Stephan Hopf, Ernst Tuchmann, Ernst Kohn, and Jakob Saemann. Between 1873 and 1919 seven Jews sat in the municipal council, and fourteen worked for the local administration.[18]

[18] Müller, *Geschichte*, 174 ff.; M. Freudenthal, *Die israelitische Kultusgemeinde Nürnberg 1874–1924* (Nuremberg, 1925), 151–3. Other Jews in local politics will figure in the next chapter.

Turning to the city's economy, Jews were predominant in the trade in hops, overrepresented in various other branches (ranging from textiles and banking to bicycle manufacture), and highly visible in the free professions. Anton Kohn, for example, founded Bavaria's largest private bank. Rudolf Bing's metal factory was the biggest of its kind in Nuremberg. By 1930 Jewish ownership reached at least ten per cent of over five dozen trades, while among the city's 742 doctors and 215 lawyers one finds 140 and 97 Jews respectively. Even without precise data on the occupational structure of Nuremberg's Jewish community, therefore, it is fair to say that within a short period of time a substantial number of Jews became established and successful members of the city's business world.[19] While this undoubtedly led to friction, I did not come across material suggesting that a majority of Gentiles were 'overwhelmed' or 'alienated' by these developments.

In fact, Jewish–Gentile relations were not so different from those of other cities before the war. The *Antisemitische Verein für Nürnberg und Umgebung*, for example, never achieved importance, and was dissolved in 1901.[20] Local historians such as Emil Reicke and Ernst Mummenhoff reported dispassionately on the history of Nuremberg's Jews, whereas a number of Protestant clerics defended them against insults and attacks.[21] To be sure, assimilation was not the norm, but we know from other places that acceptance or integration was often fragile and seldom complete. Rudolf Bing's recollections illustrate this for Nuremberg:

While at the time [turn of the century] political anti-Semitism was shunned by the working-class and the predominantly 'progressive', that is to say democratic or at least liberal bourgeoisie, the city's Jewish community, whether religious or secular, lived isolated from the rest of society . . . I am also under the impression, however, that this separation was less pronounced in my youth and became stronger as the years went by.[22]

---

[19] Müller, *Geschichte*, 202–3. According to the *Bayerische Israelitische Gemeindezeitung* of 15 February 1929, Jews made up 4.1 (1910), 5 (1912), and 1.2 (1928) per cent of the students at Erlangen University. These levels were low compared to Munich (9.3, 9.9, and 3 per cent) and Würzburg (9.6, 7.8, and 6.4 per cent). This could mean that Jews preferred more hospitable universities than Erlangen, but it also implies that Gentiles had little reason to complain about Jewish competition at their university. The low figures for 1928 indicate declining birth rates and financial problems.

[20] StAN C7/V Vd 15 1820 'Antisemitischer Verein für Nürnberg und Umgebung'.

[21] Müller, *Geschichte*, 184. See his remark that 'anti-Semitism played no special role at the time.'

[22] StAN F5 QNG 494: R. Bing, *Mein Leben in Deutschland vor und nach dem 30. Januar* (no date), 8. Bing also adds that he occasionally overheard anti-Semitic comments by his history and literature teachers and that children on the street ('Proletarierkinder auf der Straße') would taunt him with anti-Jewish slurs. Note too that Bing's father was one of Nuremberg's most successful industrialists, a member of both the municipal council and the

TABLE 3. Jewish marriage patterns in Nuremberg

	1910	1911	1912	1913	1914	1915	1916	1917/18
Number of Jews who married	66	88	78	101	58	37	25	40
Number of mixed marriages	12	9	8	13	14	13	8	8
% of mixed marriages	18	10	10	13	24	35	32	20

	1919	1920	1921	1922	1923	1924	1925	1926
Number of Jews who married	242	239	138	164	187	89	92	67
Number of mixed marriages	21	19	26	18	23	19	16	9
% of mixed marriages	9	8	19	11	12	21	17	13

	1927	1928	1929	1930	1931	1932	1933
Number of Jews who married	100	80	80	98	72	58	52
Number of mixed marriages	12	12	12	18	14	8	8
% of mixed marriages	12	15	15	18	19	14	15

Source: *Statistisches Jahrbuch der Stadt Nürnberg* 1910–33. ('Dissidents' are not included.)

The percentage of mixed marriages, which often serves as an indicator of Jewish acceptance in the Gentile world, supports Bing's assessment of the self-imposed or forced isolation of Nuremberg's Jews.

Excluding the war years, which for a number of reasons were untypical (fewer partners, fewer inhibitions in choosing a non-Jewish or non-Christian husband or wife), the percentage of mixed marriages was 13 between 1910 and 1913, 15 between 1919 and 1933, and 14 for the entire period under review. As we shall see, these levels were lower than those

chamber of commerce, and jointly responsible for the coordinated welfare effort during World War I. Integration for the Bing family must have been easier than for most other Jewish citizens of Nuremberg. See also the comments by Max Warburg in H. Krohn, *Die Juden in Hamburg. Die Politische, Soziale und Kulturelle Entwicklung einer Jüdischen Grossstadtgemeinde nach der Emanzipation 1848–1918* (Hamburg, 1974), 202.

for Düsseldorf, but whether this was a reason for Streicher's eventual success is debatable. In the first place, the numbers involved were small: in 1925, over 8000 Jews lived in the city, but only ninety-two got married, and of these sixteen chose Gentile partners. Furthermore, if we believe Bing's account (and the following chapters tend to confirm his impressions), then the relationship between both groups deteriorated in the Weimar Republic, whereas the percentage of mixed marriages actually increased slightly after 1918. Finally, Nuremberg was not an extreme case: other cities and regions had similar results but never became 'prime anti-Semitic territory'.[23]

A last factor which might explain Jewish–Gentile tensions after the war is the *Ostjudenfrage*. Max Freudenthal mentions that most Eastern European Jews came to the city in the decade before the war, although in later years their numbers stagnated or declined.[24] Unfortunately I only have statistics for 1910, but these show that Nuremberg was anything but unique in Germany. The percentage of foreign Jews within the Jewish population was higher in Karlsruhe, Bremen, Stuttgart, Chemnitz, Dresden, Leipzig, Munich, Berlin, Hanover, and Wiesbaden. The percentage of aliens who were Jewish was higher in Königsberg, Altona, Hanover, Danzig, Berlin, Leipzig, Karlsruhe, and Frankfurt.

Since most Eastern Jews were concentrated in urban centres, many Gentiles feared that 'hordes of Jewish immigrants were sweeping into the country.' Perceptions of their actual number were further distorted because *Ostjuden* were overrepresented in the total population of aliens in the Reich. This may also have been the case in Nuremberg, where 1226 Eastern Jews comprised roughly 15 per cent of both the Jewish and alien populations. Of these, many lived in extreme poverty, working as pedlars, middlemen, and small traders. But whatever their economic status, it was *during* the war that Germany's *Ostjuden* became associated with racketeering and black-market activities. From the available sources, then, Nuremberg experienced no greater and no less of a 'problem' with its Eastern Jews than comparable cities in the country.

Perhaps a combination of the above elements contributed to Nuremberg's reception of the *völkisch* movement after 1918. For instance, because Jews returned to the city at a time when economic and social change was at its height, Gentiles may have felt threatened by this rapidly

---

[23] In Germany as a whole the figures were 11.96 in 1910/11 and 19.70 per cent in 1925. The percentages of mixed marriages in large cities were: Frankfurt—14.0 per cent (1926/7); Berlin—15.06 (1901–4) and 24.74 (1925) per cent; Cologne—28.50 (1926) per cent; Breslau—16.08 (1926) per cent; Hamburg—28.83 (1906–10) and 28.83 (1925) per cent. Krohn, *Juden*, 69–70.

[24] Freudenthal, *Kultusgemeinde*, 143.

TABLE 4. Eastern Jews in German cities

	Total Jews	% of foreign Jews	% of aliens who are Jewish
Nuremberg	7,815	15.69	15.62
Munich	11,083	34.86	12.60
Cologne	12,393	13.49	17.04
Frankfurt	26,228	13.50	30.60
Düsseldorf	3,985	14.28	4.83
Leipzig	9,874	64.83	29.19
Hamburg	18,932	16.43	11.49
Mannheim	6,402	13.86	15.58
Hanover	5,386	20.26	28.84

Source: J. Wertheimer, *Unwelcome Strangers. East European Jews in Imperial Germany* (Oxford, 1987), 191–2.

growing and visibly successful group.[25] Or, since many immigrants came from Franconian villages where Jews traditionally figured as cattle-dealers and where Gentiles often resented the fact that they depended on Jewish moneylenders, Nuremberg was more likely to accept the contents of National Socialist racism. Finally, because orthodox Lutheranism was more nationalistic than other denominations, north Bavarian Protestants displayed a greater readiness to accuse the Jews of unpatriotic behaviour once such views gained currency in Germany.

There are several problems with these interpretations. First, it is impossible to establish with any accuracy a causal link between cattle-dealers in Middle Franconia and anti-Semitism in twentieth-century Nuremberg. Not only do various studies fail to single out Franconia as exceptional in this respect,[26] making it difficult to explain why Nuremberg and not Cologne or Stuttgart turned racist because of Jewish cattle-dealers and moneylenders in its vicinity, other analyses too have shown that 'reality' was often secondary when it came to anti-Jewish excesses. In the

---

[25] A similar argument, but related to the absence of a strong anti-Semitic tradition in England, was advanced by G. M. Trevelyan. See J. Katz, *Vom Vorurteil bis zur Vernichtung. Der Antisemitismus 1700–1933* (Munich, 1989), 40. On the other hand, the neighbouring town of Fürth had had a substantial Jewish population before 1850, so that Nuremberg's burghers surely were aware of the 'Jewish question' in its more immediate manifestations.

[26] M. Richarz, 'Emancipation and Continuity. German Jews in the Rural Economy', in: W. Mosse et al., *Revolution and Evolution. 1848 in German-Jewish History* (Tübingen, 1981), 96–7, 113; Verein für Socialpolitik, *Der Wucher auf dem Lande. Berichte und Gutachten* (Leipzig, 1887), 91–2, 101, 154–5, 194.

Rhineland, for example, ritual murder accusations in the 1830s occurred neither because the Jews controlled the money supply nor because credit was unavailable at the time of the protests.[27]

Second, if we substitute for these 'causes' different facts, would the outcome, everything else being equal, have been different? Would a more numerous and assertive Catholic population, a longer history of Jewish residence, or fewer *Ostjuden* have altered the picture of Jewish–Gentile relations in the Weimar Republic? Is it possible to replace single pieces of our puzzle without distorting the further course of events? Or is it necessary to put all pieces together in order to explain later developments? Whatever the interpretation, it was the suddenness of the war-time situation, that is, the radical break with the past, which transformed structures and layers into reality.

Third, there is simply no evidence to suggest that until 1914 Nuremberg was 'prime anti-Semitic territory'. What we searched for was concealed, and what revealed itself at a later stage hard to discern in normal conditions. To be sure, Jewish–Gentile relations were never ideal, but they certainly never foreshadowed Streicher and his reign of terror in the Weimar and Nazi years.

DÜSSELDORF

Religion and Class

In contrast to Nuremberg, Düsseldorf enjoyed and still enjoys the reputation of being a fairly open and tolerant city. Peter Hüttenberger, for example, claims that virulent anti-Semitism never existed in Düsseldorf, and explains this with reference to the proximity of Germany's western neighbours, the liberal and pragmatic nature of the business community, and the abundance of cultural and artistic life in the city.[28] In a similar vein, Kurt Düwell stresses the good rapport characteristic of Jewish–Gentile relations in the Rhineland.[29] This rapport is often attributed to the fact that German Catholics were sensitive both to minority positions and the anti-Christian features of racism,[30] and historians believe that this respect for the Jewish population contributed to a general hostility

---

[27] S. Rohrbacher and M. Schmidt, *Judenbilder. Kulturgeschichte antisemitischer Mythen und antisemitischer Vorurteile* (Hamburg, 1991), 325–6.

[28] P. Hüttenberger, *Düsseldorf. Geschichte von den Ursprüngen bis ins 20. Jahrhundert. Band 3: Die Industrie- und Verwaltungsstadt (20. Jahrhundert)* (Düsseldorf, 1989), 121–2.

[29] K. Düwell, *Die Rheingebiete in der Judenpolitik des Nationalsozialismus vor 1942. Beitrag zu einer vergleichenden zeitgeschichtlichen Landeskunde* (Bonn, 1968), 52–3, 79.

[30] G. Andratschke, *Nationalsozialismus und Antisemitismus in der Zentrumspresse Münsters* Staatsarbeit (Bonn, 1985), 49.

towards National Socialist policies after 1933.[31] Moreover, Rabbi Eschelbacher confirmed these impressions in his account of the Jewish community in Düsseldorf between 1904 and 1929: 'The harmonious relationship with the non-Jewish population always remained stable. Occasional anti-Semitic assaults had no effect on this.'[32]

This may seem surprising at first sight. After all, the Rhineland was known for its ritual murder 'cases', from which Düsseldorf was not spared. In December 1836, for example, the murder of a four-year-old boy led to angry demonstrations, and subsequent violence against the Jewish community was only averted through measures introduced by the Prussian government.[33] Fifty-five years later a Jew was again accused of having killed a child for ritual purposes, and although the butcher from Xanten was aquitted, the circumstances surrounding the affair further exacerbated existing tensions between Jews and Gentiles in the Rhineland.[34]

Emancipation and prejudice existed side by side. On the one hand, the provincial assembly of the Rhineland was the only one in Prussia prior to 1848 to advocate equal rights for the Jews. In May 1843 the majority of Düsseldorf's population supported equality for the Jews, and when emancipation was also favoured by the provincial assembly, Gentiles in the city responded with cheers and spontaneous demonstrations of solidarity with the Jews. On the other hand, cities like Neuss or Grevenbroich witnessed

[31] Düwell, *Rheingebiete*, 79–80; S. A. Gordon, *German Opposition to Nazi Anti-Semitic Measures Between 1933 and 1945, With Particular Reference to the Rhine-Ruhr Area*, unpublished Ph.D. thesis (Buffalo, NY, 1979), 273–4, 369; A. Voigt, *Nationalsozialistische Judenverfolgung in Düsseldorf* Hausarbeit (Düsseldorf, 1981), 29–30; R. Gelattely, *The Gestapo and German Society. Enforcing Racial Policy 1933–1945* (Oxford, 1990), 104, 109.

[32] M. Eschelbacher, *Festschrift zur Feier des 25 jährigen Bestehens der Synagoge* (Düsseldorf, 1929), 8.

[33] S. Rohrbacher, 'Ritualmordbeschuldigungen am Niederrhein. Christlicher Aberglaube und Antijüdische Agitation im 19. Jahrhundert', in: J. Schoeps (ed.), *Menora. Jahrbuch für deursch-jüdische Geschichte* (Munich, 1990), 305. Following the murder of Peter Wilhelm Hoenen in July 1834 in the district of Grevenbroich, Düsseldorf's 'lower orders' ridiculed Jews, destroyed their property, and threatened them with reprisals. A pamphlet entitled 'On the Use of Christian Blood by the Jews' reached a circulation of many thousands of copies. See B. Suchy, 'Antisemitismus in den letzten Jahren vor dem ersten Weltkrieg', in: J. Bohnke Kollwitz et al., *Köln und das rheinische Judentum. Festschrift Germania Judaica 1959–1984* (Cologne, 1984), 253. For another ritual murder 'case' in Düsseldorf, see the *Bote für Stadt und Land* of 27 Jan. 1838 quoted in Sterling, *Judenhaß*, 158.

[34] Suchy, 'Antisemitismus', 252 ff. On the Buschoff Affair, see J. Schoeps, 'Ritualmordbeschuldigung und Blutaberglaube. Die Affäre Buschoff im niederrheinischen Xanten', in: Bohnke Kollwitz, *Köln*. On Centre Party polemics comprising religious attacks on the Talmud and references to the legend of the Wandering Jew, see O. Blaschke, 'Wider die "Herrschaft des modern-jüdischen Geistes": Der Katholizismus zwischen traditionellem Antijudaismus und modernen Antisemitismus', in: W. Loth (ed.), *Deutscher Katholizismus im Umbruch zur Moderne* (Stuttgart, Berlin, and Cologne, 1991), 245.

occasional outbreaks of violence against their Jewish inhabitants.[35] Similarly, whereas the Rhineland 'assumed a character rather different from that in some remote Bavarian or Styrian valley or muddy Galician hamlet',[36] it still attracted considerable support for anti-Semitic parties in times of crisis, as in the aftermath of the Buschoff affair, when an anti-Semitic candidate in Neuss received 37.6 per cent of the Reichstag vote in 1893.[37] Accepting the 'liberal' credentials of the area therefore does not mean that those traditions qualifying the assertion that Düsseldorf was open and tolerant should be overlooked.

Düsseldorf's occupational structure was dominated by the metal sector, which employed approximately one-third of the labour force. By the mid-1890s Düsseldorf had become the city of machine manufacture, with such firms as Rheinmetall and Mannesmann gaining an ever greater share of the market. In addition, the number of white-collar jobs increased steadily from the end of the nineteenth century, giving the city its name of 'Schreibtisch des Ruhrgebiets'. However, just as the white-collar sector became more important, the proportion of those working in industry declined, reaching its nadir with 50 per cent in the inter-war years.[38] Hence 'Young, single men—some aspiring capitalists, others white-collar employees, most proletarians—became the dynamic element in a city where stalwart artisans, bureaucrats, and pensioners, overwhelmingly family men, had once set the tone.'[39]

A brief look at the class composition of Düsseldorf in 1907 reveals that over one-third of the employed population was engaged in middle-class occupations, while about three-fifths were classified as workers.[40] This changed after the war, when the proportion of workers declined to 51.2 per cent in 1925. Whatever the exact figures, however, it is clear that Düsseldorf was equally if not more *bürgerlich* than Nuremberg: in both

[35] P. Pulzer, *Jews and the German State. The Political History of a Minority, 1848–1933* (Oxford, 1992), 78; B. Suchy, 'Düsseldorf', in: J. Schoeps and L. Heid, *Wegweiser durch das jüdische Rheinland* (Berlin 1992), 70. But see the comments in Sterling, Judenhaß, 78: 'Rhenish particularists use the demand for Jewish emancipation as a weapon against the Prussian state . . . The proponents of equal rights have less the Jews in mind than the end of the system of estates, i.e., they aspire to equal rights for themselves, the up-and-coming industrial bourgeoisie of the Rhineland.' For Düsseldorf, see pages 79 and 196 n. 2.

[36] Pulzer, *Rise*, 268.

[37] Rohrbacher, *Ritualmord*, 313–14; R. Moeller, *German Peasants and Agrarian Politics 1914–1924. The Rhineland and Westphalia* (Chapel Hill, NC, 1986), 28–9.

[38] F.-W. Henning, *Düsseldorf und seine Wirtschaft. Zur Geschichte einer Region. Band 2: Von 1860 bis zur Gegenwart* (Düsseldorf, 1981), 449, 457, 584, 646–7.

[39] M. Nolan, *Social Democracy and society. Working-class Radicalism in Düsseldorf, 1890–1920* (Cambridge, 1981), 16–17.

[40] W. Köllmann, *Bevölkerung in der industriellen Revolution. Studien zur Bevölkerungsgeschichte Deutschlands* (Göttingen, 1974), 112.

TABLE 5. Employment in Düsseldorf

	1907	*1925*	*1933*
Self-employed, higher civil service	16.5%	12.8%	11.8%
White-collar, civil service	15.7%	29.7%	30.7%
Workers	57.8%	51.2%	51.6%
Household services	10.0%	6.4%	6.0%

Source: V. Franke, *Der Aufstieg der NSDAP in Düsseldorf. Die nationalsozialistische Basis in einer katholischen Großstadt* (Essen, 1987), 17. See also the figures in Köllmann, *Bevölkerung*, 123–4.

cities workers were in a majority but confronted by a substantial middle-class element; in Düsseldorf the number of persons employed in the tertiary sector was higher.

Migration was an important factor in the growth and modernization of Düsseldorf's economy. For the most part, immigrants came from the Rhineland, although the city also had a substantial intake from Westphalia and the Prussian provinces. According to Peter Hüttenberger, the majority of Düsseldorf's population hailed from these areas, with most immigrants moving to the city from nearby towns such as Krefeld, Elberfeld, Duisburg, Essen, Aachen, Barmen, Dortmund, Gelsenkirchen, and Bochum. This development, Hüttenberger argues, favoured a process of 'fusion' between the more recent arrivals and native inhabitants, both of whom were familiar with each other's customs.

Whether the religious composition of recent immigrants qualified this statement is difficult to say. As in Nuremberg, the city's main denomination (in the case of Düsseldorf, Catholicism) declined proportionately, so that by 1925 only 63.15 per cent of the population was Catholic, as compared to 80.3 per cent in 1858. The number of Protestants in Düsseldorf, by contrast, increased from 18.38 per cent in 1858 to 30.51 per cent in 1925.[41] If the new residents came from areas with largely Protestant populations like Elberfeld, Barmen, and parts of Westphalia, then again we need to ask questions about the impact of migration on the 'Jewish question' in Düsseldorf; such questions, to be sure, are impossible to answer conclusively. For example, did the influx of Protestants alter the

[41] *Jahresbericht des Statistischen Amts der Stadt Düsseldorf 1930*, 3.

TABLE 6. Origins of population in Düsseldorf (1905)

Origin of population	Absolute numbers	% of total population
Düsseldorf	111,421	43.99
Other Rhenish areas	74,795	29.53
Westphalia	20,528	8.11
Hesse-Nassau	5,305	2.10
Hanover	3,477	1.37
Other Prussian provinces	17,767	7.01
Other German states	12,533	4.95
Foreign countries (Europe)	7,182	2.84
Other foreign countries	262	0.10

Source: Hüttenberger, *Düsseldorf*, 116–17.

image of the Jew in the city? Was the influence of these immigrants greater in middle-class or proletarian neighbourhoods? Was the picture of the Jew related to economic status, or was it dependent on the religious and cultural experiences of the newly arrived immigrants?

We know that Jewish cattle-dealers and middlemen were prominent in the Rhineland and Westphalia, but historians of Düsseldorf have so far not mentioned the possibilty that anti-Semitism stemmed from this fact. Hüttenberger, for example, concedes that Judeophobia was rife in some smaller villages of the surrounding regions, but believes that this had no effect on the way Gentiles in Düsseldorf behaved towards the Jews.[42] In other words, while in Nuremberg the rural Jew of Franconia was decisive in shaping the minds of the local population (at least according to the secondary literature), the people of Düsseldorf largely ignored traditional stereotypes of Jews as pedlars, usurers, and ritual murderers. Perhaps it was the heterogeneity of Düsseldorf's population that explains why such stereotypes were absent from the Rhenish city. Compared to Nuremberg, the percentage of those born within the city and those moving to the city from the immediate countryside was low: 86.7 per cent in Nuremberg, only 71.6 per cent in Düsseldorf.[43] This point is also argued by Mary Nolan in her study of working-class radicalism in Düsseldorf:

Culture was no more conducive to working-class cohesion and politicization in Düsseldorf than was the division of labor. The multiplicity of occupations, the heterogeneity of the numerically predominant migrant group, and the ever-present religious split created a kind of cultural chaos. When the Wilhelminean era

[42] Hüttenberger, *Düsseldorf*, 121.   [43] Köllmann, *Bevölkerung*, 118–19.

opened, Düsseldorf was a patch-work of small communities, each having its own degree of permanence, and its own relationship to the surrounding society.[44]

We could thus ask whether Nuremberg was the more traditional society, whether her Rhenish counterpart was less likely to uphold older ideas and practices because her identity depended on a greater diversity of backgrounds. This must remain conjecture, however, as long as we lack information on the process and degree of adaptation by migrant elements.[45] If Nuremberg's culture was more exacting in this respect, that is, if newly arrived workers were more willing to assimilate and appropriate Franconian ways, then we still cannot account for latent tendencies without referring to events *after* the outbreak of tensions. Until 1914, therefore, Jewish–Gentile relations were relatively peaceful in both cities.

The Jews

Along with the Romans, a number of Jewish slaves, former soldiers, and merchants came to settle in the Rhineland in the first centuries of the Common Era. In Düsseldorf, however, Jews were allowed to settle permanently only in the middle of the seventeenth century, when the Pfalz-Neuburg prince, Landsherr Wolfgang Wilhelm, granted them the right to reside in the city for a period of twelve years. As elsewhere, Wilhelm extended the permit against the protests of the local guilds in order to retain the so-called *Judentribut*, a tax designed to finance his army and other expenses resulting from the responsibilities of a German prince. From then on, a small number of *Schutzjuden* lived in Düsseldorf: 81 in 1677, 215 in 1763, and 149 in 1804.[46]

At the beginning of the nineteenth century Düsseldorf's Jewish population was primarily engaged in trade, although a few members of the community were allowed to practise medicine. Jewish children attended local schools and colleges, while receiving religious instruction in their homes. By 1815 Düsseldorf had become the third largest Jewish community in the Rhineland, with 315 members, and on the whole witnessed few violent confrontations with the Christian majority. Nevertheless, Jews were well aware of their minority position in Gentile society: the

[44] Nolan, *Social Democracy*, 24.
[45] To what extent migrants gave up their earlier views and beliefs is impossible to measure. See, for example, G. Ritter and K. Tenfelde, *Arbeiter im Deutschen Kaiserreich 1871 bis 1914* (Bonn, 1992), 806.
[46] B. Suchy, *Juden in Düsseldorf. Ein geschichtlicher Überblick von den Anfängen bis zur Gegenwart*. Landschaftsverband Rheinland/Landesbildstelle Rheinland (Düsseldorf, 1990), 11–16; H. Weidenhaupt (ed.), *Düsseldorf. Geschichte von den Ursprüngen bis ins 20. Jahrhundert. Band 2: Von der Residenzstadt zur Beamtenstadt (1614–1900)* (Düsseldorf, 1988), 227–31.

synagogue, built in 1792, was situated behind the rabbi's home so as to avoid attention and possible complaints, and whatever improvements followed the Code Napoléon were curtailed or retracted during the periods of reaction after 1815 and 1848. Only with the North German Confederation of 1869 did the Jews finally enjoy equal rights as citizens of the Prussian state.[47]

In the late nineteenth and early twentieth centuries the number of Jews increased fairly rapidly, though not as fast as the population at large. In contrast to Nuremberg, the proportion of Jews living in Düsseldorf never underwent sudden shifts, as Table 7 reveals.

While around 1850 most Jews were traders, merchants, and junk dealers, by the turn of the century a majority were engaged in business, medicine, law, journalism, publishing, and art dealing.[48] As in Nuremberg, Jews became prominent members of the city's social and economic life. Jonas Herzfeld's textile firm, for example, was the largest of its kind. Many respected private banks belonged to Jews, including Scheuner und Cohn (until the late 1890s), Simons und Co., and Siegfried Falk, while the bankers Leiffmann, Simons, and Ahrweiler were active in both the municipal council and the chamber of commerce. Eduard Meyer's Getreidecommission A.G., which the corn merchant had established in 1885, was to emerge as one of Germany's most important grain firms under the leadership of his son, Hugo Meyer. The newly established theatre, the Schauspielhaus, was directed by Louise Dumont and her Jewish husband, Gustav Lindemann. Arthur Schloßmann, a convert who later became involved in local politics, and the pathologist Otto Lubarsch headed two of Düsseldorf's major hospitals, while Isaak Thalheimer owned the important *Lokalzeitung*. Finally, both Leonhard Tietz and Paul Carsch built impressive department stores in Düsseldorf's city centre in 1909 and 1915 respectively.[49]

Although Jewish wealth should not be exaggerated, it was apparent to many contemporaries that a large number of Jews could be found among the affluent members of society, a fact that was underlined by their disproportionate presence in the highest tax bracket. In 1902, for example, of the 349 people eligible to vote in the first class of the suffrage, 5 per cent were Jewish, while in the second class three-and-a-half per cent belonged to the Jewish community. Jews also lived in rather fancy neighbourhoods,

[47] Suchy, *Juden*, 25 ff. On the period after 1815, see also H. S. Schulte, 'Die Rechtslage der Juden in Köln und am Niederrhein 1815–1847', in: Bohnke Kollwitz, *Köln*, 96 ff.

[48] Suchy, 'Düsseldorf', 71.

[49] Ibid., 72 ff. The Schauspielhaus was founded in 1905. Gustav Lindemann left the Jewish community two years later. On Jews in the political life of the city, see the next chapter.

TABLE 7. Religious composition of Düsseldorf

	% of Catholics	% of Protestants	Number and % of Jews
1858	80.30	18.38	603 (1.30)
1871	76.50	22.06	919 (1.30)
1890	72.83	25.70	1401 (0.97)
1910	67.57	30.10	3985 (1.10)
1925	63.15	30.51	5130 (1.20)

Source: *Jahresbericht des Statistischen Amts der Stadt Düsseldorf 1930*, 3; Eschelbacher, *Synagoge*, 2; Hüttenberger, *Düsseldorf*, 112; Henning, *Wirtschaft*, 388. However, between 1910 and 1925, the Jewish population increased by 28.7 per cent, compared to 20.6 per cent for the entire population. See H. Silbergleit, *Die Bevölkerungs- und Berufsverhältnisse der Juden im Deutschen Reich. I Freistaat Preussen* (Berlin, 1930), 84 ff.

such as Mittelstadt (3.7 per cent of the population) and Zoologisches Gartenviertel (3.0 per cent of the population).[50] A further sign of Jewish success was the tendency to send one's children to *Gymnasien* rather than the less prestigious *Real-* or *Hauptschulen*. Although our figures refer to a later period, it is likely that this development was discernible before the war, given that the numbers declined rather than increased in the Weimar Republic. In Düsseldorf's high schools in 1924, Jews constituted over 3 per cent of the student body. At the Hindenburgschule the figures were 7.43 (1923), 5.67 (1926), and 4.94 (1931) per cent; at the Hohenzollerngymnasium 3.5 (1926/7), 2.4 (1930/1), and 2.8 (1932/3) per cent.[51] We need to remember, of course, that the vast majority of Jews did not own villas or head banks, but either lived in relative comfort like so many other members of the bourgeoisie or made their living as artisans and small shopkeepers. Despite the lack of statistical information on Jewish incomes and occupations, it is difficult to find any glaring differences between the Jews of Düsseldorf and the Jews of Nuremberg in so far as visible and outward success was concerned: in both towns there were plenty of targets for anti-Semites, but in both towns these targets rarely figured in the racist propaganda after the war.

The proportion of mixed marriages was a further indication that Düsseldorf's Jews enjoyed a certain measure of acceptance, even if it

[50] K.-P. Hennecke, *Die Vereinigung der Mittelparteien und die Liberale Vereinigung in Düsseldorf 1900–1919* Hausarbeit (Düsseldorf, 1987), 7; *Düsseldorfer Tageblatt* of 1.11.1925 'Volkszählung in Düsseldorf'. Earlier figures were not available.

[51] *Jahresbericht des Statistischen Amts der Stadt Düsseldorf 1924*, 61; Franke, *Aufstieg*, 194, 204.

TABLE 8. Jewish marriage patterns in Düsseldorf

	1907	1909	1914	1915	1916	1917	1918	1919
Number of Jews who married	47	50	67	44	31	51	66	101
Number of mixed marriages	11	12	22	10	8	21	15	27
% of mixed marriages	23	24	33	23	26	41	23	27
	1921	1922	1923	1924	1925	1926	1927	1928
Number of Jews who married	137	101	92	95	84	64	76	71
Number of mixed marriages	25	23	33	19	16	14	28	17
% of mixed marriages	18	23	36	20	19	22	37	24
				1929	1930	1931	1932	1933
Number of Jews who married				73	80	79	61	64
Number of mixed marriages				15	14	23	11	14
% of mixed marriages				21	18	29	18	22

Source: *Jahresberichte des Statistischen Amts der Stadt Düsseldorf 1907, 1909, 1914–1919, 1921–1933*. ('Dissidents' are not included.)

remains difficult to say how much this reflected the actual level of integration within Gentile society.

Again excluding the war years, the percentage of mixed marriages was 23.5 in 1907/9, 24.0 between 1919 and 1933, and 23.75 for the entire period under review. These levels were on average 10 per cent above those of Nuremberg, and within Germany only Hamburg and Cologne had slightly higher figures.[52] As in Nuremberg, the proportion of mixed marriages was not an explanation for future conflicts but a symptom of the possible acceptance of or resistance to the assimilation of the Jewish population. Furthermore, because of the low numbers, it is doubtful whether much can be said about persisting prejudices among these couples, their parents, and society at large. Even with 20 or 30 per cent mixed marriages, therefore, anti-Semitism could always resurface, often de-

[52] See footnote 23. The results for Cologne and Hamburg in the Weimar Republic were for single years only.

pending on circumstances that were wholly unrelated to the willingness of certain groups to accept Jewish men and women in their midst. Thus, while there was never need for a *Verein zur Abwehr des Antisemitismus* in Düsseldorf, the Jewish community realized that much remained to be done in order to counter the threat of anti-Semitism in the city:

In many a dispute with individuals or the authorities Jewish interests were successfully asserted. Where it was necessary and possible, this was also achieved through the press. Every year, but especially during elections, meetings were organized . . . These discussions with representatives of all parties on Jewish questions helped to clarify matters and to cool down feelings among the participants.[53]

What the words 'necessary', 'possible', 'clarify', and 'cool down feelings' signify is not the absence of Jewish–Gentile tensions in Düsseldorf, but the recognition of a fragile peace that required constant reassurance and renegotiation. Nothing is more indicative of this situation than the meetings held prior to local and national elections, when Jews had to inform politicians and the electorate on issues concerning the 'Jewish question', and it seems probable that more often than not this involved defending oneself rather than debating in an atmosphere devoid of bias and pressure.

Finally, let us turn to the presence of Eastern Jews among the Jewish population in the city. According to Rabbi Eschelbacher, most of these came to Düsseldorf at the turn of the century, usually from Galicia and Russian Poland, rarely from territories that were later to become part of the Soviet Union.[54] In 1910 14.28 per cent of the Jewish population was from the East, a figure that rose to 20.50 per cent in 1925.[55] These numbers are hardly striking. At the same time, however, the percentage of aliens who were also Jewish was extremely low in Düsseldorf: with 4.83 per cent of Jewish foreigners in the city, only Mühlheim, Krefeld, Aachen, and Hamborn had both fewer Jewish aliens and a lower proportion of *Ostjuden* in the total Jewish population.[56] In other words, Eastern Jews may have been less conspicious in Düsseldorf than in areas where they constituted a much higher percentage of the alien population. Nevertheless, this was probably more true for such Ruhr towns as Mühlheim and Hamborn, both of which had a large contingent of Polish workers in their factories, than for Düsseldorf, whose foreigners came predominantly from Holland, Belgium, and German-speaking Austria.[57] It is therefore

---

[53] Eschelbacher, *Synagoge*, 56. This does not mean that anti-Semitic organizations were absent before the war. Both a *Verein* and a newspaper, the *Deutschnationale Zeitung*, existed. Suchy, 'Düsseldorf', 272.

[54] Ibid., 3. [55] Table 4 and Silbergleit, *Berufsverhältnisse*, 24.

[56] Wertheimer, *Strangers*, 191–2. [57] Hüttenberger, *Düsseldorf*, 118–19.

not clear whether Düsseldorf's Eastern Jews were identified as such, whether they were perceived as Jews or Poles, or both, or whether Düsseldorf's Gentile population associated them with their Jewish neighbours and friends. As was the case for Nuremberg, we cannot ascertain the precise impact of the *Ostjuden* on the extent and nature of anti-Semitism in Düsseldorf.

All explanations offered in the past, as well as most of the evidence presented here, can only hint at the possible reasons for the differences between the two cities. For example, how seriously can we take the argument, put forward by Hüttenberger among others, that Düsseldorf's pragmatic business community was one factor in determining the tolerant atmosphere prevalent in the city? Could it be that Nuremberg's businessmen were so much less pragmatic? Or, to take another approach, why is it that cattle-dealers and moneylenders in Franconia should have influenced the debate on the 'Jewish question' in Nuremberg, whereas ritual murder 'cases' and other religious myths apparently played no role in Düsseldorf? Can we really ascribe this to the heterogeneity of the Rhenish town? Or is it because Catholics learned to dissociate themselves from anti-Semitism as racism came to threaten their own beliefs?

Whatever the answers to these questions, and the reader is left to decide which answers are most convincing, we must reject arguments which make sweeping statements about religious or economic factors in the development of modern anti-Semitism. This is particularly true for Düsseldorf and Nuremberg, where the transformation of the economy and population leave us with the impossible task of deciding whether one's economic status before or after arriving in the city was important, whether religion and culture were responsible for the image of the Jew, or whether political ideology became crucial in the early twentieth century. The obvious reply, namely that a combination of factors might explain what was to occur at a later date, is hardly satisfactory. In the end, however, it was the 'irrational', the unannounced and unforeseen, that would make all the difference: 'The distribution of the forces of tradition . . . cannot be grasped in any quantifiable way. As a result, great historical eruptions and their effects are as unpredictable as the behavior of people when faced with violent crises.'[58]

---

[58] L. Kolakowski, *Modernity on Endless Trial* (Chicago, 1990), 67. Modris Ecksteins has argued that the twentieth century in particular was one of unpredictability and sudden change. See M. Ecksteins, 'Der Große Krieg. Versuch einer Interpretation', in: R. Rother (ed.), *Die letzten Tage der Menschheit. Bilder des Ersten Weltkrieges* (Berlin, 1994), 16.

2

The taboo assailed
1910–1918

I have never met a German who was favourably inclined towards the Jews; and however unconditionally all cautious and politic men may have repudiated real anti-Jewism, even this caution and policy is not directed against this class of feeling itself but only against its dangerous immoderation, and especially against the distasteful and shameful way in which this immoderate feeling is expressed—one must not deceive oneself about that.

Friedrich Nietzsche, *Beyond Good and Evil* (1886 [1990])

A number of works have described the last years of Imperial Germany in terms of the growing discontent of liberals, conservatives, and socialists with an antiquated political system that served élites and notables but discriminated against the masses who demanded participation and a say in the future of the nation. What Friedrich Nietzsche called *Unmässigkeit* (immoderation) was to haunt *Honoratioren* throughout this period, and not a few members of the establishment were forced to reconsider their approach in the light of the new realities unfolding before their eyes. Despite this new quest for 'popularity' (*Volkstümlichkeit*), however, mass politics had not as yet triumphed over moderation, not the least because 'Civilised behaviour, the rule of law and liberal institutions were still expected to continue their secular progress.'[1]

This period, then, saw the rise of vanguards who subjected contemporary society to searching critiques and tried to conceptualize the felt crises of history. Years before the explosion of 1914, these men and women had developed theories and formulated ideas which after 1918 were to enter the common parlance and emerge as given forms of discourse. To take but two examples: racist anti-Semitism had already made inroads among the more radical students, agrarian pressure groups, and nationalist organizations when its impact elsewhere remained rather marginal; and the fascist synthesis, though still waiting to be articulated as a coherent and recog-

[1] E. J. Hobsbawm, *The Age of Empire 1875–1914* (London, 1989), 100.

nizable *Weltanschauung*, had been formed by a number of intellectuals dissatisfied with the strictures of bourgeois politics.[2]

On the other hand we must remember that the pre-war years did not witness the victory of these movements and ideologies. Until the outbreak of hostilities in the summer of 1914 a majority of the élites refused to accept or even accommodate dangerously new and revolutionary concepts, even if at times the opposite appeared to be true. For while groups such as the Conservative Party paid tribute to anti-Semitism by incorporating it into its programme at Tivoli in 1892, this was still regarded by many as a measure to appease rather than a statement of principle. Although Nietzsche was right in claiming that many Germans disliked the Jews, he was equally right in pointing to the persistence of a bourgeois morality which felt uncomfortable with revolution, extremism, and chaos, all the more so when these forces threatened to undermine two important pillars of traditional society, namely the idea of social harmony and the concept of a strong and stable state.[3]

I would like to suggest therefore that in the period prior to the First World War the taboo against certain forms of anti-Semitism lay embedded in a context which precluded certain forms of victory, but that at a later stage these taboo rules were deprived of their original meaning and were 'apt to appear a set of arbitrary prohibitions'.[4] Even if events showed that the taboo was wearing down, its future remained open; and even if Germans witnessed a concerted and sustained assault on this taboo, defeat was not yet final.

NUREMBERG

As elsewhere, Social Democracy posed a serious threat to the hegemony of the traditional élites in Nuremberg. With the election of Karl Grillenberger to the Reichstag in 1881, the Social Democrats scored their

[2] See J. N. Retallack, *Notables of the Right. The Conservative Party and Political Mobilization in Germany, 1876–1918* (Boston and London, 1988); N. Kampe, *Studenten und 'Judenfrage' im Deutschen Reich. Die Entstehung einer akademischen Trägerschicht des Antisemitismus* (Göttingen, 1988); G. Eley, *Reshaping the German Right. Radical Nationalism and Political Change after Bismarck* (New Haven and London, 1980); Z. Sternhell, *The Birth of Fascist Ideology. From Cultural Rebellion to Political Revolution* (Princeton, 1994).

[3] P. Kondylis, *Der Niedergang der bürgerlichen Denk- und Lebensform. Die liberale Moderne und die massendemokratische Postmoderne* (Weinheim, 1991), 23 ff. Peter Gay prefers to speak of a liberal temper, one which has the 'capacity for tolerating the maddening twists, delays, uncertainties, and disappointments attendant upon life in an open society.' Both moderation and the liberal temper offer resistance to, and oppose vehemently, all forms of aggression and extremism which challenge an ordered, reflective, and balanced life. P. Gay, *The Cultivation of Hatred. The Bourgeois Experience. Victoria to Freud*. Vol. III (New York, 1993), 526.

[4] A. MacIntyre, *After Virtue. A Study in Moral Theory* (Notre Dame, 1984), 112.

first major political success, 'though Grillenberger's election owed possibly as much to the split between the National Liberals and the Progressives as to the growing strengths of the Social Democrats'.[5] Even before the franchise reforms of 1908, which allowed Social Democrats to run for public office in Nuremberg, the party had established itself as a major force in the city: it held all four Nuremberg seats in the Bavarian Landtag, and by 1912 won two-thirds of the city's Reichstag votes.[6]

In Bavaria as a whole, Social Democracy was emerging as an accepted if not yet respected force in the political arena. On the one hand, liberalism and democratic government on a local level enabled the Left to favour reformism and the 'integration of the workers into the life of bourgeois society.'[7] On the other hand, Centre Party agitation forced liberals and socialists to band together in an effort to limit Catholic influence in the state.[8] In Nuremberg itself the SPD was characterized by a mixture of reformism and radicalism. While most of its members in the Bavarian parliament opposed the policies of Georg von Vollmar and Eduard Bernstein, socialists involved in local politics, such as Martin Treu, supported a conciliatory and cooperative approach towards the liberal elités.[9]

This situation continued into the first years of the First World War, which brought drastic changes to the city's social and economic life. Workers and members of the middle class alike confronted the collapse of many of Nuremberg's export-oriented businesses. Old markets disappeared with the cessation of international trade. Many small and medium-sized firms closed as manpower became increasingly scarce. Unemployment rose sharply, and by September 1914 Nuremberg had the highest jobless rate of any major German town.[10] Food shortages soon added to the general malaise.

As elsewhere in Bavaria, two interest groups vied for control of opinion once domestic peace had proved to be a short-lived exercise in deception. The 'producers', usually represented by the Conservative Party (or *Freie Vereinigung*) and the Centre, wished to maintain the status quo, while the

---

[5] E. G. Reiche, *The Development of the SA in Nürnberg, 1922–1934* (Cambridge, 1986), 6.

[6] D. Rossmeissl, *Arbeiterschaft und Sozialdemokratie in Nürnberg 1890–1914* (Nuremberg, 1977), 280.

[7] M. Nolan, *Social Democracy and Society. Working-class Radicalism in Düsseldorf, 1890–1914* (Cambridge, 1981), 67.

[8] W. Albrecht, *Landtag und Regierung in Bayern am Vorabend der Revolution von 1918. Studien zur gesellschaftlichen und staatlichen Entwicklung Deutschlands von 1912–1918* (Berlin, 1968), 25.

[9] K.-D. Schwarz, *Weltkrieg und Revolution in Nürnberg. Ein Beitrag zur deutschen Arbeiterbewegung* (Stuttgart, 1971), 84.

[10] Ibid., 121.

'consumers', usually represented by liberals and socialists, complained about this unyielding attitude of those who owned the land, distributed the goods, and rejected compromise.[11]

If the *Burgfrieden* could not disguise these differences, the war soon led to such levels of disenchantment among the populace that a coalition of the distraught emerged in the final years of the conflict. In the Bavarian parliament politicians from all sides of the house now attacked Prussian centralization. In Nuremberg citizens no longer trusted the authorities, who had failed to keep their promise of supplying foods and other essential goods needed to survive the coming months. Thus, while the beginning of the hostilities saw a temporary truce and the middle years a return to pre-war disputes, the final period of the war witnessed the steady erosion of confidence in the old order.[12]

It was therefore not surprising that even pillars of society like professors and clerics contributed to an atmosphere which military and civilians alike deemed to be downright dangerous.[13] The importance of these circles, however, remains difficult to assess. While it is true that many founding members of the Bavarian *Vaterlandspartei* hailed from Nuremberg, and while a high percentage of war sermons originated in the Franconian city,[14] the potential impact of radical propaganda from above was hardly more effective than popular indignation from below.[15]

This is also true in the case of anti-Semitism, where manipulation, that is, the employment of Jew-baiting by the élites to win over the masses to reactionary politics, is said to have played a prominent part.[16] Yet historians emphasizing manipulation tend to ignore two important facts, namely first, that those engaged in anti-Semitism often believed wholeheartedly in what they were professing; and second, that one and the same 'manipulatory' organization could include both committed Judeophobes and cynical politicians, whose motives and backgrounds often remained obscure, and whose relative importance within the group can no longer be established. Finally, most of the anti-Semitic material distributed in the form of postcards, pamphlets, and leaflets contains no clues as to its

---

[11] Albrecht, *Landtag*, 111.   [12] Ibid., 222; Schwarz, *Weltkrieg*, 153.

[13] See the situation report in StAN Dir. A 20 Wochenbericht 29.7.1916.

[14] Schwarz, *Weltkrieg*, 193, 195.

[15] As Karl-Ludwig Ay has demonstrated, many years of propaganda by priests and pastors had disillusioned the peasant population, who no longer trusted the clergy and its vows to stand for the nation. Hunger and poverty in the countryside replaced deference to the élites. K.-L. Ay, *Die Entstehung einer Revolution. Die Volksstimmung in Bayern während des Ersten Weltkrieges* (Berlin, 1968), 92.

[16] For an example of the 'manipulative theory' and anti-Semitism, see J. Kocka, *Klassengesellschaft im Krieg. Deutsche Sozialgeschichte 1914–1918* (Frankfurt, 1988), 139.

authorship and origin, so that who wrote, sent, and read these works cannot be reconstructed.[17]

In Nuremberg, anti-Semitic organizations such as the Pan-German League and *Reichshammerbund* were fairly weak,[18] although this did not prevent them from putting pressure on the local authorities. In his recollections of the war years, for example, Rabbi Freudenthal mentions that in October 1914 the *Hammerbund* attacked Jewish influence in the city's relief organizations. The basis for these slurs was Dr Gessler's appointment of six Jewish men as directors of the coordinated welfare effort. The *Hammerbund* thought it finally had an issue on which it might attract supporters, but the lord mayor underlined the past generosity of his new assistants and forcefully rejected the accusations.[19] A few months later, however, Freudenthal resignedly concluded that 'Jew-hatred was raising its serpent's head [*Schlangenhaupt*] more ruthlessly than ever.'[20]

In local as well as state archives one finds some evidence for this assertion. A 'poem' entitled 'The Jew in the War!', for example, contained a wide range of prejudices popular in the war years: 'Heut' sieht man auf allen Strassen / Ihre langen, krummen Nasen / Im Theater und Kaffee / Und im Eisenbahnkupee / Ueberall grinst ihr Gesicht / Nur im Schützengraben nicht.'[21] Various scattered complaints to the Bavarian War Ministry, moreover, also testify to the anti-Jewish feelings of some of Nuremberg's burghers. One such letter by Messrs Vogel, Schmidt, and Hessel accused the Jews of being shirkers who let others do the fighting for them: 'Among the local citizenry and military one finds dissatisfaction and discord because a striking number of young . . . people, especially Israelites, remain in the garrisons and occupy posts which older . . . men

[17] See, for example, BHStA Abt. I MA 97668, p. 6 'Vertraulich'.

[18] K. Scholder, 'Nürnberg und das 20. Jahrhundert', *Tutzinger Studien* 2 (1979), 67. The Nuremberg *Hammer* community counted twenty-three members with an annual budget of 94.64 marks. See also R. Lenman, *Julius Streicher and the Origins of National Socialism in Nuremberg 1918–1923*, unpublished B.Phil. thesis (Oxford, 1968), 24, who notes that only ten people attended the *Hammerbund's* founding meeting on 7 March 1912 and that this was the average number at membership meetings over the next months.

[19] M. Freudenthal, *Die israelitische Kultusgemeinde Nürnberg 1874–1924* (Nuremberg, 1925), 163. See also C. J. Ehlers, *Nuremberg, Julius Streicher and the Bourgeois Transition to Nazism. 1918–1924*, unpublished Ph.D. thesis (Colorado, 1975), 254. What Gessler had to say in private on the 'Jewish question' is of course another matter. See, for example, O. Gessler, *Reichswehrpolitik in der Weimarer Republik* (Stuttgart, 1958), 173–4.

[20] Freudenthal, *Kultusgemeinde*, 161. During the official patriotic festivities of 1915, Freudenthal gave the main talk. Again, this in itself says little about the degree to which Jews were accepted in the community, just as membership in clubs and associations or the level of intermarriage need not indicate whether integration was well advanced.

[21] BHStA Abt.I MA 97668 'Der Jude im Weltkrieg!': 'Today one sees on every street / Their long and crooked noses / In the theatre and coffee house / And in the train compartment / Everywhere their face grins / Only not in the trenches.'

could fill.'[22] A similar letter of May 1918 reminded the War Ministry that two eighteen-year-old Jews, although perfectly fit to join the army, had been exempted from military service: 'No consideration is shown for old soldiers and fathers, but this preferential treatment [*extra Wurst*] is continued [*weiter gebraten*] for understandable reasons.'[23] From the limited sources available, one cannot tell whether the myth that Jews avoided the trenches was more pronounced in Nuremberg than elsewhere; nor can one assess the popularity of anti-Semitism in the city. What one can say, however, is that at least some Jews, and in particular the rabbi of Nuremberg, Max Freudenthal, perceived the war as something of a turning-point in the relationship with the Gentile majority. In order to get a better picture of these developments, it is useful to study other areas of Jewish–Gentile intercourse.

'PROTESTANT BOURGEOISIE'

In his study of Nuremberg's liberal parties in Imperial Germany, Gerhard Nitzl notes that the local *Verein Fortschritt* was able to organize large-scale 'middle-class' support, but that this support lacked a 'qualitative basis': 'apparently the Verein was able to activate only a fraction of its members.'[24] In addition, the absence of a third political force turned Nuremberg politics into a permanent confrontation between socialist workers and bourgeois Progressives, adding fuel to the extremists of both sides: 'In Nuremberg left liberals were by far the largest and most significant group in the bourgeois camp, so that every Social Democratic victory also meant a defeat for left liberalism.'[25] Thus, despite a greater readiness to understand working-class aspirations, liberalism was forced to combat the Left to secure its own survival. Once this failed, however, Nuremberg's Progressives had trouble convincing their followers that liberalism was strong enough to stem the tide of change. Many former left liberals moved to the right as a result, the most prominent perhaps being Julius Streicher.[26]

[22] BHStA Abt. IV MKr. 13346 January 1915.
[23] BHStA Abt. IV MKr. 13359 Nürnberg 1.5.1918. See also BHStA Abt. IV Kriegsamtstelle Nürnberg Bd. 9/I Anonymous letter, October 1917; and BHStA Abt. IV MKr. 13346 January 1915, letter by R. Werner from Bamberg.
[24] G. Nitzl, *Modernisierung in den liberalen Parteien des deutschen Kaiserreichs, 1871–1914. Eine Untersuchung am Beispiel der Stadt Nürnberg, unter besonderer Berücksichtigung der Fortschrittspartei* Magisterarbeit (Erlangen-Nuremberg, 1988), 33.
[25] Ibid., 68–9.
[26] See W. Varga, *Julius Streicher: A Political Biography, 1885–1933*, unpublished Ph.D. thesis (Ohio, 1974), 7.

This did not mean that those who persisted in their advocacy of liberalism suddenly capitulated when it came to such issues as the 'Jewish question'. Indeed, Jews had been prominent members on the committees of both the Nuremberg *Fortschrittlicher Volksverein* and the *Demokratischer Verein*. In 1896, for example, at least three Jews were active in the latter organization, a number that increased to six in April 1921.[27] The *Fortschrittlicher Volksverein* counted among its committee members in 1907 Leonhard Frankenberger, Dr D. Kaufmann, Dr Josef Neuberger, and Sigmund Wertheimer.[28] Left liberalism's tolerance, at least that of its most vocal agents, was further demonstrated in its approach to the 'Jewish question' between 1910 and 1918.

This was especially the case in the run-up to the 1912 Reichstag elections, the outcome of which led to renewed attacks on the supposed subversiveness of 'international' Jewry. Conservative papers blamed liberal organizations like 'Riesser's Hansabund' for joining forces with the revolutionary Left, and referred to the elections as an assault by Jews and the Jewish spirit on Germany's national and *völkisch* foundations. In their view the time had come to 'confront that which is un-German with that which is German, the international with the national, destruction with preservation, and the deceitful struggle with the struggle of and for truth'.[29]

According to a report in the *Nordbayerische Zeitung*, the Nuremberg leader of the *Fortschrittliche Volkspartei*, Hans Häberlein,[30] stressed in a meeting of his party the need to combat 'anti-Semites, Free Conservatives, and *Mittelständler*'.[31] Both the *Nürnberger Anzeiger* and the *Fränkischer Kurier* criticized the agrarian anti-Semitic *Sauhordenton*[32] of the Conservatives. While the former warned that 'whoever contributes directly or indirectly to the election of an anti-Semite is also to blame for the brutalization that these patrons of German tradition spread,'[33] the latter condemned the Centre Party's support for an anti-Semitic

---

[27] StAN C7/V VP 3301 'Demokratischer Verein'.

[28] StAN C7/V VP 3992 'Fortschrittlicher Volksverein'.

[29] See W. T. Angress, 'The Impact of the "Judenwahlen" of 1912 on the Jewish Question. A Synthesis', *LBIY* (1983), 390. The SPD won 60.4 per cent in Nuremberg (34.8 in Germany at large); the Progressives 28.8 per cent (12.3); and the Centre Party 5.5 per cent (16.4). M. Moore-Ziegler, *The Socio-Economic and Demographic Bases of Political Behavior in Nuremberg During the Weimar Republic, 1919–1933*, unpublished Ph.D. thesis (Virginia, 1976), 305–6.

[30] Häberlein later became a founding member of the local *Verein zur Abwehr des Antisemitismus*. See *Mitteilungen aus dem Abwehrverein des Antisemitismus*, 12.6.1918, 56.

[31] *NBZ*, 6.1.1912 'Wählerversammlungen der Fortschrittlichen Volkspartei'.

[32] *NAZ*, 12.11.1911.   [33] Ibid.

candidate in Kassel.[34] Although we do not know for sure how much of this was inspired by the wish to discredit political opponents and how much was an honest disavowal of Judeophobia, the fact that anti-Semitism was repeatedly mentioned to *stigmatize* other groups illustrates the extent to which Jew-hatred was considered tasteless and disreputable.

Newspaper reports of the Beilis ritual murder trial in Kiev in the autumn of 1913 are another case in point.[35] The *Nürnberger Zeitung* spoke of a 'fairy tale', of an affront to the educated nations of western Europe.[36] The *Kurier*, though careful at first not to take sides, lashed out against the myth of ritual murder following the defendant's acquittal: 'When superstition is unleashed and people's passions are roused against members of another religion or another race, the hindrance of progess and the denial of rights are near.' [37] The prospect of religious fanaticism sweeping across Europe horrified Nuremberg's left liberals. Their press voiced nothing but outrage over the behaviour of the Russian authorities, adding that Germany's standing as a *Kulturnation* precluded such archaic practices.

Regrettably, little material exists on the political parties covering the period 1914–18. In the case of left liberalism, an article in the *Anzeiger* seems to substantiate the above findings. Written in October 1916, it was a response both to the widespread accusations that Jews undermined the existing political and social structure, either by trying to avoid the trenches or by supporting a negotiated peace and constitutional reforms, and to the announcement by the Prussian War Ministry that an inquiry was under way into the religious composition of organizations related to the coordinated war effort. As many observers noted at the time, the War Ministry's 'Jew count' was a reaction to complaints by anti-Semites, and was unique in that a group was singled out and implicitly charged with unpatriotic behaviour at a time when domestic peace was needed most:

Shirkers can be found everywhere, among all denominations and among all professions; it is therefore an unparalleled injustice to help fostering anti-Semitic

[34] *FK*, 6.1.1912 (Abend) 'Das Zentrum und die Antisemiten'.
[35] The defendant, Mendel Beilis, was accused of having murdered a young boy by the name of Andrèj Justschinskij in March 1911. The corpse was found mutilated, and the many knife wounds suggested a 'ritual murder'. Although the Ministry of Justice supported the charge against Beilis, the latter was aquitted in November 1913. K. H. Rengsdorf and S. von Kortzfleisch (eds.), *Kirche und Synagoge. Handbuch zur Geschichte von Christen und Juden. Darstellung mit Quellen*, Band 2 (Munich, 1988), 656. See also A. S. Lindemann, *The Jew Accused. Three Anti-Semitic Affairs (Dreyfus, Beilis, Frank 1894–1914)* (Cambridge, 1991), 187–8, who points out that many conservative and even anti-Semitic commentators denounced the trial as a sham.
[36] *NZ*, 10.10.1913 'Ein Ritualmordprozeß'. In the same vein, *NAZ*, 17.10.1913 'Der Kiewer Ritualmordprozeß'.
[37] *FK*, 12.11.1913 (Abend) 'Der Freispruch von Kiew'.

rumours . . . by setting up an inquiry . . . To decide this at a time when thousands and thousands of our Jewish fellow-citizens are fighting side by side with their Christian comrades on all fronts, risking their health and future, their blood and life for the protection of the fatherland, when many of them have already received the Iron Cross and countless others have died in the field of battle, means a deliberate slander of German Jewry.[38]

Although election results indicate that the Progressives had little to fear from their National Liberal rivals,[39] the latter present another interesting case for our discussion. The local National Liberal newsletter, *Die Wacht. Wochenschrift für nationale und liberale Politik*, dealt with the 'Jewish question' on a number of occasions, and the examples suggest that the party held conflicting views on the subject. When it came to 'reactionary' politics, for example, the *Wacht* complained that anti-Semitism was senseless, arguing that the latter lived off 'religious dirt' and disguised itself in 'conservative clothes'.[40] In an article on the annual conference of the Bavarian Conservative Party in Nuremberg in 1914, the paper attacked the 'unpleasant' undertone of a speech marked by 'tedious anti-Semitism' and 'anti-industrialism'.[41] Moreover, Gustav Josephsthal, chairman of the local Jewish community, played a prominent part in the local party organization.[42]

On the other hand, numerous articles applied 'mild' forms of Jew-baiting, especially against liberal newspapers like the *Berliner Tageblatt*, whose editor, Theodor Wolff, was described as having 'too much of the Heinean character to be agreeable as the head of a German paper'.[43] The *Tageblatt*'s uncompromising style in particular provoked deep misgivings: 'One can only follow with revulsion how this "Weltblatt" employs its racial over-subtlety [*rassische Spitzfindigkeit*] when it comments on every statement made by the emperor.'[44] This nasty sneer highlights what one might call the attempt to maintain a 'balance of power' in national politics. Three years later defenders of a status quo again searched for scapegoats to explain away the glaring divisions between different groups and sectors in society. Nuremberg's National Liberals discovered one such culprit in the supporters of an unconditional peace. Practitioners of high finance

[38] *NAZ*, 25.10.1916 'Verleumderische Frage nach der Konfession'.

[39] In the 1907 and 1912 Reichstag elections, the National Liberals received under 5 per cent of the vote, while the Progressives won 32.8 and 28.8 per cent respectively. Moore-Ziegler, *Political Behavior*, 305–6.

[40] *Die Wacht*, 2.3.1912 'Mit Dank abgelehnt'.

[41] Ibid., 18.4.1914 'Aus dem politischen und wirtschaftspolitischen Leben'.

[42] A. Müller, *Geschichte der Juden in Nürnberg, 1146–1945* (Nuremberg, 1968), 175.

[43] *Die Wacht*, 27.4.1912 'Die Kampfesweise des Berliner Tageblattes'. See also ibid., 3.5.1913 'Das "Berl. Tagebl." über den guten Ton'.

[44] Ibid., 28.6.1913 'Politische Wochenschau'.

were undoubtedly involved in this 'conspiracy', they believed, as was 'Great Jewry [*Großjudentum*] . . . which was related to high finance in any case'.[45] In Nuremberg, then, we find that National Liberalism, albeit opposed to so-called 'radical' and 'reactionary' anti-Semitism, practiced 'milder' forms of Jew-baiting, most of which were intended to confront the critics of national institutions and national unity.

Moving yet further to the right, the *Nürnberger Mittelstandsvereinigung* was conspicious for both its anti-capitalist and anti-socialist views. Founded in September 1904 by a group of artisans, the movement railed first and foremost against speculators, department stores, and the stock exchange.[46] A January 1912 article in the *Fränkische Mittelstandszeitung* entitled 'Hansa Election Money in Nuremberg' typified the group's resentment of, among other things, 'new' money, consisting of electrical and shipping enterprises as well as the large and still expanding commercial and investment banks with their vast international connections. It was this money, the paper argued, that was responsible for the Social Democratic victory in 1912: 'The anti-national Hansa Gold was unable to resist the fiery "red" heat [*glut-"roten" Hitze*] and so was washed away by the all-consuming waves of the red flood.'[47] Similarly, a *Mittelstand* leaflet for the 1912 Reichstag elections blamed the 'international, speculating bank and stock exchange magnates, the jobbers of big business who had no fatherland and no beliefs, and who destroyed both the man in the street and the worker', as well as the 'golden International' for upsetting traditional ways of life in town and countryside.[48] The party also suggested that the Jews would eventually control other aspects of the nation's social and political life. Claiming that the *Radauantisemitismus* of the past had given way to an anti-Semitism stemming from Jewish manipulation of the war industry, the *Mittelstandszeitung* went on to write: 'it is a fact that the Jews have even more economic power now than was already the case before the war . . . The danger is indeed imminent that the Jews are ruling the German people [*Volk*] not only economically but also spiritually.'[49]

In the case of Nuremberg, therefore, the *Mittelstandsvereinigung* resembled prevailing Conservative and Agrarian League attitudes on the 'Jewish question'. For example, the candidate of the *Bayerische Reichspartei* (Free Conservative), Tafel, denied at a party rally in Nuremberg that anti-

---

[45] *Die Wacht*, 9.12.1916 'Wie denkt man in Deutschland über den Frieden?'

[46] StAN C7/V VP 3621 'Nürnberger Mittelstandsvereinigung'. Among the forty-five founding members, there were twelve shoemakers, three bakers, and a number of tailors, carpenters, locksmiths, and bookbinders.

[47] *Fränkische Mittelstandszeitung*, 26.1.1912.

[48] Stadtbibliothek Nürnberg, Nor.547 2 o.

[49] *Süddeutsche Mittelstands-Zeitung*, 19.1.1917 'Eine Hochflut des Antisemitismus?'

Semitism was dominant among his fellow Conservatives, but conceded that 'the Israelites tend to lean towards the Left.'[50] Speakers at a meeting of the *Bund der Landwirte* in Nuremberg in 1912 stressed the 'uncanny power of this alien people', who were, unmistakably, 'the kings of our time'.[51] Like the protectors of 'middle-class ideology', Conservatives felt threatened by the victory of socialism at the polls, writing that 'cheered on by the Jewish press, the victorious "red guards" march into the Reichstag.'[52] Since liberals and socialists continued to threaten 'German ways', conservatives blamed the Jews for many of the 'ills besetting' German society: 'Not the Junker but the Jews rule our people. This we must make clear to our people, and we should not be afraid to mention the Jews in this connection, even if each time the liberal and Social Democratic press will fall upon us.'[53]

The Nuremberg Protestant Church wrote very sparingly on the issue of anti-Semitism in these years. In fact, the *Evangelisches Gemeindeblatt* had little if anything to say on the topic. In March 1910 it welcomed a Jewish convert to the Christain faith,[54] and six years later an article on the Napoleonic Wars mentioned that a 'Gesellschaft der Freunde in Berlin (meist Juden)' had donated more than 800 *Taler* to the German war effort.[55] Jew-hatred was also absent from the only racist article written before the Revolution, a piece which predicted the racial struggle between the forces of 'Germandom' on the one hand, and the dragon of 'Slavism' on the other.[56] Lacking printed sermons which might touch upon the 'Jewish question', one could speculate that the silence on the subject reflected the liberal atmosphere in Nuremberg and the subsequent desire to support the *Burgfrieden*.[57] Whatever the reason, however, Protestant clerics appear to have had little interest in the subject before 1918.

[50] *FK*, 5.1.1912 (Vormittag) 'Nürnberger Wahlversammlungen'.

[51] StAN *Nürnberger Stadtchronik 1912*, 279. In December 1906 the BdL joined forces with the *Nordbayerische Mittelstandsvereinigung* to demand a 'Deutsche Heimatpolitik'. The Agrarian League was not particularly strong in Middle Franconia, at least in comparison to Upper Franconia and Upper Bavaria. See H. J. Puhle, *Agrarische Interessenpolitik und Preussischer Konservatismus im Wilhelminischen Reich. Ein Beitrag zur Analyse des Nationalismus in Deutschland am Beispiel des Bundes der Landwirte und der Deutsch-Konservativen Partei* (Hanover, 1966), 67, 147 n. 21.

[52] *Bayerischer Volksfreund*, 6.2.1912 'Man schreibt uns'.

[53] StAN C7/V VP 1295 'Bayerische Konservative', exerpt from a speech at the Bavarian party congress of the Conservatives in Nuremberg on 15.4.1914. We need to keep in mind, however, that at the time Conservatives were extremely weak in Nuremberg: whereas in 1903 they managed to capture just over 2 per cent of the Reichstag vote, in 1907 and 1912 they were no longer represented. Moore-Ziegler, *Political Behavior*, 305–6.

[54] *EvN*, 6.3.1910 'Eine Israelitenklause'.   [55] Ibid., 5.3.1916 'Für unsere Zeit'.

[56] Ibid., 9.8.1914 'Auf zum Kampf!'

[57] Occasionally left liberals like Otto Stündt, who later led the DDP youth of north Bavaria, wrote for the Protestant weekly. See, for example, the issue of 23.3.1919.

CATHOLICISM

While the Catholic population of Nuremberg grew from 18 to 31 per
cent between 1871 and 1912,[58] the Centre Party remained weak and
insignificant. Not until 1890 did the party put up a candidate in a Nuremberg election, and the proportion of votes cast for the Centre never
exceeded 6 per cent.[59] In Bavaria the party came under the influence of its
conservative–clerical wing, which declared the struggle against Social
Democracy paramount, and which in 1901 proposed to limit the number
of Jews in German courts in order to curtail their predominance in an
especially sensitive area of social life.[60]

As elsewhere, the Centre's main opponent in Nuremberg was Social
Democracy. But while in cities like Düsseldorf the struggle between the
two was one of political power and control, in Nuremberg Catholics
fought an ideological battle, without the slightest hope of improving their
chances *vis-à-vis* socialism. In addition, the Centre Party also appealed to
disaffected members of the 'middle class' in a style reminiscent of anti-
capitalist *Mittelstandspolitik*. A January 1912 slogan, for example, read: 'A
smart merchant votes for the Centre, because this party fights against
unfair competition, because it watches the speculator's every move, because it helps to tax the department stores in line with their earnings.'[61]
Socialism's victory at the polls in 1912, moreover, was possible only
because liberalism, the *Vorfrucht* of Social Democracy, had aided and
abetted this development.[62] Like other conservative forces in Germany,

---

[58] Moore-Ziegler, *Political Behavior*, 36.

[59] Ibid. See also G. Pfeiffer (ed.), *Nürnberg. Geschichte einer europäischen Stadt* (Munich,
1971), 369.

[60] Rossmeissl, *Arbeiterschaft*, 190–1; D. L. Niewyk, 'Das Selbstverständnis der Juden und
ihre Beteiligung am politischen Leben des Kaiserreichs und der Weimarer Republik', in: M.
Treml et al., *Geschichte und Kultur der Juden in Bayern. Aufsätze* (Munich, 1988), 375:

The 'Bavarian Centre Party' . . . employed anti-Jewish slogans possibly as a means to out-
shine rival anti-Semitic organizations such as the 'Bavarian Farmers' League'. Certain
elements among the petty-bourgeois, democratic, pro-peasant faction in the Centre, including supporters of Johann Babtist Sigl's 'Bavarian Fatherland' and Georg Heim's 'Bavarian
Christian Peasant League' were much more serious in their criticism of the Jews than their
moderate party comrades.

[61] *Nürnberger Volkszeitung*, 12.1.1912 'Wer wählt am 12. Januar Zentrum?' See also ibid.,
1.2.1912 'Lokales': 'The local Mittelstandsvereinigung, which repudiates the whole-sale
capitulation [*Verschacherung*] of the bourgeois [*bürgerlichen*] voter to the party of subversion
[*Umsturzpartei*] through the great party bloc, will enter the election campaign as an independent force.' It needs to be mentioned that, whatever the differences between Nuremberg's and Düsseldorf's Catholics on the 'Jewish question', the Centre and BVP in Bavaria
were in general more conservative than their Prussian counterparts. See K. Schönhoven, *Die
Bayerische Volkspartei 1924–1932* (Düsseldorf, 1972), 17–19, 282–3.

[62] Ibid., 19.1.1912 'Lokales'.

the Nuremberg Centre Party launched a bitter attack on the 'malicious craft' [*Hetzhandwerk*] of the Progressives.

While Catholic invectives against the Left never contained anti-Semitic messages, the local party organ revealed its anti-Jewish bias when it discussed the implications of the 1916 'Jew count'. An article of 21 October still took a cautious approach: 'Often one can hear the belief that mainly Jewish businessmen are involved in . . . the war trade and that the Jews have made large profits as a result.'[63] One week later, however, in a major piece on 'Anti-Semitic Propaganda', the *Nürnberger Volkszeitung* acknowleged that rumours about Jewish influence in the war industry were at least in part justified: 'He who is not blind or deaf must know that an anti-Semitic current is on the rise in Germany. This current is underpinned by popular agitation. One reason for this is the recurring indication that an unusually large number of Jews is active in . . . war organizations.'[64] This assesssment, the paper continued, did not make the Centre Party anti-Semitic; on the contrary, the 'Jew count' in the war industries was in the best interest of German Jewry, and it was unwise of the *Berliner Tageblatt* and the *Frankfurter Zeitung* to complain about the Centre's role in putting forward the motion in parliament: 'We find this attitude, to say the least, unwise. Don't these circles tell themselves that all their excitement over this motion must make the people [*das Volk*] think that the statistics will reveal unhealthy conditions, will highlight conditions which one would rather have left in the dark . . . ?'[65] In short, the Nuremberg Centre Party explained the upcoming inquiry in terms of possible—if not likely—irregularities in the running of certain war-related organizations. It also spoke of 'hints' that rumours and accusations concerning Jewish power were based on certain elements of truth. What one can gather from the few sources available, then, is that 'official' Catholicism in Nuremberg promoted the idea that Jews were too prominent in Germany's social and political life. Whether this attitude gained ground after the war remains to be seen.

THE LEFT

After the death of Karl Grillenberger in 1897, the SPD in Nuremberg moved further to the left.[66] As Klaus-Dieter Schwarz has argued, working-class consciousness was more pronounced in the industrial town

---

[63] Ibid., 21.10.1916 'Kriegsgeschäft und Judentum'. None the less, the caption suggests that the paper possibly wished to link the two.

[64] Ibid., 27.10.1916 'Antisemitische Propaganda'.   [65] Ibid.

[66] Schwarz, *Weltkrieg*, 83.

of Nuremberg than in Munich, where 'Bebel's influence . . . was unable to prevail against the evolution of Lassallean state interventionism into Vollmarean state socialism.'[67] Nevertheless, Nuremberg Social Democracy was equally marked by a pragmatic approach to municipal affairs. Both Reichstag deputy Albert Südekum and *Magistratsrat* Martin Treu favoured reformism,[68] and both cooperated with city officials to bring about a gradual improvement of workers' conditions. Although the conflict between orthodoxy and revisionism therefore continued into the twentieth century, it never took on radical forms. This is also evident from the party's newspaper, the *Fränkische Tagespost*, whose editors could be found in both camps.

Since there are no figures on the composition of the Social Democratic leadership in Nuremberg,[69] it is difficult to reach any conclusions about 'Jewish' influence in the party. Certainly more Jews wielded power in the Nuremberg SPD than in other parties: *Tagespost* editors included Gabriel Löwenstein, Emmanuel Wurm, and Kurt Eisner, while Adolf Braun and Dr Max Süßheim shaped the party's course over the years.[70]

Surprisingly, however, the SPD paper in Nuremberg had little to say on the 'Jewish question'. We find no commentaries, for example, on either the Beilis trial or the army's *Judenzählung*; and the only article dealing with anti-Semitism in this period was written by an outside party member.[71] Perhaps we may attribute this indifference to older traditions in the party, or to the influence of Adolf Braun, a Jew who detested 'the arrogance and self-esteem' of his co-religionists: 'All Jews who feel like Jews, who would like to be something better and believe themselves to be members of a chosen people, I thoroughly dislike.'[72] Many in his party

[67] Schwarz, *Weltkrieg*, 83.

[68] Ibid., 84. Rossmeissl, *Arbeiterschaft*, 179: 'Under its new chairman Dorn, Nuremberg's SPD increasingly turned to local issues from 1904/5 onward. One gains the impression that following the victories on the state and national level and after the quarrels with the Bavarian fraction, interest in topics of more than just regional importance waned.'

[69] Rossmeissl, *Arbeiterschaft*, 243. Rossmeissl mentions that in 1904 at least 88 per cent of all SPD members belonged to the working class, a figure very similar to the composition of Düsseldorf's party. Ibid., 207.

[70] Ehlers, *Nuremberg*, 271 n. 7. Ehlers believes that the following *Tagespost* editors were also of Jewish descent: Albert Südekum (1900–2), Wilhelm Herzberg (1910–12), Emil Fischer (1920–33). No proof exists for the Jewish origin of Südekum, however. The baptized Bruno Schoenlank worked for the Nuremberg paper in the 1880s. P. Mayer, *Bruno Schoenlank 1859–1901. Reformer der sozialistischen Tagespresse* (Hanover, 1971), 33.

[71] FT, 7.2.1912 'Deutsches Reich'. The *Düsseldorfer Volkszeitung* published the same piece under the heading 'Bruhn und Heydebrand, G.m.b.H.'. While not all issues of the *Tagespost* were examined, no treatment of the 'Jewish question' was discovered in those articles most likely to contain such a discussion.

[72] Quoted in Schwarz, *Weltkrieg*, 47 n. 113. Braun edited the *Tagespost* from 1912 to 1920. Older traditions might include the influence of such important party members as Karl Grillenberger, who occasionally used anti-Jewish polemics. See, for example, Mayer,

regarded Braun as an anti-Semite,[73] perhaps a valid assessment given his occasional remarks on the subject.[74] Whether Braun alone led the discussion on the 'Jewish question', however, is another matter. Before 1918/19 at least, the SPD felt no need to face the problem of anti-Semitism, even when, as in October 1916, other parties in Nuremberg were confronting the topic.

DÜSSELDORF

Before the war, Düsseldorf's 'ruling élite' had little to fear from Social Democracy. The city council was elected under a three-class suffrage, which placed 90 per cent of the taxpayers in the lowest class; only males over the age of twenty-five who paid taxes, received no poor relief, and had resided in the city for one year were eligible for election. This precluded any socialist infiltration of the local administration, since the *Liberale Vereinigung* had a two-thirds majority, which it jealously guarded.[75]

The Centre Party, by contrast, competed against the SPD for Landtag and Reichstag seats. While the party had adapted to the emerging age of organized mass politics, it also had most to lose from a Social Democratic victory in Düsseldorf.[76] Unlike the city's liberals, it 'pitted its world view against that of the Social Democrats, appealing indiscriminately to political, religious, and social anxieties in lurid terms'.[77] Hence, the Centre also cooperated with the followers of Adolf Stöcker, the Christian Socials, prior to the 1912 Reichstag elections in order to defend its position *vis-á-vis* the SPD.[78]

Schoenlank, 34 and 123, who quotes Grillenberger as calling his fellow socialist, Parvus-Helphand, a 'dirty Polish Jew' and a Russian *Büffelochsenjude*. Schoenlank himself was not free from prejudice: see ibid., 34.

[73] Schwarz, *Weltkrieg*, 47 n. 113.

[74] At a mid-June 1919 party convention of the MSPD Braun criticized the 'talmudist method' of Bernstein's speeches. See H. A. Winkler, *Von der Revolution zur Stabilisierung. Arbeiter und Arbeiterbewegung in der Weimarer Republik 1918 bis 1924* (Bonn and Berlin, 1984), 211–12.

[75] A. Kussmann, *Das kommunale Parteiensystem in Düsseldorf beim Übergang vom Kaiserreich zur Republik. Ein Beitrag zum Kontinuitätsproblem*, unpublished MA thesis (Berlin, 1982), 37.

[76] Kussmann, *Parteiensystem*, 33: 'In 1884 the proportion of votes for the Centre was still equal to the proportion of Catholics in Düsseldorf's population; in 1912 the proportion of votes for the Centre had decreased to less than half, while the proportion of Catholics had decreased by only 8 per cent. It was the Social Democrats who benefited most from this development.'

[77] Nolan, *Social Democracy*, 47.

[78] K.-P. Hennecke, *Die Vereinigung der Mittelparteien in Düsseldorf. 1900–1919* Hausarbeit (Düsseldorf, 1987), 68.

Due to the high percentage of workers in the party and its exclusion from city government, Social Democracy saw no reason to modify its goals, theory, or tactics in the hope of attracting 'bourgeois' elements, which might have led to a more conciliatory course. Instead, Düsseldorf's Social Democrats moved from the party's 'orthodox but passive center into its activist left wing'.[79] Again, although the 'Protestant bourgeoisie' almost certainly registered this shift within the SPD with disapproval, it could react calmly, given its overwhelming majority in the city council.

Like Nuremberg, Düsseldorf suffered from the restructuring of its economy following the outbreak of war. In 'nonessential' sectors hundreds of factories and workshops closed, either because their owners were drafted or because they lacked raw materials and orders. While thousands of workers benefited from high money wages in war-related industries, the cost of living soared, causing bitterness across class lines.

The war also confirmed the Left's view that the Düsseldorf 'bourgeoisie' was unreliable, transforming its 'previous preoccupation with political Catholicism into one with the state on the one hand and the national party and unions on the other'.[80] Others thought liberalism was incapable of confronting the disintegration of both the social and political order, an impression that seemed vindicated by the inaction and ossification of 'bourgeois' organizations and parties during the war.[81]

This state of impotence did not lead to massive anti-Jewish agitation. Jew-hatred had been largely absent from politics, as the Rhenish chapter of the *Central-Verein* noted in 1913,[82] and the available sources bring little to light which would prove the opposite. Rabbi Eschelbacher, for instance, mentions Jewish assistance to the war effort in his 1929 recollections, but nowhere does he suggest that the war marked the beginning of renewed violence against the Jews.[83] Even a police report on Polish and Russian Jews in Düsseldorf's industry gives no indication as to whether there was friction between Jews and Gentiles in factories and workshops.[84]

[79] Nolan, *Social Democracy*, 197.   [80] Ibid., 251.

[81] Kussmann, *Parteiensystem*, 80.

[82] *Im Deutschen Reich*, January 1913, 7: 'Regrettably there always exist new phenomena which must be touched upon, and even if some indications suggest that official anti-Semitism is subsiding there are plenty of signs that new forms could arise.'

[83] M. Eschelbacher, *Die Synagogengemeinde Düsseldorf 1904–1929 Festschrift* (Düsseldorf, 1929), 4.

[84] HStAD Regierung Düsseldorf 15045 Polizeiverwaltung Düsseldorf, 21.6.1915. The police report mentions that most Jews were physically unfit to carry out hard labour and that some were only willing to eat kosher food. The police president of Bochum, however, reported on 2 September 1915 that foreign Jews sowed unrest among workers. See also the remarks by General von Geyl of the VII Army Corps on 5 November 1915: 'In particular one must disapprove of insulting comments referring to the . . . religious affiliation of the workers.' HStAD Reg. Düss. 9084, p. 29.

Finally, if the *Vaterlandspartei* proved instrumental in spreading national-ist hysteria, it need not have been involved in anti-Semitic propaganda. For although the party was successful in attracting support from many National Liberals, conservative Centre Party members, and nationalist workers,[85] it included men of Jewish descent such as Arthur Schloßmann and, at least officially, stood for all Germans who sided with an all-out war and rejected a compromise peace.[86]

'PROTESTANT BOURGEOISIE'

A majority of Düsseldorf's 'Protestant bourgeoisie' voted for the *Liberale Vereinigung*, an organization mainly in the hands of National Liberals.[87] Left liberalism, by contrast, had few followers in the city. This develop-ment has prompted Andreas Kussmann to describe the period 1911–12 in terms of 'a polarization of parties and voters in two blocks: socialists, democrats, and left liberals on the one side, the Centre, the Right, and National Liberals on the other'.[88] To discover whether this had any im-pact on the public discussion of anti-Semitism, let us turn first to the left liberal position in the debate.

A 1911 leaflet of the *Demokratische Vereinigung* addressed the electorate with an appeal to root out the forces of conservatism: 'If you can warm to a candidate who stands for idiotic anti-Semitism as well as the rabidly anti-tariff [*zollwütige*] Agrarian League, then vote for the so-called na-tional candidate!'[89] From the outset, Democrats opposed reactionary anti-Semitism. To what degree this was the result of 'Jewish influence' in the movement—the staff of the Progressive *Bergischer Türmer*, for example, included prominent Düsseldorf Jews such as Isaak Thalheimer, Alfred Rosenthal, and Arthur Schloßmann—can no longer be determined, but in view of Jewish proclivities to keep quiet on the issue, it is likely that most Gentile left liberals supported the party line.

[85] P. Hüttenberger, *Düsseldorf. Geschichte von den Anfängen bis ins 20. Jahrhundert.* Band 3: *Die Industrie und Verwaltungsstadt (20. Jahrhundert)* (Düsseldorf, 1989), 252.

[86] For anti-Semitism in the *Vaterlandspartei*, see Dirk Stegmann, 'Vom Neokon-servatismus zum Proto-Faschismus: Konservative Partei, Vereine und Verbände 1893–1920', in: D. Stegmann, B. J. Wendt, and P. Christian Witt (eds.), *Deutscher Konservatismus im 19. und 20. Jahrhundert* (Bonn 1983), 220–2.

[87] The 1912 Reichstag elections brought the following results: SPD—45.2 per cent; *Demokratischer Verein*—2.6 per cent; *Liberale Vereinigung*—14.9 per cent; Centre Party—34.7 per cent; Christian Social Party—2.1 per cent. In the second ballot, *LV* supporters voted overwhelmingly for the Centre Party, which received 67.0 per cent as opposed to 33.0 per cent for the SPD. Kussmann, *Parteiensystem*, 52–3.

[88] Ibid., 54.   [89] StAD XXI 251.

In the few articles discussing the matter, the *Türmer* sharply repudiated anti-Semitism. The Christian Socials, for instance, were dismissed on grounds that 'where . . . the Christian Socials have wielded power for a while . . . political decency has turned wild [*verwildert*] and become contaminated, and Jew-hatred of the lowest kind has found a home.'[90] The paper also defended Jewish minority rights. Thus, in a characteristically sarcastic tone, it criticized government indifference towards discrimination in the army:

But one must admire the resourcefulness of the government when it comes to finding new excuses for social evils . . . This of course pertains especially to the question of Jewish officers and reserve officers, who, as is well known, do not exist in Prussia, although it is equally well known that honorary posts are open to all citizens regardless of their denomination.[91]

Finally, in a prophetic statement on the consequences of the army's 'Jew count' of 1916, the *Lokalzeitung*'s Isaak Thalheimer described the dangers involved in accommodating the prejudices of a disoriented and disaffected population:

After the war it will smell of a big cleaning session [*Reinemachung*], gossips will delight in the filthy muck and from all sides the dirty linen will be laid out. The people will follow their leaders; should these make invective [*Schmähsucht*] politically respectable, a hate campaign could ensue such as the world has not yet seen.[92]

On the whole, the *Liberale Vereinigung* was equally adamant in its rejection of anti-Semitism.[93] Among its members were a number of Jews, some of whom played an increasingly important role in party committees before and during the war. This was largely the result of various agreements between the *Vereinigung* and the Jewish community. In 1906 the lawyer Samuel Cohn was elected to the city council for the *LV*, a position he held until 1918.[94] In the same year, the Jewish banker Simons joined the party's important *Tätigkeitsausschuß*. The *Vereinigung* also agreed to put forward a Jewish candidate in the first class of the electoral system in return for the community's support of liberalism in the second class. Respected Jews like the lawyer Cohen and the industrialist Gustav Herzfeld thereupon asked their co-religionists to vote for the *Liberale Vereinigung*.[95] Finally, the *LV* promised to eject all remaining Christian

[90] *Bergischer Türmer*, 16.11.1911 'Die Christlich-sozialen am Werk'.
[91] Ibid., 4.3.1911 'Die Parlamentswoche.'
[92] *LZ*, 11.11.1916 'Lokalpolitischer Brief'.
[93] The *LV* consisted of National Liberals and Free Conservatives. After 1908, left liberals also joined the party. Hüttenberger, *Düsseldorf*, 168.
[94] StAD XXI 234. [95] StAD XXI 278, XXI 283.

Socials from the organization, a move calculated to appease the Jewish electorate. (In fact, the party later dissociated itself entirely from the Stöcker movement.)[96]

The liberal press supported this stance. A *Düsseldorfer Zeitung* report on a meeting of the *Deutschnationaler Wahlausschuss* in September 1911 criticized the party's rampant anti-Semitism: 'The angry opposition which followed his very cautious attempt at anti-Semitism will have taught Mr Lattmann that such politics won't win him friends in our community.'[97] The paper further praised a Jewish teacher for speaking out against the anti-Semitic content of Lattmann's address. Likewise, an editorial on the 1912 Reichstag elections gloated over anti-Semitism's defeat at the polls: 'One learns to believe in a higher justice again when one sees how the election whirlwind [*Wahlwind*] has wreaked havoc among the reactionary demagogues.'[98]

The *Düsseldorfer Zeitung*'s treatment of the Beilis trial in 1913 closely resembles that of left liberal organs in Nuremberg. Contrasting artistic and technological progress with lingering superstitions, the paper reproached the Conservatives for deliberately spreading the myth of ritual murder, ending with an appeal to combat Conservative attempts to discriminate against the Jews: 'To combat prejudice and to repudiate unproved assertions and suspicions against a whole group of people [*Menschenklasse*] has always been a cultural duty [*Kulturpflicht*] and follows from the German way and from German conscientiousness.'[99] In short, while we find left liberalism and the *Liberale Vereinigung* on opposite ends of the Düsseldorf political spectrum,[100] both groups denounced anti-Semitism whenever they commented on the phenomenon.

Unfortunately, the Düsseldorf archives contain no material on the *Mittelstandsvereinigung* relevant to our discussion. The so-called Düsseldorf section broke away from the national movement in 1909, because the latter had tried to include in its membership social groups usually referred to as the 'new middle class'. Against this, the Düsseldorf section was determined to restrict membership of its organization to artisans and retailers only.[101] Yet this did not mean that the Düsseldorf *Mittelstandsvereinigung* was more conservative than other chapters in

---

[96] Hennecke, *Vereinigung*, 122; Hüttenberger, *Düsseldorf*, 168.

[97] DZ, 14.9.1911 (Abend) 'Städtische Nachrichten'.

[98] Ibid., 14.1.1912 'Das Wahlergebnis'.

[99] Ibid., 12.10.1913 (Morgen) 'Die Konservativen und der Ritualmord'.

[100] Kussmann, *Parteiensystem*, 54.

[101] R. Gellately, *The Politics of Economic Despair: Shopkeepers and German Politics 1890–1914* (London, 1974), 26.

the country.[102] In a piece on the history of the German *Mittelstand* movement, for example, the *Mitteilungen* described the Düsseldorf section as
liberal, refusing to cooperate with the anti-Jewish *Deutschnationaler
Handlungsgehilfen-Verband*,[103] and taking a neutral stance on religious
matters.[104] The accuracy of this assertion was further demonstrated in a
Westdeutsche Mittelstands-Zeitung article of 4 October 1913, which castigated the chairman of the *Reichsdeutscher Mittelstandsverband*, Eberle, for
currying favour with 'reactionary' attempts to redefine Germany along
the lines of a Christian as opposed to a 'materialistic' state. This, the paper
argued, would necessarily lead to anti-Semitism: 'Of course we do not
wish to show more consideration for these members [the Jews] than for
others; we only wish to prevent differences from arising in the economic
interest group between religions and denominations and wish for things
and people to be considered in the light of absolute and natural equality.'[105] Despite scant documentary evidence, the above quotations show
that the Düsseldorf *Mittelstandsvereinigung*, unlike its Nuremberg counterpart, eschewed anti-Semitism. In our discussion of Weimar politics we
shall consider whether this distinction carried over into the 'middle-class
agitation' of the *Wirtschaftspartei.*

Political conservatism seems to have had little impact in Düsseldorf.[106]
Not only was the Agrarian League weak and insignificant,[107] but the
combined efforts of the Conservatives, Free Conservatives, Christian
Socials, and agrarians produced meagre results in the area.[108] Moreover,
the importance of the Pan-German League need not have affected the

---

[102] See the speech by the chairman of Düsseldorf's *Mittelstandsvereinigung*, Stocky, at the
second general meeting in November 1909: StAD XXIII 1045: 'Now the German
Mittelstand is divided over the approach to the Hansabund. Some show enthusiasm, others
fight the organization to the bitter end. And yet the only right thing to do is to remain
neutral.'

[103] The city archive contains no material on the local *DHV*. For the Nuremberg organization, see StAN E6 261 and StAN C7/V VP 2631. The sources in the latter archive,
however, are not very helpful either.

[104] *Mitteilungen*, 5.7.1911, 100–2 'Die Mittelstandsbewegung'. See D. Stegmann, *Die
Erben Bismarcks. Parteien und Verbände in der Spätphase des Wilhelminischen Deutschlands.
Sammlungspolitik 1897–1918* (Cologne and Berlin, 1970), 46: 'the so-called Düsseldorf
section . . . also renounced anti-Semitism in its programme.' See Gellately, *Despair*, 162:
'The party-political activity of the DMV [*Deutsche Mittelstandsvereinigung*] and especially its
anti-Semitism were regarded by the Düsseldorf organization as "mistakes".'

[105] *Westdeutsche Mittelstands-Zeitung*, 4.10.1913 'Ein Wort zur Klarstellung'.

[106] Between 1871 and 1912, Conservatives were unable to attain more than 3.0 per cent
of the votes cast at Reichstag elections. H. Prokasky and K. Füllner (eds.), *Dokumentation
zur Geschichte der Stadt Düsseldorf. Düsseldorf 1850–1914. Das Zeitalter der Industrialisierung*
(Düsseldorf, no date), 447–8.

[107] HStAD Reg. Düss. 15959, 31–58.

[108] J. Retallack, *Notables of the Right. The Conservative Party and Political Mobilization
in Germany 1876–1918* (London, 1988), 199–200.

relative strength of anti-Jewish traditions. In Düsseldorf, where the pressure group was influential,[109] the national leadership's 'new' policy on the 'Jewish question' was rejected.[110] The link between the League and Jew-hatred after the war did not exist everywhere,[111] a fact that should be kept in mind when evaluating the importance of pressure groups in German politics.

The Protestant weekly in Düsseldorf discussed the 'Jewish question' far more frequently than its Nuremberg counterpart. (Between 1910 and the Revolution the paper focused on the issue seventeen times, if one excludes articles on purely religious themes or biblical exegesis.) Most of the time, Jews were mentioned in connection with 'modern life'; only thrice did the paper reflect on the future of the Protestant mission and its appeal to the Jews.

Two of these articles asked Düsseldorf's Protestants 'to show the Israelites . . . through word and deed the path to Christ'.[112] In a May 1910 meeting of the *Frauenmissionsverein für Israel*, moreover, missionary Dermer noted how important ancient Judaism was for the Church, explaining that Christianity emerged as 'the tree's crown whose trunk was already planted in Old Testament Israel'.[113] Yet there were also signs that Protestants, upon realizing the difficulty of their work, became increasingly disgruntled; keeping hopes alive that more Jews would eventually convert to Christianity, they conveniently blamed the Jews for sticking to old habits. In a speech on 'Philosemitism, Anti-Semitism, and the Jewish Mission', for example, one pastor Wagner rejected Judeophobia as anti-Christian, but warned that this did not entail unconditional love of each and every Jew. The report ended with a brief description of the ensuing discussion: 'A few Israelites (approximately five) also joined the discussion in a moderate way, but as chairman P. Schumacher rightly emphasized in his concluding remarks, their contributions revealed pride in being Jewish. Being proud—yes, that is Jewish, the nature of Christianity is humility.'[114] Not only did the paper ignore the fact that all missionary

[109] R. Chickering, *We Men Who Feel Most German. A Cultural Study of the Pan-German League, 1886–1914* (London, 1984), 143–4.

[110] *Im deutschen Reich*, November 1912, 396, where a member of the Pan-German League distances himself from the growth of anti-Semitism in his organization by referring to the fact that the Pan-Germans in Düsseldorf and Hanover had already declared 'to have nothing in common with the politics of the new course'.

[111] U. Lohalm, *Völkischer Radikalismus. Die Geschichte des Deutschvölkischen Schutz-und Trutz-Bundes 1919–1923* (Hamburg, 1970), 23–4; P. Pulzer, *The Rise of Political Anti-Semitism in Germany and Austria* (London, 1988), 224.

[112] *Düsseldorfer Sonntagsblatt*, 27.7.1913 'Jerusalems Zerstörung-Israels Fall'.

[113] Ibid., 29.5.1910 'Unter dem Zeichen der Judenmission'.

[114] Ibid., 28.5.1911 'Unter dem Zeichen der Judenmission'.

work was based precisely on the kind of pride which Düsseldorf's Jews were being accused of, but it disclosed the growing recognition that attempts to make Jews into Christians were proving futile. After the war, Düsseldorf as well as Nuremberg Protestantism no longer considered such work worthwhile.[115]

The *Düsseldorfer Sonntagsblatt* (whatever its stance on the prospects of the Christian mission) identified the Jews before and during the war with all those unfavourable aspects of modern society which threatened the 'natural order of things'. The SPD was led by 'alien' non-Germans (Marx, Singer, Frank, Bernstein, and Luxemburg);[116] the 'anti-Christian-Jewish' press was responsible for distorting reality prior to the 1912 Reichstag elections;[117] and Frankfurt had become a 'stronghold of new Jewry [*Neujudentums*]'.[118] The paper also associated Jews with prostitution,[119] atheism,[120] and finance capital.[121]

Rudy Koshar's observation that parts of the 'Protestant bourgeoisie' feared a disturbance of the 'balance of power' in Germany's social life was undoubtedly reflected in the treatment of the 'Jewish question' by the *Düsseldorfer Sonntagsblatt*.[122] A number of articles warned against the growing influence of 'Jewish plutocracy',[123] and the Protestant weekly repeatedly reminded its readers that Jews constituted a serious threat to Christian society: 'Whoever pays attention to the signs of the time must not overlook the developments within Judaism. One talks a lot about the growing influence of Catholicism. Is the influence of Judaism through capital, the press, and the manipulation of public opinion not equally great? It happens quietly and is noticed less.'[124]

Protestant clergymen in Düsseldorf were therefore more concerned with the 'Jewish question' than their counterparts in Nuremberg, and unlike their co-religionists in business and industry, believed they had to

---

[115] See also W. Altmann, *Die Judenfrage in evangelischen und katholischen Zeitschriften zwischen 1918 und 1933* (Munich, 1971), 322–3: 'Neither respected Protestant nor respected Catholic journals felt inclined to engage in a real defense of the Jewish mission.'

[116] *SB*, 8.10.1912 'Christlich-nationale Arbeiterbewegung'.

[117] Ibid., 21.4.1912 'Die Beeinflussung der Presse'.   [118] Ibid., 25.8.1912 'Allerlei'.

[119] Ibid., 15.2.1914 'Menschen-Schacher': 'According to the international Committee Against Prostitution . . . most of these criminals [pimps] are Jews!'

[120] Ibid., 26.7.1914 'Kirchliche Chronik': 'There are a number of indications that the old hatred of the Jews against Christ is in large part responsible for the fact that many people are leaving the church.'

[121] Ibid., 19.5.1918 'Kirchliche Rundschau'.

[122] R. Koshar, *Social Life, Local Politics, and Nazism. Marburg, 1880–1935* (Chapel Hill, 1986), 6.

[123] SB, 2.9.1917 'Kirchliche Rundschau'; 17.2.1918 'Kleine Bilder vom Tage'; 21.4.1918 'Kirchliche Rundschau'.

[124] Ibid., 23.12.1917 'Kirchliche Rundschau'.

protect the hegemony of 'Protestant-German' culture from all kinds of 'dubious elements'. Rhenish Protestantism, in other words, was hardly more 'liberal' than Protestantism elsewhere, and the Jews could not count on a greater degree of tolerance from this side than from, say, National Liberals or Conservatives in Franconia.

CATHOLICISM

The Centre Party in Düsseldorf faced a formidable challenge in the SPD. Especially after the turn of the century, when the Centre became an enthusiastic proponent of agrarian tariffs, many Catholic workers turned to the Social Democratic movement, where they believed they found a critique of capitalist society directly related to their everyday experiences. The Centre Party, in turn, responded by launching massive campaigns against Social Democracy.

In the run-up to the 1911 Reichstag by-election in Düsseldorf, the Catholic press asserted that the SPD was neither patriotic nor reliable enough to lead the country. An article of 24 September called on the electorate to protect 'our . . . national city Düsseldorf from the banner of subversion', and added that the city's representatives in parliament had to remain 'German and Christian'.[125] A few months later, the SPD was again accused of destroying all that was healthy in the nation: 'This party is at the same time the deadly enemy of the nation-state, it attacks everything that is dear and holy to our German hearts; Christianity and fatherland, monarchy and army . . . Democracy marches arm in arm with Social Democracy, and in its wake progessive liberalism.'[126] Following an unprecedented SPD victory at the polls, the Catholic Centre blamed left liberalism for its alleged assistance of the Left prior to the elections: 'The liberals have managed to make the party of subversion the numerically strongest fraction in the whole Reichstag.'[127]

Rarely, however, did Düsseldorf's Centre Party employ anti-Semitic stereotypes to appeal to the electorate. A 1903 pamphlet called Social Democratic leaders 'Jews', who were 'not suitable representatives of the workers' estate'.[128] An article in the *Düsseldorfer Tageblatt* of 10 September 1911, moreover, tried to establish a connection between high finance and

[125] *Düsseldorfer Tageblatt*, 24.9.1911 'Christliche Deutsche Wähler!'
[126] *Wahl-Glocken. Beilage zum Düsseldorfer Tageblatt*, 11.1.1912. See also *DT*, 16.1.1912 'Auf zum Stichkampf!': 'The magic word "fatherland" has always had its impact in times of danger.'
[127] *DT*, 30.1.1912 'Ein roter Präsident?'
[128] StAD III 6397 'Herunter mit der Maske! Eine praktische Abrechnung mit der Sozialdemokratie.'

socialism: 'Of the 8000 shares owned by the paper [*Humanité*] 3/4 are in the hands of big capitalists, one of the big shareholders is—Rothschild.'[129]

Yet on the whole, direct references to 'Jews' were absent, even if attacks on liberalism were not free from anti-Semitic connotations whether uttered in private or at conferences. The Centre Party leader Wilhelm Marx, for example, raged against the 'un-German spirit' of the *Berliner Tageblatt*, which consisted of 'aliens who are poisoning the German people and inciting Catholics and Protestants against one another'.[130] In addition, the treatment of the Beilis trial in the *Tageblatt* could hardly be regarded as an espousal of the defendant's cause. On the contrary, the paper either remained uncommitted or remarked that the case was 'not without . . . negative overtones [*Beigeschmack*], since Jews argue that the ritual murder accusation has been invented to provoke pogroms'.[131]

During the war, Centre Party *Honoratioren* joined National Liberals and Conservatives to found the local chapter of the *Vaterlandspartei*.[132] The party organ also sharply criticized Matthias Erzberger's behaviour in the Reichstag, where the latter fought for peace and democratic reforms.[133] Political Catholicism in Düsseldorf thus embraced conservative policies between 1910 and 1918, mainly for fear of losing ground to Social Democracy. Occasionally this involved appeals to anti-Semitism, but Jew-hatred never entered the party's programme.

THE LEFT

Mary Nolan has pointed out that the SPD recruited almost entirely from the migrant element, which, unlike the city's native working class, had broken with traditional authority patterns and social relationships, as well as pre-industrial modes of existence. What is more, the comparatively 'young members, like the young leaders, were new to politics and venerated neither the established party and union organizations nor the grand old men of the movement. They were unencumbered by the vested interests and anxious conservatism that characterized older Social Democrats, and as a result were more receptive to radicalism.'[134] Finally, because workers dominated the movement, the Düsseldorf SPD 'catered exclusively to working-class interests'.[135]

---

[129] *DT*, 10.9.1911 'Zur Reichstagswahl'.   [130] *Mitteilungen*, 31.1.1912, 23.
[131] *DT*, 10.10.1913 'Ausland'.   [132] Hüttenberger, *Düsseldorf*, 251–2.
[133] W. Stump, *Geschichte und Organisation der Zentrumspartei in Düsseldorf, 1917–1933* (Düsseldorf, 1971), 18.
[134] Nolan, *Social Democracy*, 113, 121.
[135] Kussmann, *Parteiensystem*, 20; Nolan, *Social Democracy*, 102.

At least before the war, these aspects of Düsseldorf Social Democracy seem to have influenced its stance on racism. At a Lower Rhine party congress in October 1907, for example, the SPD put forward a strongly anti-colonialist resolution, which stated that 'the party congress rejects any socialist colonial policy which would base a right of "guardianship" on the differences in cultural levels among various people.'[136] Similarly, the party's approach to the problem of anti-Semitism was mainly one of opposition, and only occasionally tainted by attempts to demonstrate that conservative Jew-baiters were insincere in their attacks on the Jews.

A February 1912 article in the *Volkszeitung* castigated the anti-Semitism of the *Kreuzzeitung*, but hinted that Jew-baiting could never really take hold of the Conservative Party: 'And as for the struggle against Judaism, there are too many conservative Junkers whose mothers or wives are wealthy Jewesses for there to be no restraining elements.'[137] Likewise, after reporting on the rabid anti-Semitism prevalent at a *Bund der Landwirte* meeting in Berlin, the paper concluded: 'In all these hateful remarks one can detect something like yearning for love [*Liebessehnsucht*], similar to the statement supposedly made by a Viennese anti-Semitic leader: "Our business can only revive if a thrifty Jew assumes control of the matter." '[138] To be sure, such remarks were intended to discredit conservatism's anti-Semitic leaders, but they probably had a desensitizing effect on Social Democratic supporters, who may have gained the impression that Jew-baiting was merely a tactical device to bolster one's position.

By and large, however, the Düsseldorf SPD was adamant in its rejection of anti-Semitism. German conservatives were 'worthy cousins of the Russian reactionaries',[139] and the Beilis trial was further proof of lingering religious fanaticism in the Russian Empire: 'Not an individual fate is decided here, a whole people's fate is threatened . . . From the darkest Middle Ages the ritual murder accusation was recalled to life so as to incite the fanatic mobs even more against the Jews.'[140]

To sum up: Social Democrats repeatedly poured moral indignation on anti-Semitic politicians. Although the Düsseldorf SPD made statements to the effect that conservative Jew-baiting was nothing but rhetoric, the party never used anti-Jewish imagery to appeal to its constituency.

[136] Nolan, *Social Democracy*, 181.
[137] *VZ*, 2.2.1912 'Die Junker als Radauantisemiten'.
[138] Ibid., 20.2.1912 'Kriegsrat der Geschlagenen'.   [139] Ibid., 7.2.1912.
[140] Ibid., 13.10.1913; see also ibid., 18.10.1913 'Zur Kulturschmach in Kiew' and 29.10.1913 'Der Blutprozeß zu Kiew'.

SUMMARY

Seldom did the parties and organizations examined above devote their time to the 'Jewish question'. Yet what they wrote or said on the issue was read and discussed by the public, and this in turn determined how the less articulate saw or judged the respective positions taken by opinion leaders in both cities. To be sure, the historian can never settle the exact interplay between older traditions, recent developments, and the impact of outside forces on the daily lives of the people. But to discover why certain regions were more likely to support anti-Semitism we need to move beyond 'legends' and 'reputations'. While quantitative data will tell us what we already know, namely that the 'Jewish question' was never all-important to most Germans, qualitative data will show how it was more important to some than to others.

If we compare Düsseldorf and Nuremberg in the years 1910–18, a number of striking differences appear. First, although political conservatism was weak in both cities, Nuremberg's Catholics and middle-class apologists held anti-modernist views, of which anti-Semitism was an integral part. In Düsseldorf, by contrast, Catholics limited their attacks to Social Democracy and liberalism, without succumbing to all-out anti-Semitism, while the *Mittelstandsvereinigung* went so far as to criticize the movement's national leader for his anti-Jewish insinuations. National Liberalism, it seems, was more 'national' in Nuremberg than liberal, which led to occasional gibes against representatives of 'Jewish' culture. In Düsseldorf, neither National Liberals nor Progressives resorted to anti-Semitism, the former because they needed Jewish votes and could overlook the rise of Social Democracy, the latter because they catered to a numerically insignificant electorate which renounced Jew-hatred. The Protestant Church in Nuremberg was much less concerned with the 'Jewish question' than its counterpart in Düsseldorf. Why this is so we cannot really say, but whatever the reasons, 'orthodox Lutheranism' was never the monolithic block its detractors wish to portray.

Finally, the SPD in Düsseldorf was much more outspoken in its rejection of racism than socialists in Nuremberg, a fact we may attribute to the radicalism of the former and to the influence of party leaders on the latter. However, as is true for all of the above statements, much remains guesswork, and the overall nature of our material makes it difficult to establish causal connections between, say, reformism and anti-Semitism, since moderation could have existed without and need not have led to Jew-hatred.

If we analyse the 'meaning' accorded to the 'Jewish question' in this period, we can conclude that those who employed anti-Semitic imagery usually associated the Jews with forces threatening 'tradition': the SPD, left liberalism, the press, finance capital, cultural innovation; whereas those who opposed anti-Semitism did so because they favoured 'progress' and fought 'reaction'. Whatever the influence of such organizations as the Agrarian League and the DHV, therefore, it was not very visible in either city, where the nature of anti-Semitism usually remained conservative and where right-wing politics lay embedded within the context of moderation.[141] The terms of the debate, in other words, were still very much familiar ones—the 'Left' versus the 'Right'—and it was the war and its aftermath which were to bring about a qualitative and quantitative change in this respect.

[141] The very fact that evidence is hard to come by for this period suggests that anti-Semitism was never regarded as crucial for most parties and organizations under review. Without the war and its disruptions, therefore, the 'Jewish question' may have occasionally assumed a character of importance, never becoming the deadly serious matter it did after 1918.

3
Floodgates opened
1918–1921

Man kaufe nicht bei Juden, man lese nichts von Juden
Geschriebenes, man gehe nicht in ein jüdisches Theaterstück und
nehme keinen jüdischen Arzt und Rechtsanwalt. Wenn das alle 60
Millionen Deutschen täten, ja, wenn es nur diejenigen täten, die am
liebsten jeden Tag einen Juden totschlügen, dann wäre die jüdische
Gefahr schon gebannt.

DNVP Statement

There is widespread agreement that the war and its effects had an enormous impact on German society, and that its outcome marked 'the great
discontinuity in modern German history that brought to the fore the more
negative and destructive components of its political culture at the expense
of its more promising ones'.[1] Both the civilian and military population had
become so brutalized that the years following 1918 were marked by a
quantitative and qualitative shift in the nation's political discourse.[2] As
Richard Bessel has argued, political struggle 'took on a new meaning in
the wake of the First World War, as violence left its mark on almost
all aspects of civil society. A line had been crossed: physical violence
had become part of the political armoury which, increasingly, Germans

[1] G. D. Feldmann, *Army, Industry, and Labor in Germany, 1914–1918* (Oxford, 1992),
XV.
[2] See G. L. Mosse, *Fallen Soldiers. Reshaping the Memory of the World Wars* (Oxford,
1990), 172: 'The dehumanization of the enemy was one of the most fateful consequences
of this process of brutalization.' P. Fussell, *The Great War and Modern Memory* (London,
1975), 79:

The physical confrontation between 'us' and 'them' is an obvious figure of gross dichotomy.
But less predictably the mode of gross dichotomy came to dominate perception and expres-
sion elsewhere, encouraging finally what we can call the modern versus habit: one thing
opposed to another, not with some Hegelian hope of synthesis involving a dissolution of both
extremes (that would suggest a 'negotiated peace,' which is anathema), but with a sense that
one of the poles embodies so wicked a deficiency or flaw or perversion that its total submis-
sion is called for.

See also N. Elias, *Studien über die Deutschen. Machtkämpfe und Habitusentwicklung im 19. und
20. Jahrhundert* (Frankfurt, 1989), 232 n. 6.

habitually employed.'[3] Even though, as we have seen in the previous chapter, extreme groups had already tried to destabilize society by employing uncompromising language before the war, the period 1914–18 accelerated and exacerbated existing tensions in 'an abrupt way', so that various sources of legitimacy dissolved too quickly for there to emerge adequate alternatives at a time of widespread and profound disorientation.[4] Thus, while before the war 'crisis' meant for many radical nationalists a disenchantment with the way 'things were going', after the war 'the term "crisis" became an understatement; much broader social strata were (now) affected, and the threat was not to their claims to embody culture or authority, but rather to their very social existence'.[5]

The events surrounding the Revolution also gave rise to questions about Jews in prominent positions of leadership.[6] If before 1914 complaints had centred on 'Jewish influence' in the media or the arts, in the period after 1918 it was far easier to preserve, invent, and inculcate anti-Semitic stereotypes. Names like Luxemburg, Eisner, Toller, Preuß, and Rathenau, among others, testified to anti-Semitic suspicions. Beyond this, earlier fears and hints concerning Jewish 'unreliability', sentiments which had become more widespread as the war progressed, now found growing support among disillusioned Germans of all stripes. For many Germans it was tempting to replace war-time nationalism with a post-war anti-Semitism, not least because feelings of aggression and the desire for cohesion could not be so easily discarded.

Because the post-war era was also characterized by higher levels of violence, less respect for traditional forms of authority, and a general lack of natural purpose and direction,[7] propaganda against the Jews could more easily be disseminated and later accepted. Whereas earlier the radical anti-Semites had occupied marginal positions in society, after the war they became respected members in the German polity.[8] In short, the context of moderation prevailing before the war was now deprived of its basis, and

[3] R. Bessel, *Germany after the First World War* (Oxford, 1993), 262.

[4] W. Mommsen, 'Der Erste Weltkrieg und die Krise Europas', in: G. Hirschfeld and G. Krumeich, *Keiner fühlt sich hier als Mensch . . . : Erlebnis und Wirkung des Ersten Weltkriegs* (Essen, 1993), 30.

[5] R. Chickering, *We Men Who Feel Most German. A Cultural Study of the Pan-German League, 1886–1914* (London, 1984), 300.

[6] On Jews in the Revolution, see W. T. Angress, 'Juden im politischen Leben der Revolutionszeit', in: W. E. Mosse and A. Paucker (eds), *Deutsches Judentum in Krieg und Revolution 1916–1923* (Tübingen, 1971).

[7] Fussell, *Great War*, 270: 'The atmosphere of emergency and the proximity of violence will always promote a relaxing of inhibition ending in a special hedonism and lasciviousness.' Elias, *Studien*, 49.

[8] D. L. Niewyk, 'Solving the "Jewish Problem": Continuity and Change in German Antisemitism, 1871–1945', in: *LBIY* (1990), 369.

collaped under the strains of a radically new situation. To see how these developments affected different localities in the country, let us turn to a discussion of Düsseldorf and Nuremberg between 1918 and 1921.

NUREMBERG

Unusual as this may seem, Kurt Eisner, the leader of the Bavarian Revolution, enjoyed enormous prestige during the first few weeks of November 1918: 'He was personally unknown, but "the revolution" was everywhere accepted. All of the major political groups in Bavaria were quick to align themselves "on the basis of the facts," even though the facts were still only vaguely apparent.'[9] Bavarians in general, and the Munich population in particular, had experienced an SPD that was reformist rather than radical, and therefore they expected the new rulers to install democratic policies that eschewed radicalism and violence. Yet in the eyes of most Bavarians the actions taken by the Eisner regime, however moderate in comparison with revolutionary movements elsewhere, assumed forms that were frightening to say the least.[10] The past weakness of orthodox Marxism in Bavarian politics made the upheaval look all the more threatening, and reasons were sought to account for the unbelievable fact that a radical Jewish journalist had apparently overthrown the old and stable Wittelsbach monarchy.[11]

It was above all Eisner's reluctance to accept the unpopularity of his leadership, as well as his attempt to document German responsibility for the outbreak of the war, that helped the *völkisch* cause in 1918/19. Even if Eisner's revelations had little or no impact on the course of the Versailles Conference, his behaviour gave rise to public fury: 'Disappointed nationalist and patriotic liberals had discovered in Eisner a scapegoat, even the "Father of the shameful Versailles Peace Treaty".'[12] Since many considered Eisner guilty of treason rather than insurrection, anti-Semites could point to his Jewish origin and assert that every Jew in Germany was unreliable, potentially dangerous, and ultimately incapable of grasping 'German' sensibilities.

---

[9] A. Mitchell, *Revolution in Bavaria 1918–1919. The Eisner Regime and the Soviet Republic* (Princeton, 1965), 109.

[10] A. J. Nicholls, 'Hitler and the Bavarian Background to National Socialism', in: E. Matthias and A. J. Nicholls (eds), *German Democracy and the Triumph of Hitler. Essays in Recent German History* (London, 1971), 104–5.

[11] Ibid., 107.

[12] F. Wiesemann, 'Kurt Eisner. Studie zu seiner politischen Biographie', in: K. Bosl (ed.), *Bayern im Umbruch. Die Revolution von 1918. Ihre Voraussetzungen, ihr Verlauf und ihre Folgen* (Munich, 1969), 411. For another view on Eisner, see F. Schade, *Kurt Eisner und die bayerische Sozialdemokratie* (Hanover, 1961). Eisner hailed from Berlin. He was neither a 'Galician' Jew nor was his real name 'Kosmanowski', as the canard had it.

The Revolution was greeted in Nuremberg with some enthusiasm, and resistance to the developments of late 1918 was virtually absent.[13] Gessler's tendency to favour cooperation over confrontation helped to prevent the more radical sections of the population from gaining ground. The administration agreed to work with the newly constituted workers' and soldiers' councils, and in the first few weeks after the Revolution Nuremberg witnessed a relatively smooth transition to democracy. The elections to the National Assembly in January 1919, moreover, reflected the belief of the electorate that moderate politics was in their best interest. Winning more than 51 per cent, the MSPD achieved an absolute majority; the party's main rival on the Left, the Independent Socialists, received only 7.5 per cent. Nearly 30 per cent went to the left liberals, leaving the Catholic BVP with just over 9 per cent of all votes cast.[14]

That same month, however, saw the first instances of political violence since the Revolution. The Communist uprising led to the occupation of the *Fränkische Tagespost* building, and in mid-February the offices of the *Fränkischer Kurier*, as well as the *Deutschhaus* barracks, seat of the deputy high command of Army Corps III, were stormed by demonstrators supporting the USPD. The brief existence of the Bavarian Soviet Republic resulted in further violence in Nuremberg, culminating in a clash between Spartacists and the army on 26 April, which killed five and wounded ten.[15]

Nevertheless, we must be careful not to overestimate the importance of these events; Nuremberg was not Munich. The workers' and soldiers' councils rejected a motion calling for the proclamation of a soviet republic in Nuremberg,[16] and on the whole the city's workers followed a less radical course than revolutionaries elsewhere: 'In Nuremberg the independent workers are more peaceful and more sensible than the workers of the majority party here [Munich]. The reason is that Nuremberg has no bohemian society, no Schwabing.'[17] Nuremberg experienced occasional outbreaks of violence, but in comparison with other cities the number of casualties and the extent of suffering were low. By April, moreover, unemployment declined and food shortages were kept to a minimum.[18] Perhaps it was the previous absence of any form of radicalism that

[13] K.-D. Schwarz, *Weltkrieg und Revolution in Nürnberg. Ein Beitrag zur Geschichte der deutschen Arbeiterbewegung* (Stuttgart, 1971), 282.

[14] E. C. Reiche, *The Development of the SA in Nürnberg, 1922–1934* (Cambridge, 1986), 8–9.

[15] Schwarz, *Weltkrieg*, 323.   [16] Ibid., 322.

[17] J. Hofmiller, *Revolutionstagebuch* (Leipzig, 1938), 167, quoted in Schwarz, *Weltkrieg*, 324.

[18] Schwarz, *Weltkrieg*, 324.

accounted for much of the hostility of those who had been used to the stability of a city run by reformist liberals. The remainder of this section will examine the effects this disappointment with the Revolution had on the 'Jewish question'.

'PROTESTANT BOURGEOISIE'

The *Fränkischer Kurier*, Nuremberg's most influential 'bourgeois' newspaper, generally welcomed the Revolution and indicated some willingness to support the Eisner government.[19] At the same time, however, the paper asked the provisional regime for a guarantee 'that the statements by the workers' and soldiers' councils do not apply to Bavaria . . . Bavarian Social Democracy . . . cannot want radical alien [*landfremde*] elements to destroy all that the party has accomplished in many years of hard work.'[20] Ten days later, the *Kurier* demanded Eisner's resignation, because he was seen as lacking the leadership qualities necessary to head the Bavarian state: 'Just as someone who can read the Bible or the Talmud in the original need not have sufficient qualities to be a great politician, so too Eisner lacks what it takes to lead a state like Bavaria in these fateful times.'[21] We see then that a respected daily, whose managing director was a founding member of the local *Verein zur Abwehr des Antisemitismus*,[22] could claim that Eisner was able to read Hebrew without having to fear being labelled anti-Semitic. A strange paradox resulted from this. Language crept into the press that at first appeared harmless and later assumed forms of vilification and hatred.

The *Kurier* was perhaps unaware of this, for it continued to castigate intolerance and anti-Semitism. For example, in an article of 8 January 1919 entitled 'Why do I vote for the candidate of the German People's Party?' the paper commented: 'The German People's Party stands for absolute tolerance; it repudiates attempts to blame a great community for the faults of a few . . . We therefore reject and condemn anti-Semitic propaganda.'[23]

The paradox, in fact, involved the very nature of the *Kurier* itself. When USPD-led workers occupied the newspaper's headquarters in mid-February, onlookers belonging to the 'bourgeoisie' (*Bürgerstande*)

---

[19] See, for example, *FK*, 13.11.1918 (Abend) 'Zur neuen Lage'.
[20] Ibid., 20.11.1918 (Abend) 'Der Kampf um das freie Wort'.
[21] Ibid., 30.11.1918 (Morgen) 'Bayern in Gefahr?'   [22] *Mitteilungen*, 12.6.1918, 56.
[23] See also *FK*, 10.1.1919 (Morgen) 'Wider Rassen- und Glaubenhaß', in which the *FK* cites a leaflet by the *Abwehrverein* responding to accusations that the Jews had caused war and revolution. The *Deutsche Volkspartei in Bayern* was the Bavarian equivalent of the DDP.

remarked that the 'Jew paper' deserved such treatment.[24] The *Kurier* was judged in the light of its pre-war readership, as well as its support of left liberalism; but times had changed, and the paper had to face the problem of anti-Semitism from a new angle. While carrying on with its fight against Jew-hatred, the *Kurier* still spoke of 'the Levine's, Mühsam's, Landauer's, Toller's and other alien [*volks- und landfremden*] literary figures',[25] knowing full well that this implied more than just a particularistic opinion on the 'non-Bavarian' leadership of the Revolution.

By contrast, the radical liberal *Nürnberger Anzeiger* and the more moderate *Nürnberger Zeitung* condemned Eisner without ever referring to his background.[26] While the *Anzeiger* refrained from commenting on anti-Semitism in this period (a fact that shows how fearful left liberals and Jews were of attracting too much attention in this regard), the *Nürnberger Zeitung* occasionally warned against the dangers of *völkisch* racism.[27] Both newspapers, however, agreed that the credibility of the newly founded *Deutsche Volkspartei in Bayern* was being threatened by former *Vaterlandspartei* members and other 'conservative elements' who hoped to influence the policies of the then largest 'bourgeois' party in Nuremberg. The *Anzeiger* reminded the *Fränkischer Kurier* of this when it wrote: 'Is the "F.K." really so naïve as to believe that a democratic party . . . could emerge from a mixture of such heterogeneous elements as National Liberals, Progressives, and members of the Fatherland Party?'[28] In other words, it seemed that the *Kurier* was willing to accommodate certain aspects of German politics, which, according to the other liberal papers in Nuremberg, seriously undermined the prospect of a truly liberal and democratic party taking root in post-war Bavaria.

While the growing resonance of anti-Semitism troubled many contemporaries in the immediate post-war months, the real apogee of Jew-baiting occurred in 1919/20. Early in 1919 the former *Vaterlandspartei* member, Carl Maerz, founded the local *Deutschvölkischer Schutz- und Trutz-Bund*,[29] and in the following weeks huge amounts of anti-Semitic propa-

[24] *FK*, 18.2.1919 (Abend) 'Die Ausschreitungen gegen den "Fränk. Kurier".'

[25] Ibid., 17.3.1919 (Abend) 'Die Münchener Literaten-Diktatur soll bleiben'. On the other hand we must remember that Bavarians dismissed 'foreigners' of all sorts. See Julie Meyer Frank, 'Erinnerungen an meine Schulzeit', in: H. Lamm, *Von Juden in München. Ein Gedenkbuch* (Munich, 1958), 158. See also the contribution by Moritz Julius Bonn, 'Meine Beziehungen zu München', 173–4.

[26] See, for example, *NAZ*, 9.12.1918 'Wahnsinnspolitik an der Isar' and *NZ*, 28.11.1918 'Torheiten'.

[27] See, for example, *NZ*, 24.11.1918 'Vorsicht!'

[28] *NZ*, 22.11.1918 'Vorsicht!'; *NAZ*, 22.11.1918 'In Abwehr!'

[29] Schwarz, *Weltkrieg*, 326–7.

ganda material flooded the streets of Nuremberg.[30] A climax was reached in the autumn of that year when the Jewish community recommended 'that conspicious behaviour be avoided on the streets and that before services no one ought to promenade in front of the synagogue or on the streets.'[31] A police report of November 1919 described the charged atmosphere between Jews and Gentiles in similar terms: 'always and everywhere, on the street, in shops and restaurants, and on the train one can hear angry comments about the Jews.'[32]

It was the police, however, that not only ignored Jewish fears but contributed to the general feeling of helplessness and isolation among Nuremberg's Jews. Although the authorities registered that anti-Semitism was everywhere on the rise,[33] they tended to accept the racist argument that 'Germans' and 'Jews' were two separate entities:

> The most important reasons for the anti-Jewish atmosphere spreading through the *Volk* lie very deep, they are rooted in the never quite to be bridged racial difference [*Rassengegensatz*] which separates the Jewish tribe [*Stamm*] from our people [*Volk*] . . . a difference which must lead naturally to an inborn mistrust of the local population against their alien [*stammesfremden*] fellow citizens.[34]

The police, in other words, understood the anti-Semites so well precisely because they accepted the underlying 'reasons' for the *völkisch* agitation after the war. Tragically, this was going to have considerable influence on the reactions to Julius Streicher and the rise of National Socialism in the later years of the Republic.

The *Fränkischer Kurier*'s conflicting views on the 'Jewish question' persisted in 1920/1. On the one hand, the paper protested against the

[30] R. Hambrecht, *Der Aufstieg der NSDAP in Mittel- und Oberfranken (1925–1933)* (Nuremberg, 1976), 18–19. See also the *Abwehrverein*'s statement in the 19.1.1919 morning edition of the *FK*: 'In the past few weeks malicious agitators have tried to disrupt and undermine religious peace in our home town. So far all denominations have lived together in peace and harmony, and have contributed to the common good. Now leaflets and special newspapers of a truly vile nature are being distributed.' In 1920 the *Schutz- und Trutz-Bund* produced 7.6 million leaflets, 4.8 million handbills, and 7.9 million stickers. See U. Lohalm, *Völkischer Radikalismus. Die Geschichte des Deutschvölkischen Schutz- und Trutz-Bundes 1919–1923* (Hamburg, 1970), 123.

[31] *Protokollbuch der Israelitischen Gemeinde*, IV, 7.11.1919, 97–8.

[32] BStAN Rep. 218/1 I Nr 332 Wochenbericht Nr 1124. For rural areas, see BHStA Abt.I MK 19290, 16.9.1919 'Über Stimmungen und Wünsche bäuerlichen [*sic*] Kreisen [*sic*] Frankens': 'One is of the opinion that local organizations and Jewish merchants make all the money and that the peasant gets nothing.'

[33] NSDAP Hauptarchiv Reel 64, Folder 1477 'Auszug aus dem Bericht der Polizeistelle für Nordbayern' of 17.1.1920: 'The anti-Semitic movement is growing by the hour. In almost every meeting, whether organized by the unemployed, by war veterans and invalids, by leftist or rightest parties, one hears agitated and resentful shouts against Judah.'

[34] BStAN Rep. 218/1 I Nr 332 Wochenbericht Nr 1124, 21.11.1919. For further examples of anti-Semitism in the police, see Nr 336 Allgeminer Bericht Nr 41/1921, 5 and Allgemeiner Bericht Nr 31/1921, 2.

disruption of a DDP meeting by 'German-*völkisch* intrigues',[35] on the other, it employed anti-Semitic imagery when it condemned 'socialist terror'.[36] Both belonged to the inventory of 'bourgeois' respectability: the rejection of *Radauantisemitismus* was seen as imperative to 'peace and order and Germany's recovery', the attack on the east European 'plague' as a matter of national self-defence.

The effects of the Kapp Putsch possibly heightened the sense of disappointment with the course of German history found among members of the 'Protestant bourgeoisie'.[37] The general strike called in response to the Putsch lasted longer than elsewhere. More important, however, clashes between radical strikers and the army under the command of captain Heiß caused the deaths of over twenty insurgents and bystanders. The events of 15–17 March 1920 therefore led to a general hardening of positions: while for many workers the strike had not yielded any tangible results, the Right, but also the more moderate *Fränkischer Kurier*, was furious over Mayor Luppe's attempts to integrate socialists into the Civil Guard so as to prevent further violence.

Even though the *Fränkischer Kurier* still supported the DDP in this period, it was slowly drifting towards a more conservative line, following the general swing to the right after the June 1920 elections. A former employee of the newspaper noted this development with particular reference to the problem of anti-Semitism:

Chief editor Thomsen's attempts to curb anti-Semitism proved ineffective and his endeavour to act as a restraining element in debates on the 'Jewish question' was equally unsuccessful; although registered by the public, his efforts were hardly acknowledged with a gentle smile, as when in one of his few articles he somewhat cautiously included the sentence: 'The Jews weren't responsible for World War One!'[38]

Armin Groß's comments suggest that the *Kurier* was never quite sure how to respond to Jew-baiting, a fact we need to discuss later in relation to the paper's portrayal of National Socialism.

As we saw above, the other liberal organs in Nuremberg criticized the *Fränkischer Kurier* for wanting to be all things to all people. Ironically, the DDP used similar language in this period, at a time when the party was

[35] *FK*, 21.9.1920.
[36] Ibid., 20.5.1920 (Morgen) 'Sozialistischer Terror oder Bürgerblock?': 'Out of this emerged black marketeering and usury, supported by the revolutionary East Galician rabble [*Gesindel*], whose expulsion was rejected mainly by the socialist leadership.'
[37] The following is based on Reiche, *Development*, 13 and H. Hanschel, *Oberbürgermeister Hermann Luppe. Nürnberger Kommunalpolitik in der Weimarer Republik* (Nuremberg, 1977), 136–43.
[38] A. Groß, *Glück und Elend des 'Frankischen Kuriers'* (Nuremberg, 1967), 22.

still in a powerful position *vis-à-vis* its main political rivals. Prior to the January 1919 Reichstag elections, for example, the DDP/*Bauernbund* list printed an appeal in which it denounced the 'aliens' (*Fremdlinge*) ruling Bavaria;[39] a parallel address in the *Nürnberger Zeitung* of 11 January voiced dismay over the fact that 'a radical, confused dreamer [*Phantast*], a foreigner has placed himself at the head of the government.' It may be that the Democratic Party was forced to make concessions to its diverse constituency, but it is equally possible that the party, perhaps unwittingly, adopted terms that were becoming increasingly common at the time.

The DDP eventually lost many of its members to other, more conservative parties. The National Liberals, for instance, who had never attracted much support before the war and only reluctantly joined the DDP following the collapse of the Empire, now decided to form a People's Party that distinguished between 'Bavarian democracy' and the 'democracy of the *Frankfurter Zeitung*'.[40] The Nuremberg leader of the DVP, Hans Sachs, clarified this point at a meeting in Fürth: 'Regarding the "Jewish question" his party is concerned that one professes one's faith in the idea of a German state and not in that of an international citizenry.'[41]

It is very likely that from an early period onward support for the DDP dwindled rapidly. Rudolf Bing regarded this development as inevitable, given the party's erstwhile role as a place of hiding for compromised nationalists, and Hermann Luppe sketched the process very graphically in his later recollections: 'First industry withdrew [its support], . . . then the factory-owners Heinrichsen and Schmidt, finally the national-liberal intelligensia.'[42] It remains to be seen whether this decline enabled the Democrats to launch an uncompromising attack on anti-Semitism—now that they were unencumbered by reactionary ties—or whether they rather chose to avoid the topic so as not to be labelled a *Judenpartei*.

Unfortunately, little material exists on the *Mittelstandsvereinigung* for this period. In the 1919 elections it joined the *Bayerische Mittelpartei* (DNVP) list,[43] only to become the Nuremberg *Wirtschaftspartei* some

---

[39] StAN *Stadtchronik* 1919, p. 417 'Aufruf'.

[40] *NBZ*, 15.5.1920 'Nürnberger Nachrichten'.

[41] Ibid., 5.6.1920 'Fürther Nachrichten'. The party, its leader's pronouncements notwithstanding, seems to have attracted anti-Semites. See the *NAZ* of 5.6.1920 'Zur Wahlkundgebung': 'Later then I found anti-Semitic handbills of the DVP pasted on buildings and shop windows.' On the DVP in Bavaria, see Lohalm, *Völkischer Radikalismus*, 199: 'The German People's Party . . . was also not completely immune to anti-Semitic propaganda. This was especially the case in Bavaria.'

[42] StAN F5 QNG 494: R. Bing, *Mein Leben in Deutschland vor und nach dem 30. Januar* (no date), 30: 'In the end the Democratic Party consisted of a handful of loyal followers. Its voters were mainly Jews.' H. Luppe, *Mein Leben* (Nuremberg, 1977), 145.

[43] Hanschel, *Luppe*, 33.

time later. We do have, however, three articles in the *Süddeutsche Mittelstandszeitung* of May and June 1920—right before the Reichstag elections—which indicate a continuation of pre-war opinions on the 'Jewish question'.

The DDP, for example, was dismissed as 'the representative of money [*Geldmächte*], especially of wholesale trade, the department stores and large banks, and thus not suited for the man in the street. At the same time the party is international in nature, even if for appearance sake it calls itself German.'[44] Socialization, furthermore, would leave Germans as 'an object of exploitation by unscrupulous Jewry and big business'.[45] Finally, one day before the elections, voters were reminded once again that the Democratic Party was in the hands of Jews and high finance.[46]

The *Mittelpartei*, by contrast, which was founded on 10 December 1918 in the *Lehrerheim* of Nuremberg, represented the most right-wing elements of the 'Protestant bourgeoisie': 'Aside from the Bavarian Agrarian League founding members included the Middle Franconian Farmers' League, the *Völkisch Schutzbund*, the Nürnberg *Mittelstandsvereinigung*, Bavarian Conservatives, the *Reichspartei*, and a number of university professors from Erlangen.'[47] Anti-Semitism, moreover, became an integral part of the party's programme.

For example, the *Bayerischer Volksfreund* time and again pointed to the inherent differences between 'Germans' and 'Jews.' In a leading article of April 1919 on 'Anti-Semitism and Jew-baiting', the paper argued that the former was 'not a backward principle but for us Germans and Christians a necessary defence and even a moral duty [*sittliche Pflicht*]!' The party organ also suggested that the CV was not made up of German citizens 'who are merely of the Jewish persuasion but of Jewish citizens, that is, citizens of the international Jewish state who happen to carry a German name! Germandom and Jewry are mutually exclusive [*schließen sich gegenseitig aus*], like water and fire.'[48] In addition, the Jews were held responsible for causing Germany's defeat in the First World War,[49] and

---

[44] *Süddeutsche Mittelstanszeitung*, 8.5.1920 'Ist eine neue Partei notwendig?'

[45] Ibid., 24.5.1920 'An unsere Landtagswähler!'

[46] Ibid., 5.6.1920 'An den gesamten Mittelstand!'

[47] W. Liebe, *Die Deutschnationale Volkspartei 1918–1924* (Düsseldorf, 1956), 40. See also H. Fenske, *Konservatismus und Rechtsradikalismus in Bayern nach 1918* (Bad Homburg, 1969), 68–73.

[48] *Bayerischer Volksfreund*, 24.4.1919. Eisner was almost always a 'Berlin' or 'Polish' Jew. See 16.11.1918 'Wochenschau'; 20.11.1918 'Jubelt Bayern?' An article of 30.11.1918 tried to link politics with 'Jewish' trade practices: 'Since a Jewish cattle trader and a Jewish prime minister always follow the same methods and never say what they really mean to do . . .'

[49] *Bayerische Tageszeitung*, 10.5.1920 'Ein Wort zur Judenfrage'. The *Bayerische Tageszeitung* succeeded the *Volksfreund*.

the *Mittelpartei* noted that German-speaking and German-writing Jews, not 'Hungarians, Galicians and other tribal comrades [*Stammesgenossen*] from the East' had prepared and led the Revolution, so that it was fallacious to distinguish between 'German' and 'Eastern' Jews.

The official party correspondence leaves us in no doubt that the 'Jewish question' was taken very seriously by the *Mittelpartei*. Both the 'Jewish press' and 'Jewish Marxism' figured prominently in its newsletters; 'racially alien' men and women were in control of the nation's destiny, and any German government 'which shies away from fighting this devastating alien [*fremdrassigen*] influence sins terribly against its own people!'[50] The party also offered some advice as to how Germans could rid themselves of this 'awful disease': 'Buy nothing from Jews, read nothing written by Jews, refuse to watch a Jewish play, refuse to have a Jewish doctor or lawyer. If all 60 million Germans followed this advice, in fact, if only those did so who claim they would like to kill a Jew every day, then the Jewish danger would already be averted.'[51] If words are like 'small doses of arsenic',[52] then it may well be that the language used by the *Mittelpartei* in this period prepared the path for Hitler's discrimination against the Jews in the Third Reich.[53]

Ending our survey of the 'Protestant bourgeoisie' from 1918 to 1921, we need to look briefly at the Church itself to determine whether the Revolution also affected the clergy's approach to the 'Jewish question'. Again, we rely on the *Evangelisches Gemeindeblatt*, the only source available in the context of our study.

As we recall, the Protestant weekly showed very little interest in the issue before the war. Surprisingly, given the massive circulation of anti-Jewish propaganda at the time, the paper continued to ignore the question after 1918. Between the Revolution and March 1922, it focused on 'Jews' and 'anti-Semitism' only seven times. While rejecting modern anti-Semitism as a fateful step towards an un-Christian world,[54] the *Gemeindeblatt*, like the *Fränkischer Kurier*, incorporated language which emphasized the background of some of the revolutionary figures. 'Bela Kuhn' [*sic*], for example, was the 'Jew' Bela Kuhn,[55] profiteers and rack-

---

[50] *Blätter der Bayerischen Mittelpartei* (Nuremberg), Universitätsbibliothek Erlangen 40. Hist. 525: *1919*—Nos 2, 14; *1920*—Nos 11, 12, 17, 20, 21, 22, 35, 51, 56; *1921*—Nos 15, 28, 32, 37, 60, 62, 71, 74, 97.

[51] Ibid., *1921*—No. 104.

[52] V. Klemperer, *LTI. Die Sprache des Dritten Reiches. Notizbuch eines Philologen* (Leipzig, 1991), 21.

[53] *Mittelpartei* leaflets and pamphlets also contained such language. See, for example, Stadtbibliothek Nürnberg StA AV o 3 and BHStA Abt.V FlSlg 65.

[54] *EvN*, 12.3.1922 'Rundschau'.   [55] Ibid., 25.1.1920 'Rundschau'.

eteers were 'Jewish',[56] and the Berlin lecturer Nikolei, a former 'pacifist and traitor to his country', had once been known by the name of Löwenstein.[57] These were minor examples compared to the anti-Jewish hysteria of the *Mittelpartei*, but they do indicate that the Revolution brought about a shift in the rhetoric and perception of the 'Jewish question' among Church officials. As yet still muted, this change would take on more pronounced forms in the future.

CATHOLICISM

Bavaria's Catholics witnessed the immediate post-war era with a profound sense of helplessness. How could they, so concerned with the fate of their state, suddenly be ruled by a 'gang of thieves and hooligans', they asked. It was this feeling of impotence, according to Allan Mitchell, which largely shaped the course of Bavarian politics after the collapse of the Empire: 'This was . . . attributable to the abruptly altered circumstances of a state previously dominated by a Catholic political establishment.'[58]

In Nuremberg itself, where political Catholicism had always remained weak, the BVP attempted to improve its lot by lashing out against socialism and its supposed 'leaders', the Jews. In fact, nowhere do we find as much interest in the 'Jewish question' as in the party's organ, the *Bayerische Volkszeitung* (later *Nürnberger Volkszeitung*). In the weeks leading up to the 1919 National Assembly elections, the paper touched on the issue over a dozen times, mostly in connection with the new ruler of Bavaria, Kurt Eisner.

While the pre-war Centre Party in Nuremberg had alluded to the growing influence of Jewry in German political life,[59] the BVP extended this claim to include language of the kind discussed above. Again, the Jews had won the 'economic and political battle', and the only way for Christians to restore the balance of power was to strengthen their position in the realms of politics, trade and industry, and the world of finance.[60] The *Bayerische Volkszeitung*, moreover, repeatedly referred to Eisner as 'the Galician Jew', whose tribal disposition (*Stammeseigenschaften*) precluded any knowledge of the Bavarian psyche.[61] But not only Eisner, 80 per cent of all revolutionaries were 'of the Jewish race.' Like the *Mittelpartei*, then,

[56] Ibid., 14.3.1920 'Rundschau'.   [57] Ibid., 8.8.1920 'Rundschau'.
[58] Mitchell, *Revolution*, 124.   [59] See the previous chapter.
[60] *Bayerische Volkszeitung*, 12.11.1918 'Antisemitismus'.
[61] Ibid., 16.11.1918 'Der galizische Jude, der erste Mann in Bayern?'; 18.11.1918 'Säuberung'; 25.11.1918 'Die Fremdherrschaft in Bayern'; 3.12.1918 'Rücktritt Eisners?' See also BHStA Abt.V FlSlg 58, BVP leaflets 'Warnung!', 'Bayerische Bürger und Bauern!', 'Die Segnungen der Revolution!', 'Der Bolschewismus'.

the BVP fought the 'golden chains' of international Jewry, even if it officially distanced itself from such 'Jew-baiting.'[62]

Political Catholicism also revived the myth that the Jews had benefited from both war and revolution. A 1919 leaflet 'directed especially at soldiers', for example, stated that 'a number of Jewish war profiteers managed, through the help of the Revolution and its Jewish instigators, to put their profits safely away in neutral Switzerland'.[63] Similarly, the *Volkszeitung* felt that the ever-growing chorus of Jew-hatred was more than justified: 'For the Jews have collected plenty of war profits. While Christian soldiers fought in the trenches, Jews were prominent among the indispensable at home [*Unabkömmlichen*] and thus war profiteers. And at the end of the war we witness the saddest sight: we seem to have become the vassals of Jewry.'[64] Although the party rejected racial fanaticism and pogroms, this did not entail a defence of the Jews as such, since 'real' Germans had every right to 'foam with rage' over their subjugation by a small minority.[65]

Over a year later, the BVP was still employing anti-Semitic language in some of its election material. A leaflet of 6 June 1920, for instance, used poetry to bring home a distinct message: 'Who ruled? Only tricksters, / Foreigners, Jews and Berliners. / Come now, you upright Bavarians, / Don't let yourself be deceived.'[66] Another leaflet of that day warned that only the BVP could prevent 'Berlin Jewry' from becoming the master of Germany.[67] Finally, in a revealing passage on the expulsion of foreign Jews from Bavaria, the party's city councillor, Johann Adam Jäckel, responded to accusations that the Jews had been mocked by saying: 'If someone's called Moses he cannot be called Hans.'[68]

We see, then, how easily political Catholicism resorted to Jew-baiting. Never a mere reaction to the events in Berlin, BVP anti-Semitism reflected the post-war consensus that the Jews had somehow used defeat and revolution for their own purposes. A few rumours during the war, a few 'Jewish' protagonists in the Revolution, could never have led to this massive outburst of anti-Semitism. Loss of power and orientation too gave rise to forms of discourse on the 'Jewish question' which had been largely absent from such debates in pre-war Nuremberg. In subsequent

[62] *BV*, 14.12.1918 'Christliche Pogromhetze'.

[63] Staatsbibliothek München 2 o H. Un. App. 28 n 'Ein offenes Wort an alle besonders die Frontsoldaten!'

[64] *BV*, 24.12.1918 'Gerechtigkeit gegen alle, auch gegen die Juden!'   [65] Ibid.

[66] Staatsbibliothek München 2 o H. Un. App. 28 n 'Was will die Bayerische Volkspartei'.

[67] BHStA Abt.V FlSlg 58 'Die Entscheidungsstunde ist da!'

[68] *NBZ*, 6.10.1920 'Aus dem Nürnberger Verwaltungs- und Polizeisenat'. The paper added that Jäckel's comments caused amusement among the assembled company.

chapters we shall discover whether political recovery in Bavaria as a whole was to alter the BVP's stance on the 'Jewish question.'

THE LEFT

As elsewhere, the split within the Socialist camp led to the founding of an Independent Social Democratic Party (USPD) in April 1917. In Nuremberg, however, this did not have the immediate effect of dividing the working class. The *Fränkische Tagespost*, for instance, remained the sole organ of the Left until July 1918, and differences between the two parties revolved around questions of tactics rather than principle.[69] By contrast, the KPD's more radical course had a relatively small impact at the time; by September 1919 the party's membership was estimated at only 600–2000 persons, of which many were members of the so-called 'old *Mittelstand*'.[70] A majority of socialists in Nuremberg thus preferred moderation to revolution, a fact that has prompted some historians to seek explanations in the city's conservative labour force: 'The largely traditional working-class . . . showed few radical leanings.'[71]

The MSPD leadership included a number of prominent Jews, among whom were the veteran Social Democrats Dr Max Süßheim and Adolf Braun, as well as the new head of the soldiers' council, the lawyer Dr Hermann Ewinger. It is doubtful, however, whether the party's composition served as a pretext for Nurembergers to become anti-Semites: the pre-war SPD had also seen Jews in prominent positions, and there was no basis whatever for the oppostion to speak of sudden 'Jewish domination' in the SPD. In the previous chapter we noted the strange absence of comment on the 'Jewish question' by the *Fränkische Tagespost*, and suggested that Adolf Braun was possibly responsible for this. After 1920, however, Braun no longer controlled the party organ, and it remains to be seen whether the SPD's stance changed as a result.

In a December 1918 article entitled 'Christliche Pogromhetze', the *Tagespost* attacked the BVP for wanting to 'send the Jews into the desert'. This witch-hunt was not only demagogic but un-Christian, the paper

---

[69] Schwarz, *Weltkrieg*, 278: 'Shortly before the Revolution majority socialists stood for "peace and continual democratization", while the independents favoured "peace and radical democratization".' See also G. Rückel, *Die Fränkische Tagespost. Geschichte einer Parteizeitung* (Nuremberg, 1964), 80, where he comments on the rather benevolent treatment of the MSPD by the Independents and vice versa.

[70] Ibid., 319–20. See also Hartmut Mehringer, 'Die KPD in Bayern 1919–1945. Vorgeschichte, Verfolgung und Widerstand', in: M. Broszat and H. Mehringer (eds), *Bayern in der NS-Zeit. Die Parteien KPD, SPD, BVP in Verfolgung und Widerstand* (Munich, 1983), 7.

[71] U. Neuhäußer-Wespy, *Die KPD in Nordbayern 1919–1933* (Nuremberg, 1981), 237.

added. At the same time, however, the MSPD organ wished to dispel any belief in a 'Jewish-socialist' plot: 'No one can suspect us of defending Jewish interests. Our paper has included many a word against our Jewish citizens, not because they are Jewish but rather because they neglected their duties *vis-à-vis* the common good.'[72] Three weeks later, the paper again wrote of the dangers of anti-Semitism, this time noting that the consequences for Germany's reputation would be grave.[73]

But the *Tagespost* also learned from experience in town and countryside how helpful occasional references to the 'Jewish' background of Eisner and comrades could be: 'But the likes of Landauer, Mühsam, Wadler, Lipp, and comrades do not act for the public good but for their own benefit . . . People like Wadler, who left the Jewish community to become a Catholic for purely opportunistic reasons, . . . have no time for the pains and sufferings of the people [*Volk*].'[74]

A further indication of Social Democratic uncertainty regarding the 'Jewish question' was a meeting of the 'SPD Wahlverein Nürnberg-Altdorf' in April 1919. Judging from a brief summary of the proceedings, we may conclude that the party reacted to the growing tensions between Gentiles and Jews by accommodating the majority position:

Three weeks ago the government was trusted. Who are its enemies now? People like Landauer, Mühsam, Boenheim; people who weren't party members before 9 November, individualists . . . (Shout: Jews!) Yes, also some Eastern Jews. These unfortunate Jews seem to want revenge for all the injustice their people has had to endure over the centuries. Levien lived through the war years as inspector of provisions; Dr Walder was responsible for bringing [*Importierung*] Belgian workers to Bavaria . . . We must be extremely wary of these people who suddenly pretend to be leaders of the proletariat.[75]

The speaker, first attempting to distinguish between German and Eastern Jews, then pointing to a history of persecution, finally echoed the audience's view that too many Jews exercised too much power in Bavaria.

One year later, when the BVP launched an anti-Semitic campaign against Dr Süßheim for his refusal in parliament to grant the Wittelsbach dynasty any form of compensation, the *Tagespost*'s response was one of unequivocal support for Süßheim, who had been elected 'as a Social Democrat and not as a Jew by fully eligible Bavarian voters and not by

---

[72] *FT*, 13.12.1918 'Nürnberger Chronik'.

[73] Ibid., 3.1.1919 'Antisemitismus': 'Should this [spirit of violence] manifest itself again in the suppression of a minority, the German people won't regain the trust of the world. Without this trust, however, a recovery is impossible.'

[74] Ibid., 15.4.1919 'Das schwelende Feuer in München'. These three articles are the only ones touching on the 'Jewish question' from the beginning of November 1918 to the end of April 1919.

[75] StAN *Stadtchronik* 1919, 381. The speaker was a Dr Heimreich.

Jews.'[76] None the less, there remained an element of apology in this defence, possibly because the party still recognized the continuing appeal of the anti-Jewish message.[77]

This appeal was certainly evident to the leaders of the USPD in 1919/20.[78] A police report of late November 1919, for example, observed that 'the aversion for the Jewish leaders is also growing among the ranks of the radical left parties.'[79] The Independent Socialist Fritz Soldmann, moreover, confirmed this assessment. In a meeting of his party on 23 November 1919 he argued that 'only through working-class unity and power . . . can one defend oneself against monarchical reaction, Jewish impudence [*Juden-Frechheit*], and the over-confidence [*Übermut*] of the military.'[80] Another UPSD leader, Neumann, contributed to the discussion by asking: 'Where does Helferich get his money from if not from Jews and war profiteers?'[81] Jews were not only war profiteers, according to this account, but also the financiers of the right-wing DNVP. In addition, the police recorded the words of one of the party's representatives in the Nuremberg municipal council, Fischer, at a rally in March 1920, in which the latter deplored the fact that some workers were 'hoarding goods for the Jews'.[82] The USPD, then, felt obliged to play the racist card whenever it sensed the prevalence of anti-Semitism among its supporters. How often this was the case we do not know, but in the period under review Independent Socialists gave in more than once to the sway of post-war xenophobia.

From its inception in February 1919, the Nuremberg KPD was confronted with the ascendancy of *völkisch* thought in the city. The *Schutz- und Trutz-Bund*'s Carl Maerz, for example, attended Communist meetings, attempting to spread the anti-Semitic bacillus in the ensuing discussions.[83] Similarly, when Dietrich Eckart and Gottfried Feder came to Nuremberg in the autumn of 1919 to give a speech on finance capital,

---

[76] *FT*, 12.5.1920 'Die Juden und die Wittelsbacher'.

[77] In an article of 21 September 1920 ('Nürnberger Chronik') the *FT* commented on the disruption of a DDP meeting by right-wing hooligans: 'We regret that a few workers who still haven't perceived their class status were also among the German-*völkisch* agitators.'

[78] At least two prominent Jews were members of the USPD: Hugo Freund, third mayor of Nuremberg, who left the city in 1921; and E. E. Neumann, who edited the *Sozialdemokrat*. Both, however, seldom or never figured in the hate campaigns of the extreme Right. Hanschel, *Luppe*, 47; Rückel, *Tagespost*, 80.

[79] BStAN Rep. 218/1 I Nr 332 Wochenbericht Nr 1124, 21.11.1919.

[80] BStAN Rep. 218/1 I Nr 330 'Bericht'. See also Nr 1156, 29.11.1919: 'It is also of interest that Soldmann made very critical remarks about the Jews; proof, therefore, that the anti-Semitic movement is not confined to "reactionary" groups.'

[81] Ibid.   [82] BStAN Rep. 218/1 I Nr 565, 31.3.1920.

[83] Schwarz, *Weltkrieg*, 327. See also Lohalm, *Völkischer Radikalismus*, 113: 'The history of the Nuremberg section is important in so far as it is the only significant case where the Schutz- und Trutz-Bund made serious inroads in the working class.'

the audience included 'approximately 2000 persons, mainly *völkisch* supporters, but also very many U. [*independents*], S. [*socialists*] and communists'.[84] This right-wing agitation bore fruit a few months later with the creation of a *Deutschsozialistische Partei* by two former communists, Vey and Kleinlein.[85]

In April 1920 rumours surfaced that the KPD entertained links with the *Deutsch-völkischer Bund*;[86] moreover, the party leader, Karl Grönsfelder, was reproached with his allegedly 'Jewish' background.[87] This post-war truce between communism and anti-Semitism undoubtedly desensitized left-wing supporters, who were never made to believe, as far as one can tell, that Jew-baiting was a serious problem.[88] When the local leadership warned its members in May 1921 that continued fraternization with *völkisch* circles would result in expulsion from the party, the KPD indirectly acknowledged the influence anti-Semitism had had on the movement and, by implication, on parts of the working class.[89]

DÜSSELDORF

If Nuremberg experienced sudden change as a threat to gradualism and 'bourgeois' tranquillity, Düsseldorf experienced violence and disorder as a challenge to growth and progress. The middle classes (*Bürgertum*) especially, who had witnessed an almost 'inexorable advancement of civilization' and who had been accustomed to a fashionable lifestyle, felt cheated by the events surrounding the Revolution of 1918/19.[90] Unlike the burghers of Nuremberg, therefore, who were astonished to find that revolution meant more than just a government decree, Düsseldorf's population had to deal with economic and social dislocation of a different kind.

Already in the summer of 1918 a number of strikes had indicated the unwillingness of most workers to accept the demands of war industry.[91] What is more, while the split in the working-class movement was a national phenomenon, in Düsseldorf the USPD represented the majority of socialist supporters, controlling the party organ as well as the party's funds and associations.[92] During the initial stages of the Revolution the

---

[84] Schwarz, *Weltkrieg*, 327.   [85] Ibid., 328.   [86] Neuhäußer-Wespy, *KPD*, 42.
[87] Ibid., 44. Jews never headed the Nuremberg KPD.
[88] This is also argued by Neuhäußer-Wespy, who only very briefly examines anti-Semitism in the KPD. Ibid., 45.
[89] Ibid., 65.   [90] Hüttenberger, *Düsseldorf*, 264.
[91] S. Lispki, *Dokumentation zur Geschichte der Stadt Düsseldorf. Düsseldorf während der Revolution 1918–1919 (November 1918 bis März 1919). Quellensammlung* (Düsseldorf, no date), 2.
[92] Ibid., 3.

'middle class' was thus confronted with a far more radical alternative to the existing order than was the case elsewhere.

The tenuous alliance between 'right' and 'left' socialism, for example, collapsed earlier in Düsseldorf, where leading Independents 'were angry that the provisional government had not reformed the bureaucracy and military or instituted partial socialization'.[93] The 'bourgeoisie', however, far from being hostile to the early developments of the Revolution, was ready to cooperate with the new rulers if that meant peace and stability. As Peter Hüttenberger pointed out, the workers' council was far from unpopular in December 1918, especially among the Protestant workforce, but also among civil servants and white-collar workers, who resented the well-off and who were no longer willing to suffer as a result of war and economic mismanagement.[94]

The first act of violence that was to seriously undermine the prospects of continued support for the Revolution occurred in January 1919. The local KPD, which had virtually no organization of its own but which enjoyed growing support in the workers' council, occupied the offices of the 'bourgeois newspapers', the railway station, the telegraph, and the police headquarters. Mayor Adalbert Oehler and District President Alfred Kruse fled across the Rhine to Belgian-occupied territory. The KPD arrested several city notables, dissolved the city council, and took over the municipal transportation system.[95] When, on 10 January 1919, a protest by the DDP and MSPD against the new regime resulted in the killing of fourteen demonstrators, the Communist-led workers' council introduced a number of measures to quell the resistance. To the surprise of many workers and the dismay of the 'middle classes', the new regime had survived its difficult birth.

The elections to the National Assembly, moreover, seemed to vindicate left-wing radicalism: the USPD gained nearly 25 per cent of the vote, leaving the MPSD a distant third, with only 14.4 per cent. But there were troubling signs too. The combined support of the MSPD and USPD amounted to just over 40 per cent, compared to the SPD's 56 per cent in 1912. As a result, the Centre Party again emerged as the strongest force in Düsseldorf politics. Growing differences between the KPD and USPD also boded ill. Despite the city council's decision to hold municipal elections on 23 February, the Communists, who feared a 'bourgeois' majority, first closed all non-socialist papers and then seized and destroyed the ballots. Furious over these actions, the USPD declared that the Commu-

---

[93] Nolan, *Social Democracy*, 278.   [94] Hüttenberger, *Düsseldorf*, 283.
[95] The following is based on Nolan, *Social Democracy*, 284–99; Hüttenberger, *Düsseldorf*, 291; Lipski, *Dokumentation*, 56.

nists had 'betrayed the ideas of Luxemburg and Liebknecht', and insisted that they could no longer support the alliance. The KPD's final demise, however, came a few days later, when the Free Corps Lichtenstrahl marched into Düsseldorf. The workers' council immediately abolished the KPD executive council and elected a USPD–MSPD one; peaceful elections took place in mid-March. Finally, towards the end of April, the last remnants of the Revolution disappeared: the general strike that had been called earlier and claimed the lives of thirty-nine people ended in failure, the workers' council was dismantled, and the military reasserted control over the city.

As is evident from the above, Düsseldorf's transition to democracy was marked by a confrontation very different from that experienced in Nuremberg. What is more, the occupation of the city by Belgian, French, and British forces between 1918 and 1923 created further problems for a city already hard-hit by the effects of the post-war crisis. According to Uwe Lohalm, it was precisely this uninterrupted period of confusion and disorder that proved so helpful for anti-Semites in the Rhineland and Westphalia.[96]

'PROTESTANT BOURGEOISIE'

The German Democratic Party, founded in Düsseldorf by Professor Schloßmann in late November 1918, was from the outset compromised by a number of former National Liberals and Free Conservatives, 'who did not dare to declare their continued allegiance for Bismarckian and chauvinistic liberalism but rather found temporary shelter in left liberalism'.[97] More serious still for the DDP in this period was the fact that the city's main liberal paper, the *Düsseldorfer Zeitung*, soon began to support the German People's Party (DVP). Left liberals had to rely on the *Lokalzeitung* instead, a paper that never officially endorsed the DDP and one that often remained aloof from party politics.[98] Given all these impediments, as well as left liberalism's insignificance before the war, it surprised no one that the Düsseldorf vote for the DDP in January 1919 was well below the national average.[99]

---

[96] Lohalm, *Völkischer Radikalismus*, 317–18.   [97] Hüttenberger, *Düsseldorf*, 305.
[98] K. Koszyk, *Deutsche Presse 1914–1945. Geschichte der deutschen Presse*. Teil III (Berlin, 1972), 174. The *Düsseldorfer Zeitung* was owned by the National Liberal publisher, Heinrich Droste. See also A. Kussmann, *Das kommunale Parteiensystem in Düsseldorf beim Übergang vom Kaiserreich zur Republik. Ein Beitrag zum Kontinuitätsproblem*, unpublished MA thesis (Berlin, 1982), 144 n. 4.
[99] The DDP gained 12 per cent in Düsseldorf, 18.6 per cent in the Reich as a whole. Nolan, *Social Democracy*, 289.

As elsewhere, the Democratic Party in Düsseldorf had to respond to charges that it catered exclusively to Jewish interests. The local CV, for instance, placed an advertisement in the *Düsseldorfer Nachrichten* of 26 January 1919 denying links between the Jewish community and any one party: 'Jews! Co-religionists! The yellow poster which has been distrib- uted in town today and which reads: "The Democratic Party is the party of Jewry" is a flagrant election manoeuvre [*Wahlmanöver*]. We as Jews have only one slogan: "No vote for an anti-Semite or for a party in which anti-Semites have found a home." '

For the most part, the DDP tried to avoid the topic; only occasionally do we find scattered remarks alluding to the 'Jewish question'. An early election leaflet aimed against the DVP, for example, accused the People's Party of inciting 'the lowest instincts' with its anti-Semitic propaganda.[100] A similar leaflet directed at the DNVP ridiculed the assertion that a small minority—the Jews—could 'terrorize' the German people: 'And this tiny minority is supposed to control Germany's destiny? What an insult to the great German people! . . . Therefore, don't vote for the DNVP, the party of anti-Semites.'[101]

If the DDP attacked political opponents for their anti-Semitism, it also hoped to rid itself of the *Judenpartei* label. *Der Weckruf*, for example, a special pre-election paper of 25 January 1919, answered the DNVP's attempts to stigmatize the Democratic Party by questioning its motives: 'To conceal the fact that the German-national Party likes to accept Jews, and that the Centre in Cologne is supposed to have established a special campaign committee to attract Jewish voters is—German-national.'[102]

Since hardly any material exists that could further elucidate the DDP's stance on the issue, we may conclude from the above that most left liberals in Düsseldorf, although weak and on the defensive, never gave in to the anti-Semitic message. A possible explanation for this is the relatively early departure of the more conservative elements from the party, a process that took longer in Nuremberg, where the alternative to left liberalism was not so much the DVP but the right-wing *Mittelpartei*.

Compared to the Democrats, the DVP entered the field of post-war politics on a better footing, since the city of Düsseldorf had always been a stronghold of National Liberalism.[103] Founded in March 1919, the local party branch represented the city's industrialists, various economic

[100] StAD XXI 228 (1919?).   [101] Ibid.

[102] StAD Plakatsammlung Mappe 1 'Von den Konservativen in Düsseldorf'.

[103] W. Hartenstein, *Die Anfänge der Deutschen Volkspartei, 1918–1920* (Düsseldorf, 1962), 70; H. Romeyk, 'Die Deutsche Volkspartei in Rheinland und Westfalen 1918–1933', in: *Rheinische Vierteljahrsblätter* (Bonn, 1975), 193.

interest groups and trade guilds, as well as better-situated white-collar employees and civil servants.[104] In the first few months after the Revolution, the DVP received its propaganda material from the party's Rhenish headquarters in Essen. It also cooperated with the DNVP in an electoral alliance prior to the 1919 National Assembly and Prussian state elections, in order to forestall a possible left liberal triumph.

The material distributed in this period abounded in nationalistic phraseology; often, though not always, this included anti-Semitic remarks. 'Where are German loyalty, German morality, German law, German freedom?' the party asked,[105] and in early January 1919 it reminded its followers: 'Remember that which resides in your *own breast*! Not imitation of the different [*des Fremden*], not emulation of foreign stuff!'[106] A letter to the former members of the Elberfeld *Nationalliberaler Verein*, moreover, stressed the differences of the DVP and DDP in their perception of *völkisch* ideology: 'We reject the pacifist, international spirit of the *Berliner Tageblatt* which undermines the German-*völkisch* tribal nature [*Stammesart*].'[107]

But it was the election campaign of the DVP/DNVP *Liste Koch* in January 1919 that showed most clearly how far the DVP was willing to go in its endeavour to discredit the DDP. The latter,[108] representing the *Berliner Tageblatt* and the *Frankfurter Zeitung*, was made responsible for the 'poisoning of the German soul [*Volksseele*]. This international society must be exposed and then eliminated from the political stage of our fatherland.'[109] Even more ominous was the leaflet 'of a loyal Eckart', which supported the DVP/DNVP platform without officially endorsing it. Again, 'aliens' (*Fremdstämmige*), whose 'racial peculiarity' (*Rasseneigentümlichkeit*) precluded 'German feeling', controlled the press. But that was not all: 'How much longer will the German worker be led by the Jews, how much longer will the German be influenced to his detriment by the press of the "Jerusalemstraße"? How much longer will Bavaria be governed by Eisner? How much longer will German art and German creative work be belittled and corrupted by aliens?'[110] Even if one concedes that the DNVP had a greater interest in spreading the anti-Semitic bacillus than the People's Party, it is also evident that the latter's

[104] Hüttenberger, *Düsseldorf*, 306.   [105] StAD XXI 306.
[106] StAD Plakatsammlung Mappe 18, 26.1.1919 'Deutsche Volkspartei'.
[107] StAD XXI 305, 4.1.1919 'An die Mitglieder des früheren Nationalliberalen Vereins'.
[108] The DVP liked to refer to the DDP as the ' "deutsche" Demokratische Partei'. See, for example, StAD XXI 320 (no date). For Nazi language and inverted commas, see Klemperer, *LTI*, 79: 'Chamberlain, Churchill, and Roosevelt are merely "statesmen" in inverted commas, Einstein is a "scientist", Rathenau a "German", and Heine a "German" poet.'
[109] StAD XXI 306.   [110] StAD XXI 305.

consent to such slanderous talk could only have underpinned the *völkisch* cause in Düsseldorf.

The city's most respected daily, the *Düsseldorfer Zeitung*, seems to have rejected the anti-Jewish agitation of 1918/19. Sharply critical of Eisner, the paper none the less refrained from carping at him for his alleged lack of 'German' qualities. Only twice does the reader encounter references to Eisner's background: in late November the liberal organ mentioned an article in the *Jüdisches Echo* which accused him of harming Jewish interests; and a few days later the paper quoted another outside force, this time the notorious *Miesbacher Anzeiger*, to speculate on the Bavarian leader's 'actual' name.[111] On the whole, however, the *Düsseldorfer Zeitung* maintained a low profile on the 'Jewish question', neither condemning anti-Semitism by others nor succumbing to racist language itself.

The equally distinguished *Düsseldorfer Nachrichten*, on the other hand, very quickly joined the post-war chorus of anti-Semitism. Eisner, 'alias Salomon Kusnewski', for example, could not share German fears and anxieties 'since [he] isn't of German descent'.[112] The paper also blamed Jewish revolutionaries for inciting the workers against the bourgeoisie: 'Don't our workers . . . have other and better models than such real Russian [*echt-russischen*] men as Trotzki-Brorstein [*sic*], Kamenev-Rosenthal, and Radek-Sobelsohn?'[113] The *Nachrichten*'s word games culminated in an article of 17 May 1919 on the Hungarian leadership taken from the *Neue Zürcher Zeitung*:

'Béla Kun, alias Kohn, was at one time editor of small provincial papers . . . The true dictator of present-day Hungary is Béla Bágó, alias Weißmann, by profession Commissar of the Interior . . . Psychologically the most interesting case is Tibor Szamuelly, alias Samuel, . . . A weak and tubercular young boy of twenty, very Semitic in appearance.'[114]

---

[111] *DZ*, 27.11.1918 (Mittag) 'Aus Bayern'; 30.11.1918 (Mittag) 'Eisners Ende?': 'The Miesbacher Anzeiger writes that Kurt Eisner's real name is supposedly Salomon Kusnowski. The paper doesn't know if this is true. Whether the prime minister's name is from the Old or the New Testament doesn't matter as long as his politics are wise and beneficial for all the people. This, however, is not the case.'

[112] *DN*, 1.12.1918 (Morgen) 'Ein Rückblick'; 7.12.1918 (Morgen) 'Eisner als Franzosenfreund'; 26.11.1918 (Abend) 'Phantasien des Präsidenten Eisner'. The *Nachrichten*, although officially neutral, reported favourably on the DVP.

[113] Ibid., 29.12.1918 (Morgen) 'Ein Rückblick'. See also 1.5.1919 (Morgen) 'National oder international': 'Doesn't the whole world laugh about the short-sighted Germans who are being provoked into fighting each other by alien Russians, Poles, and Galicians (who like Radek, Lewin, Leviné (!), Axelrod, Toller, and many others have changed their names to count as "real" Russians).' For an instructive analysis of the use of names and their role in isolating the Jews, see D. Bering, *Der Name als Stigma. Antisemitismus im deutschen Alltag 1812–1933* (Stuttgart, 1987).

[114] *DN*, 17.5.1919 'Die Bolschewistenführer in Ungarn'.

The *Düsseldorfer Nachrichten*, before the war a *General-Anzeiger*-type paper, time and time again used language of this sort to distinguish between 'German' politicians and 'eastern' radicals. This language, however, did not creep into the news coverage at some unguarded moment; it was there from the start, separating Jews from non-Jews in an attempt to explain the momentous events of 1918/19.

As in Nuremberg, the Kapp Putsch further exacerbated existing tensions between left-wing organizations and their political opponents. Even though a majority of the Düsseldorf population seems to have rejected the short-lived regime in Berlin,[115] the ensuing strike, which led to violent clashes with the army under Major von Rudorff, gave rise to renewed fears that left-wing radicalism was about to resurface in Düsseldorf. The working class too felt it had been betrayed. Whether 'class relations had come full circle' with the Kapp Putsch, as Peter Fritzsche contends, 'returning—after the nationalist euphoria of August 1914 and the populist promise of November 1918—to the mutual hostility and shattered community of the prewar era' is a question we cannot answer here,[116] but the events of March 1920 undoubtedly confirmed deeply held views about the rebelliousness of the 'working class' on one hand and 'bourgeois' repression on the other.

It is of course difficult to establish any direct relationship between the outcome of the Kapp Putsch and anti-Semitism. In spite of this, however, we can observe that the 'Jewish question' remained on the agenda a few months later, in the run-up to the Reichstag elections of June 1920. This was especially the case for the DNVP. Nevertheless, other more moderate parties also believed in the importance of the issue. The DVP's *Düsseldorfer Zeitung*, for example, overturned its past refusal to employ anti-Semitic imagery when it questioned the loyalty of the Democratic Party in an article entitled 'We and the Others': 'It is good that the party calls itself "German"—otherwise one could easily forget that it is supposed to defend German beliefs [*Gesinnung*] and German culture! But we of course understand that a party which receives its guidelines from the *Berliner Tageblatt* cannot emphasize German interests unreservedly.'[117]

This change of policy was highlighted by the local DDP in an advertisement of 5 June, which contrasted the DVP's position in 1919 with its most recent statement on the 'Jewish question': 'The German People's

[115] HStAD Reg. Düss. 15980, 30.4.1920: 'News about the Kapp Putsch has surprised the population. Even in rightist circles it was received with mixed feelings.'

[116] Fritzsche, *Rehearsals*, 61–2; B. Brücher et al., *Dokumentation zur Geschichte der Stadt Düsseldorf. Düsseldorf während der Weimarer Republik 1919–1933. Quellensammlung* (Düsseldorf, 1985), 84. Major von Rudorff's attempt to quell the strike killed six workers.

[117] *DZ*, 3.6.1920.

Party in 1919 . . . We are determined opponents of anti-Semitism. The People's Party in 1920 . . . We are opponents of anti-Semitism, but fight the corrosive influence of the Jews.'[118] Although the Democratic Party's assessment was somewhat off the mark, it did underline the continued role of anti-Semitism in the election propaganda of the DVP.

A possible explanation for this is the growing rivalry between the People's Party and the DNVP. In the internal correspondence of the former we find hints that both parties were hoping to outdo each other in the 'art' of Jew-baiting:

In a DNVP meeting in Haan the speaker strongly attacked the German People's Party. The DVP's leadership was in Jewish hands, leading members included the Jew Riesser and Stresemann, whose wife was a Jew, the party was therefore dominated by Jews . . . First of all Stresemann's wife is *not* Jewish, her father was Protestant, though it's true that her mother was of Jewish descent. In other words, Mrs Stresemann cannot be addressed as a Jew. By suggesting a relationship between Jewry and the People's Party the speaker intended to discredit the latter as unreliable in German matters, as un-German, and as responsible for the great misfortune which has befallen our people.[119]

The DNVP speaker surely erred in his judgement of the People's Party, for the latter tried very hard to uphold its *völkisch* image. Prior to the February 1921 Prussian state elections, for example, a number of DVP leaflets appealed to the anti-Semitic prejudices of the electorate. The DDP, as well as a host of revolutionary figures, served Jewish interests, according to one such flyer, and the working class was advised not to trust 'the old myth of class warfare'. Subtler forms of racist thinking also appeared. A leaflet entitled 'Where was this written?' quoted a *Kreuzzeitung* article which pronounced the Reformation the work not of 'the peasantry and various alliances aimed at eliminating Jewish usury . . . not the work of *völkisch* and social movements, but merely that of the local lords'. This emphasis by the newspaper on the non-*völkisch* causes of the Reformation, the leaflet intimated, had specific reasons. Thus the DVP flyer ended with the rhetorical question: 'But why?', implying that the DNVP-led *Kreuzzeitung* could not afford to upset its 'Jewish supporters' and therefore had to suppress the '*völkisch* bases' of

---

[118] *DN*, 5.6.1920 (Morgen) 'Die deutsche Volkspartei ist die Partei der Widersprüche'.
[119] StAD XXI 308 Deutsche Volkspartei—Landesverband Düsseldorf-Ost, 1.2.1921. See also ibid., 14.2.1921: 'In Elberfeld DNVP youths pasted small black and white bills on DVP posters Friday evening. These read: Who still votes DVP??? The Prussian bloc is Jew-free [*judenfrei*]! Is a more spiteful method of struggle imaginable? Even the Democrats and majority socialists fight more honestly! More honestly? Yes! For the German-national People's Party has itself Jews in its ranks!'

the Reformation.[120] Finally, the DVP depicted the Russian Communist 'Sinowjew-Apfelbaum' as a 'typical' Jew, with large ears, voluptuous lips, and a crooked nose.[121] This caricature was a final illustration of the party's willingness to resort to anti-Semitic imagery in its election campaign. As the DDP no longer presented a serious threat, the People's Party had to contest the votes of its new political rival, the DNVP. If the former recognized the potential appeal of anti-Semitism in this period, it was above all because Jew-baiting seemed to improve the chances of the latter.

The Düsseldorf branch of the *Deutschnationale Volkspartei* was founded by the 'Superintendent' of Düsseldorf, Gustav Meinberg, and the former Christian Social, Karl Neuhaus, in November 1918.[122] The DNVP immediately emerged as the representative of Protestant interests in the city; a number of prominent clergymen (eight altogether) soon joined the party, including Eugen Funke, chairman of the *Evangelischer Bund*, and Pfarrer Harney, editor of the *Sonntagsblatt*.[123]

The DNVP also attracted former members of conservative and nationalist groups like the *Konservative Vereinigung*, the *Nationale Vereinigung*, and the *Vaterlandspartei*. Moreover, whereas civil servants, clerics, and teachers filled the ranks of the party, the working class remained underrepresented. Various *völkisch* organizations found refuge in the party too. According to Gisbert Gemein, however, anti-Semitism in the DNVP was not racist, 'but corresponded to widespread prejudices and antipathies against the Jews found among all bourgeois parties, although the DNVP articulated these more sharply and more frequently. Statements of this kind were not, however, directed at the Jew as such, but rather focused on the image of the Jew'.[124] Leaving aside the question of whether the struggle against absolute abstracts such as 'world Jewry' or the 'Jewish International' was less pernicious than personal attacks against individual Jews, we need to consider the accuracy of Gemein's assertion that racism was absent from the DNVP.

In both the press and the election material of the party we can discern a wide range of anti-Semitic stereotypes. At a meeting in December 1918, for example, a DNVP speaker proclaimed that Germany had denied its true spirit by accepting the leadership of the Jews.[125] We read of 'Jewry's

---

[120] StAD XXI 308 'Wo steht das geschrieben?'

[121] Ibid., 'An ihren Früchten sollt ihr sie erkennen!'

[122] G. J. Gemein, *Die DNVP in Düsseldorf 1918–1933*, unpublished Ph.D. thesis (Cologne, 1969), 2.

[123] Hüttenberger, *Düsseldorf*, 307.

[124] Gemein, *DNVP*, 183. Also Hüttenberger, *Düsseldorf*, 311. For the relatively low number of workers in the party, see Gemein, *DNVP*, 117.

[125] Newspaper article in StAD XXI 306, no date or title.

omnipotence', of 'Jewry's army', or of 'Jewish devotion to Mammon'.[126] DNVP advertisements attacked 'every corrosive, un-German spirit, whether emanating from Jewish or other sources'.[127] In short, in 1919 and 1920 countless examples of this kind circulated among Nationalists in Düsseldorf; most of these anti-Jewish jeers, moreover, were not limited to 'traditional' forms of prejudice found in the 'bourgeoisie'.

In fact, the above claim that Jews as such were never subject to defamation is far from true. The *Wacht*, for example, responded to complaints about *völkisch* policies and tactics by the *Central-Verein* in March 1920 with the following warning: 'We recommend that the gentlemen of the Central-Verein show more restraint. Otherwise they shouldn't be surprised to encounter an outraged public which repudiates the Revolution and its eastern origins . . . They would then have to accept the consequences.'[128] Racism, moreover, was never shunned when it came to portraying the 'enemy of the German people', the Jews.[129] The women's section of the DNVP advised its members to avoid extremes of the 'Type Resi [*sic*] Wolfstein, who thank goodness [*Gottlob*] isn't German'.[130] Similarly, the DDP was 'no party of the "middle" but rather, owing to its Jewish blood [*Einschlages*], one-sided in its leftist "orient"-ation'. It goes without saying that this pun was directed not only against 'the enemy within', but also against a specific target, namely the 'Semites' in the Democratic Party, and, by extension, the 'Semites' in all of Germany.[131] Finally, in the autumn of 1920, a number of articles described the insurmountable differences between 'Germandom and Jewry'. The 'Jewish question' could never be solved through legal means, one such piece explained, for Jewish influence threatened all walks of life and therefore continued to present a 'spiritual danger'. In the end, the paper concluded,

---

[126] *Die Wacht am Niederrhein*, 14.1.1919 'Auf wen rechnen wir?'; 14.1.1919 'Wen soll ich wählen?'; 24.1.1919 'An die evangelischen Einwohner in Stadt und Land'.

[127] *DN*, 11.5.1920 (Morgen).

[128] *Die Wacht*, 6.3.1920 'Die "anständige" Kampfesweise'.

[129] Ibid., 17.4.1920 'Wer macht die zweite, die kommunistische Revolution?': 'If the Hungarians managed to rid themselves of these unwelcome aliens . . . fairly easily and quickly, sixty million Germans should be able to do the same with its one million Jews.' The *Wacht*, it will be noted, multiplied the existing number of German Jews by two.

[130] Ibid., 29.4.1920 'Liebe Parteifreundinnen und Mitschwestern!' Rosi Wolfstein was a member of the Duisburg *Spartakusbund*. She briefly joined the Düsseldorf workers' and soldiers' council in 1918/19, and from 1921 to 1924 was a member of the Prussian parliament. In 1924 she was expelled from the KPD, and until her emigration in 1933 worked for various communist splinter groups. There are no signs that other Jews were active in the Düsseldorf workers' and soldiers' council. S. Lispki, *Der Arbeiter- und Soldatenrat in Düsseldorf (Zwischen den Novemberereignissen und dem Zweiten Rätekongreß, November 1918 bis April 1919). Vom politischen Organ zur wirtschaftlichen Interessenvertretung*, unpublished Ph.D. thesis (Düsseldorf, 1978), 11 n. 65, 15 n. 86, 121–2.

[131] Ibid., 15.5.1920 'Der 16. Mai ein deutschnationaler Opfertag!'

it was up to the German people to oust the Jewish peril from its soil: 'If Siegfried shall prevail Judah must perish!'[132]

We need to keep in mind that listing these examples is not a tedious exercise in inculpation; it should merely alert us to the fact that one of the most powerful 'bourgeois' parties in Düsseldorf repeatedly appealed to anti-Semitic sentiments without expressing any qualms or doubts.[133] Like the *Mittelpartei* in Nuremberg, the DNVP demanded the exclusion of the Jews from German life; and even if the party was not in a position to practise what it preached, its words soon formed part of the daily discourse on the 'Jewish question'.

As noted earlier, the Protestant Church in Düsseldorf identified the Jews before and during the war with all those unfavourable aspects of 'modernity' which seemed to threaten the hegemony of Protestant German culture. Between 1918 and 1921, the *Düsseldorfer Sonntagsblatt* published approximately thirty articles dealing with the 'Jewish question', most of which went beyond older forms of anti-Semitism to include racist language of the sort found in right-wing parties such as the DNVP.

Already in December 1918 the paper advised 'Christian women' to vote only for parties that had no links with Jews;[134] a month later *völkisch* despair erupted even more forcefully in an article on Germany's political life: 'Admittedly, when one sees German workers with their Germanic skulls adoring a Mr Levi or a Röschen Wollstein [*sic*], that Russian Jewess, then nothing can shock one any longer . . . Lord God, forgive them, they are ignorant, help them so that they may think German, act German, live German, German and Christian.'[135]

While the Protestant weekly continued to criticize 'Jewish influence' in numerous areas of German culture, it now revelled in language which called for the separation of Gentiles and Jews. Marx, for example, became Mordechai, Lassalle Feist Lasals, and Maximilian Harden Isidor Wittkowski.[136] 'Aliens' (*Fremdstämmige*) were mentioned by name—'the Jews'—and described as the 'gravediggers of German life and ways' (*Totengräber der deutschen Volkssittlichkeit*).[137] Even where the paper distanced itself from racist Christians, it made sure not to sympathize with the Jews: 'God didn't make the Jews his people because they were inherently the noblest or the most religious, but to demonstrate his boundless

[132] *Die Wacht*, 30.10.1920 'Deutschtum und Judentum'; 13.11.1920 'Volkstum und deutsche Zukunft'; 11.12.1920 'Wider den Antichrist'.

[133] The DNVP gained 9.5 per cent of the vote in June 1920, the DVP 11.8 per cent, and the DDP 3.6 per cent. Brücher, *Dokumentation*, 194.

[134] *SB*, 22.12.1918 'Wie wählt die christliche Frau?'   [135]Ibid., 19.1.1919 'Zeitschau'.

[136] Ibid., 26.1.1919 'Dein Tänzer ist der Tod'; 1.6.1919 'Zeitschau'.

[137] Ibid., 18.7.1920 'Zeitschau'; 23.11.1919 'Kleine Pfeile'.

pity for a people which in its history always wanted to choose the wrong path . . . It is a deep and hidden truth that God made this in so many ways dangerous people the source of revelation.'[138] In short, the *Sonntagsblatt* tried to steer clear of both the 'Scylla of Jewry' and the 'Charybdis of racial anti-Semitism' without recognizing that it had long since succumbed to the language of the latter.[139] Confronted with the consequences of its own undoing, the Protestant weekly tried to distinguish between different kinds of racism in order to defend the Church from more radical influences. For unlike the DNVP, which could emphasize or play down its *völkisch* character whenever it saw fit, the Protestant Church was forced to remain within the bounds of religious orthodoxy if it wanted to protect traditional articles of faith.

CATHOLICISM

The Centre Party in Düsseldorf was divided into two opposing factions: on the one hand a conservative wing that was willing to cooperate with the 'bourgeois parties of the right', and on the other a group representing the Christian unions that supported closer links with Social Democracy. While the former included *Vaterlandspartei* members and the owner of the annexationist *Düsseldorfer Tageblatt*, the latter consisted of more liberal-minded politicians who called for an end to the Prussian electoral system. Although the conservatives in the party had to accept the Revolution as a fact of life, they were still able to control much of the policy-making of the Centre after the war. This was especially true for the 1919 election campaign, as Wolfgang Stump has noted: 'The socialist Left as well as the newly founded German Democratic Party were mainly attacked on cultural grounds. Towards the newly-formed Right, the German National Party, the Centre's propaganda was more reserved.'[140]

Moreover, in October 1919 a member of the old guard, Clemens Adams, took over the local party leadership to accommodate those in the 'bourgeoisie' who had expressed fears about the growing power of the unions in the Centre Party. According to Peter Hüttenberger, Adams's policies in the following months created conditions for a secret deal with

[138] Ibid., 11.7.1920 'Kirchliche Rundschau'. The article attacked Friedrich Delitzsche's attempt to eliminate the Old Testament from Christian liturgy. See also ibid., 10.10.1920 'Zeitschau': 'In my [Pfarrer Harney's] opinion the Jew isn't a disaster for us because he is a Jew, but because there is a curse on him which he has until this day been unable to overcome.' However, the *Sonnagsblatt* time and again blamed the Jews for being Jews.

[139] Ibid., 2.1.1921 'Wider das Christentum—für das Deutschtum!'

[140] W. Stump, *Geschichte und Organisation der Zentrumspartei in Düsseldorf 1917–1933* (Düsseldorf, 1971), 39.

conservative and liberal forces, similar to the one that had existed since 1914 and which was to underpin conservative influence in the city.[141]

Using the *Düsseldorfer Tageblatt* to analyse Catholic opinion on the 'Jewish question' is no doubt problematic, given the ideological rift in the party following the collapse of the Empire. None the less, it may be helpful to discover whether the most conservative elements in the Düsseldorf Centre Party employed anti-Semitism at a time when they were challenged from both within and outside the movement.

At least before January 1919, the *Tageblatt* rejected Jew-baiting. In its many commentaries on the Eisner Regime, for example, the paper never referred to the Bavarian leaders' Jewish background. The only hint of anti-Semitism found for this period is a November 1918 article on 'Concerned Jewish voices' which quoted one Rahel Rabinowitz as having said: 'He [Eisner] is not to be blamed for being Jewish and thus forever incapable of appreciating Germandom, but for being so outrageously presumptuous as to dare to head the state in spite of these facts.'[142] Since no such articles appeared again, we can conclude that the *Tageblatt* refused to capitalize on existing anti-Jewish sentiments in the first few months after the Revolution.

In the run-up to the 1919 National Assembly elections, however, the Centre Party's stance on the issue became more ambiguous. While leaflets directed against the DDP contained no anti-Semitism,[143] propaganda material about the Social Democrats mentioned the Left's past and present 'dependence' on the financial support of Bleichröder, 'Galician industrialists', and Rothschild capital.[144] What is more, the *Tageblatt's* language changed markedly between March and May 1919. In an article entitled 'Civil War in Munich', for example, the Centre organ wondered how it was possible for the Bavarians to tolerate the machinations of a group of shady alien literary figures: 'It will remain one of the greatest mysteries how the Bavarian people, usually so insistent on its *völkisch* nature, could accept the rule of persons whose unscrupulous practices and whose pernicious [*volksverderblichen*] convictions were apparent from their Russian-Jewish background.'[145] A number of further pieces on the Bavarian events spoke of 'Jew-infiltrated art and literary circles', of 'a

---

[141] Clemens Adams headed the Centre Party fraction in the municipal council. He was also a former *Vaterlandspartei* member. Hüttenberger, *Düsseldorf*, 315–16.

[142] *DT*, 28.11.1918.

[143] StAD Plakatsammlung Mappe 16 'Was will die Deutsche demokratische Partei?'

[144] *Düsseldorfer Volkswille. Wahlflugblätter der Düsseldorfer Zentrumspartei*, 18.1.1919 (in the *DT* of that day).

[145] *DT*, 16.4.1919.

horde of foreign and racial aliens', of 'Russian-Jewish leaders'.[146] The *Tageblatt*'s approach to the problem of anti-Semitism thus took a turn for the worse, although it never quite reached the level of hatred found in the *Düsseldorfer Nachrichten*.

At the same time, however, the Centre Party repudiated extremism and *völkisch* hysteria. Düsseldorf's Catholics, for instance, described the Kapp Putsch as a 'criminal military attack' and called for a restructuring of the army so as to protect the accomplishments of the Republic.[147] An article of June 1920 on anti-Semitism among high-school students, moreover, accused the DNVP of inciting young boys and girls to disrupt CV meetings and insult their fellow students 'in a most loutish manner'.[148] Likewise, the paper mentioned Siegfried von Kardorff's break with the DNVP in the context of his disapproval of racial and religious anti-Semitism, which for the Centre Party was one important reason not to vote for the German Nationalists.[149]

The language of 1919 re-emerged briefly in February 1921, prior to the Prussian state elections. Although the party ridiculed the 'cheering and real German bard chants by the only real nationalists', it criticized the 'fantasies of a Bolshevist paradise à la Sobelsohn and Mandelbaum'.[150] In a similar appeal to the Prussian electorate, the Centre Party also attacked the DNVP, 'which has elected the Jew Weyl, leader of the Independent Socialists, as Lord Mayor of Berlin', as well as the '*Berliner Tageblatt* and the like' (i.e. the DDP) for being the enemies of the Christian state.[151]

Düsseldorf's Catholics, in other words, held conflicting views on the subject: while discrediting the anti-Semitism of political opponents, they condoned racism within their own ranks; while *völkisch* thought was largely absent from the party's programme, occasional anti-Jewish remarks were put to its service; while the actions of fanatical Jew-baiters were held in disrepute, revolutionary agitators provoked feelings of disgust and hatred. On the whole, therefore, the Düsseldorf Centre Party neither accepted whole-heartedly nor rejected unambiguously the anti-Semitic appeal.

---

[146] Ibid., 17.4.1919 'Die Anarchie in München'; 18.4.1919 'Spartakusprogramm und Intellektuelle'; 3.5.1919 'Der bayerische Bürgerkrieg'; 5.5.1919 'Der Kampf in München'; 6.5.1919 'Ruhe in München'.

[147] Stump, *Geschichte*, 39.

[148] *DT*, 27.6.1920 'Politisierung der Jugend an Düsseldorfs höh. Schulen'.

[149] Ibid., 27.5.1920 'Warum nicht deutschnational?' Von Kardorff left the DNVP following the Kapp Putsch; he later joined the DVP.

[150] StAD XXI 18, 13.2.1921 Election appeal.

[151] StAD XXI 18 'Wähler in Preussen'.

THE LEFT

Both the Independent and Majority Social Democrats of Düsseldorf were most adamant in their opposition to anti-Semitism in this period. The MSPD paper, for example, carried a number of articles in 1918/19 that attacked 'pogromists' like the *Deutsche Tageszeitung* for spreading the anti-Semitic venom. The *Freie Presse* also reported on 'persecutions of Jews' and 'new ritual murder campaigns', and warned that nothing could harm the German people more than a victory of reactionary Jew-hatred.[152] In particular, both parties condemned the anti-Semitism of the DNVP. The USPD's *Volkszeitung*, for example, dismissed right-wing attempts to distinguish between 'acceptable' and *Radauantisemitismus*:

The party tries to distance itself from *Radauantisemitismus* by declaring that it fights any corrosive, un-German spirit, whether Jewish or not . . . In the German-national 'Election Handbook for Everyone' the DNVP explains that it is the only party which does not admit Jews. Thus there is no sign whatever of a real dissociation from *Radauantisemitismus*.[153]

Similarly, the MSPD wrote of 'this nastiest marsh plant [*Sumpfpflanze*] of our political life' being rehabilitated by the Nationalists in an attempt to divert attention from the real culprits, the 'warmongers of conservative and national liberal opinion'.[154] Both parties, moreover, went beyond the usual assaults on political enemies to include little-known *völkisch* groups, the police, and the Bavarian Civil Guard. Finally, the Düsseldorf Left declared its solidarity with foreign workers in Germany—Poles, Jews, and Lithuanians—who were threatened with expulsion after having been carried off from their homes in the East to work under appalling conditions in German factories.[155] It was above all this defence of potential competitors of the native workforce (and the socialist constituency!) that showed how little the Left was willing to give in to the racist onslaught.

To sum up, the socialist parties in Düsseldorf never felt obliged to make concessions to the anti-Jewish feelings of the electorate. Not only was this possible because the working class was largely immune to racism, but also—and more important—because the socialist movement was radical enough not to allow for alternative explanations of social and economic

---

[152] *Freie Presse*, 13.12.1918 'Die Deutschen Pogromisten'; 11.2.1919 'Ein antisemitisches Witzblatt'; 8.5.1919 'Neue Ritualmordhetze'; 18.5.1919 'Judenverfolgungen'. There is no material on the 'KPD and anti-Semitism' in this period.

[153] *VZ*, 17.5.1920 'Die Partei der Gegenrevolution'.

[154] *Freie Presse*, 26.5.1920 'Deutschnationale Antisemitenpartei'; 31.5.1920 'Die deutsch-rassige Einwohnerwehr'; 4.6.1920 'Düsseldorfer Nachrichten'; 6.6.1920 'Deutschnationale Flegel'.

[155] *VZ*, 2.12.1920 'Ein Ausnahmegesetz gegen ausländische Arbeiter'.

disorder. This also explains why the now insignificant MSPD continued to hold the same views on the issue as its powerful rival to the left, the USPD, even though there was a slight chance for it to improve its position by appealing to the 'middle-class' anti-Semitism of this period.

SUMMARY

We are left with a number of conclusions after our comparison of Düsseldorf and Nuremberg between 1918 and 1921. First, while the Düsseldorf Centre Party resorted to anti-Semitism, it did so less frequently and less viciously than its Nuremberg counterpart, the BVP. While the former gave up its pre-war restraint when fighting political opponents, the latter moved beyond pre-war economic and cultural prejudice to include racism of the worst kind.

Second, while in Düsseldorf both moderate and radical socialists rejected anti-Semitism throughout the period, Nuremberg's Left either accommodated or played down the *völkisch* appeal. Pre-war traditions were largely confirmed here, with the former continuing to be hostile, and the latter continuing to be indifferent to the anti-Jewish message.

Third, in both cities the 'Protestant bourgeoisie' resorted to anti-Semitic imagery after 1918. While Nuremberg's National Liberals had done so before the war, Düsseldorf's *Honoratioren*, deploring its sudden absence of prestige and power, now did the same. The far Right, moreover, showed little moderation in either city, calling for measures to exclude the Jews from German political and social life.

Fourth, the Protestant Church in Nuremberg altered its pre-war approach to the 'Jewish question' through its use of occasional racist rhetoric, a development very similar to that of the *Fränkischer Kurier*. By contrast, Düsseldorf's Protestants no longer limited their attacks to 'Jewish' modernity, as had been the case before the war, but felt compelled to distinguish between 'Jews' and 'Germans' as two completely different entities.

Fifth, both cities witnessed a number of troubling incidents between 1918 and 1921, which makes it difficult to judge the significance of anti-Semitism on the basis of levels of hardship and suffering. While Nuremberg was both less prepared for, as well as somewhat closer to the 'disgraceful' events of Munich, the Revolution in Düsseldorf caused unprecedented violence and was followed by the occupation of parts of the city by foreign troops.

Sixth, accounts which stress the anti-Prussian or anti-socialist strains of Jew-hatred need to be qualified in so far as anti-Semitism prevailed among both left-wing supporters and those who voted for parties alleged to be Prussian, such as the DVP or the DNVP in Nuremberg. While Jew-baiting often coexisted with such tendencies, most material suggests that the connection is tenuous at best.

Seventh, if we take language to be a 'flag which signals the desirability of using a certain vocabulary when trying to cope with certain kinds of organisms', then the language used after the war by wide sections of the German public was an attempt to redefine the 'Jewish question' along the lines of inherent differences between 'Germans' and 'Jews'.[156] The causes for this change may lie in the effects of the war or in the impact of the Revolution, but whatever the reasons, many Gentiles now believed that *the* 'Jews'—and not just a few of them—were somehow responsible for the misery and dislocation that was post-war Germany.

Eighth, one can speak of a 'new anti-Semitism' emerging in this period, which built on already existing stereotypes and whose spiritual ancestors were long since dead, but whose significance lay in the way it pushed other forms of prejudice—'cultural' or 'economic'—to one side, establishing itself as the predominant form of discourse on the 'Jewish question'.[157] What is more, this 'new anti-Semitism' was not restricted to certain groups in society, but permeated wide sections of the populace, including individuals not normally associated with Jew-hatred. It is this fact, namely that men like Max Pechstein and Walter Gropius, both followers of the Left after the war, could blame the Jews for revolution and military defeat, that illustrates the changed atmosphere in regard to the 'Jewish question' following the momentous events of 1914–19.[158]

---

[156] See R. Rorty, *Contingency, Irony, and Solidarity* (Cambridge, 1989), 15.

[157] What this means is not that other aspects of anti-Semitism disappeared; rather, it means that one form gained influence over and against the others. See also the view taken by Quentin Skinner in relation to political theory: J. Tully (ed.), *Meaning and Context. Quentin Skinner and his Critics* (Cambridge and Oxford, 1988), 14:

Thus the problem facing an agent who wishes to legitimate what he is doing at the same time as gaining what he wants cannot simply be the instrumental problem of tailoring his normative language in order to fit his projects. It must in part be the problem of tailoring his projects in order to fit the available normative language ... An ideologist changes one part of an ideology by holding another part fast; by appealing to and so reinforcing convention.

[158] See J. Weinstein, *The End of Expressionism. Art and the November Revolution in Germany, 1918–19* (Chicago and London, 1990), 53, 64.

4
Exclusion confirmed
1922–1924

We stabilize our ideals like Platonic-Pythagorean ideas, immoveable
and unchangeable, and if reality does not follow them, then we are in
a position to claim precisely this as a proof of their ideality, of which
reality is only their 'impure' realization.

> Robert Musil in *Die neue Rundschau* (December 1921) quoted
> in D. S. Luft, *Robert Musil and the Crisis of European Culture*
> *1880–1942* (1980)

If the immediate post-war era was marked by revolutionary turmoil and a
high degree of uncertainty, the years 1922–4 witnessed equally disturbing
developments, including the murder of Walther Rathenau, the Ruhr occupation, and the Hitler Putsch. These and other events in Germany
indicated that the Weimar Republic faced the impossible task of being all
things to all people, especially since a majority of these people rejected the
constitution and a great many were unaccustomed to any form of political
compromise.

In this situation, the 'conceptual Jew' became part of the political
discourse of the nation. Unlike Zygmunt Baumann, however, I would
argue that 'modernity' allowed for different approaches to the 'Jewish
question', and that the abstract Jew he outlines emerged, more than
anywhere else, in post-war Germany, where the notion of the racially
'other', devoid of any personal traits, became increasingly common.[1]
Thus, although it must have been apparent that there was little correlation
between the concrete Jewish neighbour and the abstract 'Jewish Jew',
many Germans came to internalize the latter concept as a given fact of life.

On the other hand, the exclusion of Germany's Jews from the rest of
society was never a one-sided affair, where the 'conceptual Jew' emerged
with equal force and affected all Germans at the same time. Rather, it

---

[1] Z. Baumann, *Modernity and the Holocaust* (Cambridge, 1989), 39: 'The age of modernity
inherited "the Jew" already firmly separated from the Jewish men and women who inhabited
its towns and villages.'

became a widespread phenomenon both among those who supported the parties of the Protestant middle and those whose Catholicism was more traditional and conservative in nature. In order to examine these differences, as well as tracing the development toward the 'conceptual Jew', let us turn to the representatives of political opinion in the country, the parties, churches, and the press.

NUREMBERG

The murder of the German foreign minister, Walther Rathenau, on 24 June 1922 added to an already tense situation in Nuremberg. Rathenau's assassination coincided with a right-wing agricultural festival which had led to anti-republican incidents and subsequent protests by the city council. When the news of the murder was announced in the festival's main tent, those present broke out into the *Deutschlandlied*, prompting Hermann Luppe to speak of the 'low level of morality which hatred against the Republic and also against Jewry has engendered'.[2] In the furious outcry which followed, the festival's imperial flags were torn down by workers and its costume parade was transformed into a memorial procession for Rathenau. In addition the city council, against the votes of all 'bourgeois' parties, decided to rename the Hindenburgplatz after the deceased foreign minister in a move which was bound to alienate a majority of the city's burghers, who already 'experienced an unprecedented interference of government in their social and political lives'.[3]

It was at this time, too, that the political Right was gaining ground in the city. The first indication of this trend had occurred after the war, when a branch of the *Deutsche Sozialistische Partei*, which had links with the *Schutz- und Trutz-Bund* as well as the extreme right-wing Thule Society, was founded in November 1919.[4] The *DSP* soon attracted the primary schoolteacher, Julius Streicher, whose name became synonymous with the rise of the *völkisch* movement in Franconia.

---

[2] H. Luppe, *Mein Leben* (Nuremberg, 1977), 116. Whether Rathenau was murdered as a Jew, an *Erfüllungspolitiker*, or a representative of the Weimar 'system' is not the issue here. Many Germans believed that his death was at least in part related to his Jewish background, and we therefore need to look at the response by newspapers and parties to the murder in order to examine one particular way of confronting the problem of anti-Semitism in this period.

[3] R. Lenman, *Julius Streicher and the Origins of National Socialism in Nuremberg 1918–1923*, unpublished B.Phil. thesis (Oxford, 1968), 60; H. Hanschel, *Oberbürgermeister Hermann Luppe. Nürnberger Kommunalpolitik in der Weimarer Republik* (Nuremberg, 1975), 162–3.

[4] Lenman, *Streicher*, 42.

Born in 1885 in the Bavarian village of Fleinshausen near Augsburg, Streicher's political career until 1919 gave little hint of his future notoriety. In 1911 he joined the Progressives, for whom he gave frequent electoral speeches, and held a number of prominent positions within the *Verein Jung Fortschritt*. After returning from the war with the rank of lieutenant, he attended meetings of former officers, as well as those of the three socialist parties, only to find himself convinced that the real problem facing Germany was the racial struggle against 'world Jewry'.[5] In 1919 he joined the *Schutz- und Trutz-Bund*, a year later the *DSP*. In June 1920 he became editor of the *Deutscher Sozialist*, whose first issue carried a front-page article appealing to 'Our Brothers of the USP, MSP, and KPD'.[6]

Yet Streicher was too radical for the the party's leadership, who preferred *völkisch* 'high culture' to the radicalism of mass politics. The former therefore decided to leave the party in October 1921 for the more promising *Deutsche Werkgemeinschaft*. Streicher's involvement there, however, was of even shorter duration, again owing to an extremism which other members found too compromising. Finally, in October 1922, Streicher founded the first local branch of the NSDAP.[7]

The autumn of 1922 seemed an appropriate time for the appearance of National Socialism in Nuremberg. The show of strength by the Left following the Rathenau murder, as well as the reunion of the SPD and USPD in late September, alarmed many opponents of socialism. Streicher capitalized on these developments by concentrating his efforts on the 'Jewish question' which he saw as the key to solving Germany's problems.

The Nuremberg Nazi leader also benefited from the rather lenient attitude taken by the authorities. Heinrich Gareis, head of the state police and, after 1 November 1923, police director of Nuremberg-Fürth, especially sympathized with the *völkisch* movement. This is evident in a letter of April 1922 in which he commented on Streicher's anti-Semitic agitation in the *Werkgemeinschaft*: 'It is only natural that *Werkgemeinschaft* meetings, announced on striking posters, aroused protest and excitement

---

[5] R. Hambrecht, *Der Aufstieg der NSDAP in Mittel- und Oberfranken (1925–1933)* (Nuremberg, 1976), 24; E. Reiche, *The Development of the SA in Nürnberg, 1922–1933* (Cambridge, 1986), 15. See also W. P.Varga, *Julius Streicher: A Political Biography, 1885–1933*, unpublished Ph.D. thesis (Ohio State University, 1974), 12: 'When questioned later about this dramatic shift in his political attitude, Streicher explained that his interest in anti-Semitism was kindled when he read Theodor Fritsch's "Handbook on the Jewish Question" during the closing months of the war.' H. Preiß, *Die Anfänge der Völkischen Bewegung in Franken* (Nuremberg, 1937), p. 43 dates Streicher's 'conversion' after the war.

[6] Lenman, *Sreicher*, 46.   [7] Ibid., 53–4, 63–5.

in Jewish circles, yet concern is much more justified in response to left-wing political rallies, during which Jewish speakers often incite the audience.'[8]

In his autobiography, Ernst Röhm praised both Gareis and his assistant, Friedrich Schachinger, for providing vital support to right-wing groups in spite of opposition from city officials under Mayor Luppe; both men, according to Ernst Röhm, proved 'just as effective as their Munich colleagues, Ernst Pöhner and Wilhelm Frick'.[9] Not surprisingly, then, many Jews felt more deserted than ever. In October 1922, for example, the local Jewish paper reported a number of anti-Semitic incidents in high schools,[10] and a few months later the community had to fear attacks on individual members as the Passover festival was approaching: 'How bad the situation was for Nuremberg's and Franconia's Jews is evident from the fact that, as a result of Streicher's ritual murder accusations, the community expected an attack on the synagogue during the Passover holiday of 1923. Anxiety was running so high that other Jews and I stayed in the cellar of the synagogue at night for an entire week.'[11]

Meanwhile, Hitler's plans for a coup matured that summer, and his self-confidence was apparent at the German Day in Nuremberg on 1 and 2 September 1923. Though similar to other meetings of this kind, the Nuremberg demonstration differed from them in both size and scope. Virtually every *völkisch* and paramilitary organization participated, and speakers included Adolf Hitler, Theodor Fritsch, and General Ludendorff.[12] Monninger and other right-wing publishers produced a mass of *völkisch* literature for the occasion, distributing the 'Protocols of the Elders of Zion' in various forms and producing postcards in honour of Hermann Ehrhardt and Graf Anton Arco-Valley.[13]

---

[8] BStAN Rep. 270 IV K.d.I. II 714, 28.4.1922. For similar views by the Bavarian government, see BHStA MA 10016 and BHStA MA 100403.

[9] Hambrecht, *Aufstieg*, 42–3. See also *NAZ*, 6.4.1923: 'The representative of the Bavarian Ministry of the Interior in the Franconian towns of Nuremberg and Fürth, State Commissar Gareis, takes rough action against Communist meetings but tolerates the worst excesses of anti-Semitic gatherings.'

[10] *Nürnberger Israelitisches Gemeindeblatt*, 1.10.1922 'Aus dem Abwehrkampfe'.

[11] StAN QNG 404a: B. Kolb, *Die Juden in Nürnberg. Tausendjährige Geschichte einer Judengemeinde von ihren Anfängen bis zum Einmarsch der amerikanischen Truppen am 20. April 1945* (Nuremberg, 1946), 25–6. See also *NIG*, 1.6.1923.

[12] See the programme in NSDAP Hauptarchiv Reel 4.

[13] Lenman, *Streicher*, 146 n. 2. See also StAN C7/I GR 2982 'Bekanntmachung': 'We national workers are unwilling to tolerate the Jewish terror employed by our misguided colleagues. We have suffered and remained silent for many years. Now it's enough.' Ehrhardt, who headed various free corps in the aftermath of the Revolution, also led the *Organisation Consul*, a secret organization responsible for the deaths of Erzberger and Rathenau. Arco-Valley assassinated Kurt Eisner in February 1919.

Nuremberg's right-wing circles described the German Day as a complete success. Gareis, in his official report, claimed that the idea of '*völkisch* freedom had defeated the International',[14] and the attitudes of both the press and police illuminated the extent to which Nuremberg welcomed the nationalist cause in the early twenties.

The days prior to and following the Hitler Putsch further exacerbated Jewish–Gentile tensions in the city. Thus, two days before the coup, the *Jüdische Volkspartei* introduced a resolution in a community meeting protesting against the continued attacks on Nuremberg's Jewish citizens:

The mass expulsion of Jews from Munich, the continued assaults on Jewish inhabitants in Nuremberg, the unhindered stirring up of passions [*Volksleidenschaften*] against the Jews in meetings and the press, the unscrupulous Jew-baiting in schools: all this discloses a situation in which citizen rights no longer exist for the Jews. The Jewish community of Nuremberg protests against this abandonment of Bavarian Jewry by the state authorities, and in the name of justice and humanity demands full legal protection.[15]

The following sections will describe the reactions by non-*völkisch* groups within the population to these and other events.

'PROTESTANT BOURGEOISIE'

Left Liberals in Nuremberg consistently opposed all forms of anti-Semitism. Although membership lists no longer exist, it is likely that by 1923 Jews formed a vocal element within the DDP.[16] In May of that year, for example, Mayor Luppe was able to found the *Nürnberg-Fürther Morgenpresse* only with the help of Jewish financial support,[17] and throughout the Weimar Republic a number of Jews held prominent positions within the party leadership.[18]

---

[14] Reiche, *Development*, 42. On anti-Semitic incidents during the German Day, see StAN C7/I GR 2982 'Bemerkenswerte Vorkommnisse beim "Deutschen Tag"'. For anti-Semitic agitation in October, see StAN C7/I GR 2980, letter by Dr Heinrich Orthal of 26.10.1923. See also Luppe's complaints to Gareis: 'Such events would, if they were repeated, seriously undermine the local population's sense of justice and security.'

[15] *Protokollbuch der Israelitischen Gemeinde*, V, 7.11.1923, 166–70.

[16] StAN F5 QND 494: R. Bing, *Mein Leben in Deutschland vor und nach dem 30. Januar* (no date), 30. Jews also played some part in the creation of the local *Reichsbanner*. See Jacob Toury, 'Jewish Aspects as Contributing Factors to the Genesis of the Reichsbanner Schwarz-Rot-Gold', in: *LBIY*, 1992, 247.

[17] Luppe, *Mein Leben*, 145.

[18] Julie Meyer, who later joined the SPD, was a leading member of the *Jung-Demokraten*. Dr Richard Kohn was in the party executive. Luppe himself was not free from certain prejudices, as some of his comments reveal. See, for example, *Mein Leben*, 53, where he calls Dr Richard Kohn 'a Jew of perfectly noble beliefs'; p. 55, where he calls Süßheim 'a Jew of

This was reflected in the party press and propaganda material. In early November 1922, for example, the Nuremberg DDP sent a letter to the *Regierung Mittelfranken* complaining about Nazi anti-Semitism and warning that the *völkisch* movement had made considerable strides in the region.[19] Moreover, most Democratic papers linked Rathenau's murder to the growing anti-Semitic movement spreading throughout the country, a connection other groups were unwilling to make. While the *Nürnberger Zeitung* bitterly remarked that 'everything which is Jewish is being spat at, and everything which is to the left of the German People's Party is being derided', the *Anzeiger* argued that hate-inspired refrains like 'Shoot down Walther Rathenau / The goddamned Jewish swine!' ('Schießt ab den Walther Rathenau / Die gottverfluchte Judensau!') were responsible for the moral abyss Germany found itself in: 'The call to treacherous murder [*Meuchelmord*], which is present in this criminal and venomous hymn, has now been followed.'[20] Similarly, a December 1922 article in the DDP youth organ reminded its readers that true patriotism could do without 'cheap Jew-baiting':[21] 'Baron von Stein refrained from searching for scapegoats for Prussia's misfortune; thus he neither invented a stab-in-the-back legend nor provoked an anti-Jewish hate campaign.'[22] Finally, the Democratic Party was the only non-socialist group in Nuremberg to disapprove of the events surrounding the German Day in September 1923,[23] including the anti-Jewish propaganda that followed it.[24]

The *Fränkischer Kurier*, by contrast, ever more cautious not to upset its nationalist readership, both rejected anti-Semitism and welcomed *völkisch* thought. In a piece on National Socialism, for example, the *Kurier* noted that 'it is unworthy of a morally superior people to make political and economic recovery conditional upon the question of race,' only to close the article by advising the state to utilize the 'decent national core' inherent in the Nazi movement.[25] Likewise, the paper's ambivalent reaction to the Rathenau murder revealed how far the *Kurier* had drifted to the right.

the softer, delicate kind'; or p. 112, where he calls Julie Meyer a 'smart and tenacious Jewess'. Lenman, *Streicher*, 107 mentions that Luppe prevented his daughter from marrying a Jew.

[19] BStAN Rep. 270 IV K.d.I. II 714, 3.11.1922.

[20] *NZ*, 26.6.1922; *NAZ*, 26.6.1922 'Meuchelmord an Rathenau'. See also *NAZ*, 15.11.1922 'Revolution im November?': 'In Franconia the teacher Julius Streicher attacks our Jewish fellow citizens in a way that takes some beating. Each and every decent person must repudiate . . . such behaviour.'

[21] *Echo*, 4/1924, p. 83. This article shows how much anti-Semitism was regarded as a given in extreme right-wing thought: 'That the German *völkisch* also railed against the Jews in their usual cheap way goes without saying, so that it is mentioned only in passing.'

[22] Ibid., 12/1924, p. 178.   [23] *NFM*, 3.9.1923 'Zum "Deutschen Tag"'.

[24] Ibid., 24.9.1923 'Eine Erklärung'.

[25] *FK*, 2./3.12.1922 'Der Nationalsozialismus'.

On the one hand, the racist 'clique which had reproached him for his denomination' was to be eliminated,[26] yet on the other, the 'hideous act' was not to be used as a pretext for undermining the country's efforts at revising the Versailles Treaty.[27]

The German Day as well as the Hitler Putsch further underlined this approach to the *völkisch* movement. The former, for instance, was greeted enthusiastically by Nuremberg's main 'bourgeois' paper: 'Unconcious, bleeding from thousands of wounds, the German body politic [*Volkskörper*] lies deeply humiliated. Vain and misguided people pursued international illusions, believed in enticing promises by smooth-talking pharisees; worship of the golden calf commenced and now ends in the most shameless deception.'[28] The failed coup occasioned bathos of a similar kind: 'No, we just experienced the deaths of twenty men in Munich, all of whom were intent on ending German suffering but instead let the bullets speak another language . . . Oh, had these bullets only struck our enemies.'[29] Even if the *Kurier* believed that Hitler was incapable of leading the country, such words idealized his motives and ignored his racist fanaticism. Even if, therefore, the paper now and then condemned Jew-baiting as unworthy of the German *Kulturnation*, it disclosed on the whole a rather cavalier treatment of the potential threat emanating from the extreme Right. Anti-Semitism was still regarded as somewhat distasteful, but the post-war consensus that *völkisch* ideals were fruitful and justified soon made nought of any remaining scruples *vis-à-vis* the 'Jewish question'.

As we may recall from our analysis of the group's activities after the war, the Nuremberg *Mittelstandsvereinigung* had no reason to show any restraint in this respect. Thus the renamed *Wirtschaftspartei* continued to attack Jewish influence in German social and political life, a policy evident from a number of articles in the party's newspaper. In April 1922, for example, the *Süddeutsche Mittelstandszeitung* advised the Jews to distance themselves from their East European brethren, who were compared to fleas and lice: 'Do we have to accept such lice? . . . Indeed, it is high time we used a long comb to rid ourselves of these creatures.'[30] This theme was repeatedly invoked following the *Deutscher Tag* in September 1923. An

---

[26] Ibid., 28.6.1922 (Abend) 'An der Bahre Rathenaus'.

[27] Ibid., 26.6.1922 (Abend) 'Die Pflicht der Stunde'.

[28] Ibid., 2.9.1923 'Willkommen in Nürnbergs Mauern'.

[29] Ibid., 11.11.1923 'Das deutsche Ziel in Bayern'. See also the 'neutral' *NBZ*, 10.11.1923: 'The putsch was an extremely regrettable episode. Although it cannot be excused, it is explicable in terms of the hopeless emotional state of the German people.'

[30] *Süddeutsche Mittelstandszeitung*, 29.4.1922 'Die ostjüdische Einwanderung eine Gefahr für den Mittelstand'.

article at the end of October, for instance, used language which threatened both local and Eastern Jewry: 'The Eastern Jewish vermin [*Geschmeiß*] must leave the land. Like parasites [*Zecken*] it sucks dry our economy and fills itself with our blood until bursting at the seams . . . We have already pointed out that if German Jewry fails to dissociate itself radically from Eastern Jewry it shouldn't be surprised at being lumped together with the latter.'³¹ All this culminated in a warning that if the authorities failed to halt the 'influx' of Eastern Jews, the German people would be forced to take matters into its own hands. The paper therefore greeted the looting and violence in the Scheunenviertel of Berlin, where angry crowds had attacked Polish and Russian Jews held responsible for illicit trading and racketeering: 'And as in Berlin it must come to nation-wide pogroms where the authorities fail.'³² The Nuremberg *Wirtschaftspartei* thus accepted the possibility of pogroms, implied that German Jews could be the next target of popular discontent, and showed how far 'traditional middle-class ideology' had adjusted to the wave of *völkisch* hysteria in the years 1922–3.

The Bayerische *Mittelpartei*, it will be remembered, was well known for its anti-Semitic platform, and it continued to pursue this line after 1922. While the party distanced itself from the notion that anti-Semites were 'fanatics, thieves, or mass murderers', it insisted that anti-Semitism was justified as a means of eliminating 'Jewish' influence: 'Germany's leaders shall be Germans!' it proclaimed.³³ Although very little material exists for this period, all evidence points to the fact that the Bavarian DNVP saw 'Jews everywhere!'³⁴ and believed that every party, including the KPD, should recognize the importance of destroying the 'Jewish peril'.³⁵ While the anti-Jewish propaganda was not quite as heated as in the immediate post-war era (possibly owing to a cross-party consensus that something had to be done against the 'Jews'), the *Mittelpartei* persisted in its advocacy of the *völkisch* cause.

The disastrous outcome of the Hitler Putsch failed to paralyse the *völkisch* movement. In December 1923 Streicher founded the *Deutsche Arbeiterpartei* (DAP), one of many heirs to the now defunct NSDAP. Streicher also joined the *Grossdeutsche Volksgemeinschaft* after his release from pretrial detention in February 1924. Predictably, the *DAP* proved

³¹ *Süddeutsche Mittelstandszeitung*, 31.10.1923 'Der Eiserne Besen'. See also 22.9.1923 'Wird der Berliner Augiasstall ausgemistet?' and 5.9.1923 'Der Deutsche Tag': 'Stepping on to the "Hindenburgplatz"—despite everything Hindenburgplatz, Mosjö Süßheim—the roaring cheers for father Hindenburg resumed their force in unit after unit.'
³² Ibid., 10.11.1923 'Pogromstimmung in Berlin'.
³³ *Blätter der Bayerischen Mittelpartei* (Nuremberg), Universitätsbibliothek Erlangen 40 Hist. 525: *1922*—No. 39 'Antisemitismus'.
³⁴ Ibid., *1922*—No. 33.   ³⁵ Ibid., *1922*—No. 68 'Verein oder Partei?'

too moderate for Streicher's taste, leading him to create a local branch of the *Grossdeutsche Volksgemeinschaft* a few months later, whose meetings soon drew audiences of two to three thousand.[36] The results of the Bavarian state elections, moreover, indicated that the right-wing appeal in the city had hardly subsided. With 57,000 votes, representing 28 per cent of the electorate, the *Völkischer Block* received only 700 fewer votes than the SPD; the Democratic Party, by contrast, once the second strongest force in Nuremberg, suffered even more drastically than the Social Democrats. With 9300 votes, representing 4.5 per cent, the DDP now ranked last of all the major parties.[37]

The *völkisch* success in the state elections, repeated in the Reichstag elections of May, resulted in part both from publicity accorded to the trial of Hitler and Ludendorff and to social and economic dissatisfaction. While inflation had been largely conquered by 1924, many Nuremberg citizens still suffered from the effects of unemployment. At the beginning of December 1923, for example, more than 16,000 were without jobs, a number three times as high as the October figures. Although 1924 witnessed a steady decline in unemployment, this positive trend came too late to overcome widespread discontent.[38]

A further cause for the charged atmosphere in Nuremberg was the confrontation between the Right and the city administration. As early as 1922 Streicher had been convinced, against all evidence, that Mayor Luppe was of Jewish descent,[39] and by 1925 the Mayor had sued Streicher on a number of occasions. The March 1923 Luppe–Streicher trial, moreover, disclosed how readily *völkisch* anti-Semitism was viewed as a mitigating circumstance, for both the prosecution and the public at large believed that Streicher was acting out of firm, even honourable, convictions. Luppe himself expressed outrage at the way in which the 'Jewish question' was being used to discredit his leadership: 'It is simply humiliating how I have to stand here before this court and elucidate my family tree in public. But it is even more humiliating how Streicher, upon hearing my evidence ... was able to exclaim that my testimony had no value since I hadn't had the courage to admit that I was really a Jew.'[40]

---

[36] Hambrecht, *Aufstieg*, 61; Reiche, *Development*, 52–3. The *GVG* invited Communists to mass meetings, but any cooperation between the two failed to materialize because of differences over the 'Jewish question' and the disapproval of many *GVG* supporters of working with Communists. G. Pridham, *Hitler's Rise to Power. The Nazi Movement in Bavaria, 1923–1933* (London, 1973), 29.

[37] Hambrecht, *Aufstieg*, 70–1; Reiche, *Development*, 53.

[38] Reiche, *Development*, 54.   [39] Hanschel, *Luppe*, 190.

[40] StAN *Stadtchronik* 1924, 107. For the significance of the Luppe–Streicher trials, see Hanschel, *Luppe*, 204–16. For anti-Semitic incidents at the time, see *NIG*, 1.12.1923 'Aus

Despite Nazi losses in the December 1924 Reichstag elections, the Right remained strong. For while the DDP gained 6.6 per cent of the vote, thereby increasing its support by 3 per cent, the *Mittelpartei* more than doubled its vote to 16.1 per cent. At the same time, the *völkisch* movement managed to secure over 10 per cent, more than three times the national average, a clear sign of the continued appeal of right-wing ideology in the city.[41] Even if Nuremberg was controlled by a Left/liberal alliance, therefore, it remained a stronghold of the anti-Republican Right.

Nuremberg's Democratic Party, though heavily burdened by electoral setbacks and financial problems, refused to reverse its policy on the 'Jewish question'. The *Nürnberger Zeitung*, for example, reminded its readers that religion and politics needed to be kept apart: 'We shall read Goethe's *Faust* again instead of Dinter's *Sünde wider das Blut*. We shall be a free people in a free country, not one which calls for dictators and blood samples!'[42] The *Nürnberg-Fürther Morgenpresse* condemned anti-Semitism even more forcefully in an article prior to the May 1924 Reichstag elections:

Germany's Jews have a right to Germany, for they were born here and didn't immigrate. They must defend themselves against those who deny them a right to *Heimat*, to a mother tongue, to feelings for their fatherland [*Heimatgefühle*]; defend themselves as if confronted with a murderer. Whoever has a sound mind and a righteous heart must support them in their struggle and reject those who want to spread Jew-hatred among the people.[43]

In addition, left liberals castigated other parties for supporting the racist cause. The *Mittelpartei*, for example, 'has carried its anti-Semtism to extremes', while the *Wirtschafispartei* had shamelessly employed Jew-baiting in its election propaganda.[44] Similarly, the National Liberals, who

dem Abwehrkampfe', and the May and October issues under the same heading. Interestingly enough, a number of Nuremberg citizens whom the author consulted in the summer of 1991 were utterly convinced that Luppe was a Jew. For all its extremism, then, Streicher's propaganda seems to have created new realities.

[41] Reiche, *Development*, 84. The *Wirtschafispartei* (or *Mittelstandsbund*), clearly opposed to the Republic and a bitter enemy of the Jews, received 6.4 per cent, whereas the DVP, relatively weak in Bavaria as a whole, gained 1.2 per cent. Overall support for the Right thus amounted to 34.2 per cent, as opposed to 41 per cent for the SPD, 7.2 per cent for the KPD, and 6.6 per cent for the DDP.

[42] *NZ*, 19.4.1924 'Religion und Politik'. See also 17.4.1924 'Politische Chronik' and 2.5.1924 'Aus der Geschichte des Antisemitismus'.

[43] *NFM*, 22.4.1924 'Die antisemitische Taktik'. The article can also be read as an attempt to distinguish between native and Eastern Jews.

[44] Ibid., 9.4.1924 'Lehren aus der Wahl'; 15.4.1924 'Politische Streiflichter'; and the election appeal by the *Deutscher Block in Bayern* (DDP and *Bauernbund*) in the *NBZ* of 5.4.1924.

had hoped to join the DNVP in the run-up to the Bavarian state elections, were fiercely attacked for asking Jewish members to leave the party.[45] This stance was equally prominent in November and December 1924. An election appeal directed at women stressed the need for racial tolerance,[46] and the *Nürnberg-Fürther Morgenpresse*, in a comparison of election material, highlighted the effectiveness of a *Bund jüdischer Frontsoldaten* poster, which showed death spreading swastikas on Jewish graves just as a mother was bemoaning the victims of the war, 'whom *völkisch* racism was slandering to their graves'.[47] In sum, the DDP stressed the dangers involved in racist anti-Semitism, knowing full well that this policy was far from popular.

The *Fränkischer Kurier*, on the other hand, was firmly in nationalist hands. Already visible after 1920, this development was compounded by a financial deal in 1923 which enabled the MAN firm to secure a minority holding in the paper, with the understanding that the *Kurier* followed a 'national' course.[48] Yet the paper never needed such encouragement, as we may recall from earlier observations. In 1924, moreover, the *Fränkischer Kurier* shifted even further to the right.

One example of this 'new policy' was the sympathy accorded to the *völkisch* movement. In April 1924, for example, one of the *Kurier*'s reporters visited Hitler in Landsberg, where he encountered an 'honest, decent, and courageous man', and came to the 'terrible' conclusion that 'one can lose ones's freedom if one struggles for one's people's freedom.'[49] A few days later, in the run-up to the Reichstag elections, a *Kurier* headline put this in similar terms: 'German men, German women, call the traitors [*Dolchstößler*] of 1918 to account! Vote national!'[50] Nuremberg's most important 'bourgeois' newspaper clearly opposed the events of 1918, an approach repeatedly confirmed throughout 1924.[51] The apogee of rightwing propaganda, however, was reached in December 1924, when the

---

[45] Ibid.   [46] Stadtbibliothek Nürnberg Nor. 547 2 0 'An alle Frauen'.

[47] *NFM*, 1.12.1924 'Der Wahlkampf im Bild'. See also 28.11.1924 'Grundsätzliches zum Wahlkampf'; 30.11.1924 'Die Deutschnationalen 1919 und 1924'; and the *NZ* of 3.12.1924 'Zum Kampfe um die Republik'.

[48] K. Koszyk, *Deutsche Presse 1914–1945. Geschichte der deutschen Presse*. Teil III (Berlin, 1972), 202; T. Hübner, *Nürnberg im Kommunikationszentrum der Zeit des Nationalsozialismus unter besonderer Berücksichtigung der Tagespresse* Diplomarbeit (Nuremberg, 1991), 39; C. Dittrich, *Pressegeschichtliche Aspekte zum Aufstieg der NSDAP in Franken, aufgezeigt am Beispiel Nürnberger Zeitungen*, unpublished Ph.D. thesis (Erlangen, 1983), 30–6. The MAN firm in turn was owned by the Gutehoffnungshütte, the Ruhr steel firm, whose managing director was Paul Reusch. In 1929 the *Kurier* was taken over by MAN.

[49] *FK*, 27.4.1924 'Hitler und Landsberg'. See also 9.4.1924 'Ludendorff und die deutsche Bewegung', where the *FK* called the DDP 'undeutsch'.

[50] Ibid., 3.5.1924.

[51] See especially *FK*, 11.8.1924 'Verfassungsfeiern in Nürnberg'.

Kurier asked its readers to create a *Volksgemeinschaft*: 'Therefore German, fulfil your duty on December 7th, vote *völkisch*! Help to create the great German *Volksgemeinschaft*!'[52]

The question of anti-Semitism itself was rarely mentioned, owing perhaps to the fact that the *Kurier* received advertisements from Jewish businesses.[53] Nevertheless, in its support of the *völkisch* movement, the *Kurier* alienated large sections of the Jewish community, who came to realize that the once Progressive paper was a serious threat to peace and stability in the city. As if to underline this judgement, the *Kurier* some years later (1926) refused to publish a Bamberg police report which refuted Streicher's claim that a Mr Schlesinger was of Jewish origin. As the CV bitterly noted, the *Kurier* found even this too compromising: 'Unfortunately Nuremberg's most widely read paper, the *Fränkischer Kurier*, refused to accept the disclaimer "as a matter of principle".'[54]

Turning to the extreme Right, we find that the *Nationalliberale Landespartei Bayern*,[55] the *Wirtschaftspartei*, and the *Mittelpartei* continued to stress their *völkisch* commitments. The National Liberals, for example, who had emerged just left of the DNVP in 1924, demanded the absence of Jews from *Bürgerblock* lists if the party was to join such alliances in the future,[56] a request fully in line with its programme.[57] The *Wirtschaftspartei* was equally supportive of the nationalist cause. Hitler and his comrades were 'men of honour . . . from head to toe . . . These men have our full support. It's with them in the dock and will join them when they go to jail.'[58] The campaign for the Bavarian state elections in April 1924, moreover, showed how little the Nuremberg *Wirtschaftspartei* was willing to scale down its anti-Semitic agitation. While the party was somewhat less vociferous than in 1923, it showed no signs of remorse. Thus it insisted that Eastern Jews be expelled in order to secure Germany's *völkisch* recovery,[59] and ridiculed the DDP for having changed

---

[52] *FK*, 6.12.1924 'Deutscher, tue Deine Pflicht!' See also various articles in November and December that emphasize Christian as opposed to democratic and socialist values.

[53] A. Groß, *Glück und Ende des 'Fränkischen Kuriers'* (Nuremberg, 1967), 22.

[54] NSDAP Hauptarchiv Reel 91, Folder 378.

[55] The party was founded by Professor Friedrich Lent of Erlangen University, after the leaders of the DVP's district organization in Franconia no longer wished to be associated with the policies of Stresemann. See L. E. Jones, *German Liberalism and the Dissolution of the Weimar Party System, 1918–1933* (Chapel Hill, 1988), 199. On Lent and anti-Semitism at the university, see M. Franze, *Die Erlanger Studentenschaft 1918–1945* (Würzburg, 1972), 19, 65, 112, 404.

[56] *NIG*, 1.11.1924 'Aus der Abwehrbewegung'.

[57] *FK*, 4.4.1924 'Ziele der Parteien': 'Since its inception the National Liberal Party of Bavaria . . . has made it its task to combat the influence of international Jewry.' Jews were excluded from the party.

[58] *Süddeutsche Mittelstandszeitung*, 1.3.1924 'Hitler vor dem Münchener Volksgericht'.

[59] Ibid., 'Handwerker, Gewerbetreibende.'

its name to *Deutscher Block in Bayern*: '[Luppe] was kept in the background during the elections, but that helped the Democrats as little as the utterly ridiculous name change [*Umtaufe*] which nearly cost them the votes of the naturalized Galicians, who were informed about the change just in time and then told that the party was one of "ours" ["*Es wären 'unsere Lait'* "].'[60]

The *Mittelpartei*'s (DNVP) election material for 1924 included similar statements. Germany's capitulation to the Entente, for example, was linked to 'international Jewry, that exploiter of nations',[61] and an appeal to white-collar workers warned that 'banks and stock exchanges, Jews and black marketeers, trusts and syndicates' were in control of the economy.[62] *Mittelpartei* leaflets proclaimed the need for 'positive *völkisch* work' through the elimination of 'everything alien [*Fremdblütigen und Artfremden*], especially everything Jewish, by maintaining our Germanic heritage'. In an attempt to demonstrate its *völkisch* credentials following the secession of a more radical group under Albert von Graefe and Reinhold Wulle, the party also listed its past achievements and future plans concerning the 'Jewish question': 'All the old champions of anti-Semitism in parliament belong to the DNVP; such a seasoned veteran as the leader of the *völkisch Schutz- und Trutzbund*, Alfred Roth, will, alongside other *völkisch* fighters, represent our party in the new Reichstag.'[63]

Finally, the Protestant Church in Nuremberg, which had close ties to the *Mittelpartei*, remained surprisingly silent on the issue between 1922 and 1924. To be sure, there were occasional references to the immigration of *Ostjuden* or the racial background of the Social Democrat, Rudolf Hilferding,[64] but on the whole the Protestant weekly remained aloof on the question, relying perhaps on other groups to deal with the issue. Only once, in August 1924, does the reader find a detailed account of the 'Jewish question', which discussed such things as the murder of Christ— 'From now on something restless, vacillating, and dogged enters Jewish history'—and argued that 'the Jew, despite everything, remains a Jew'.[65] These examples suggest that the Church continued to oppose 'Jewish' influence and power, but that at the same time it felt no need to confront

---

[60] Ibid., 9.4.1924 'Was lehren uns diese Zahlen?' See also 5.4.1924 'Wen sollen wir wählen?': 'The Democrats must really think they are finished for good if they suddenly decided to rename [*umtaufen*] themselves "German block in Bavaria" (if it is at all appropriate to speak of renaming [*taufen*] in this case).'

[61] *NBZ*, 2.5.1924 DNVP election appeal 'Was uns bevorsteht'.

[62] *NZ*, 3.5.1924 DNVP election appeal 'Angestellte . . .'

[63] BHStA Abt.V FlSlg 65 'Positive deutschvölkische Arbeit' and 'Was wir wollen'.

[64] *EvN*, 4.6.1922 'Rundschau'; 9./16.9.1923 'Rundschau'.

[65] Ibid., 28.4.1924 'Die Lösung der Judenfrage'.

the subject too often, since Nuremberg's Protestant community had other sources to keep itself informed on the matter. More important still, the Church was rather anxious to avoid too great an involvement in the debate lest *völkisch* ideology sweep away important tenets of Lutheran orthodoxy.

CATHOLICISM

As may be remembered from the previous chapter, the BVP was one of the harshest critics of the Revolution in Nuremberg and, together with the *Mittelpartei*, the most anti-Semitic party. This changed after 1922, for the party now perceived National Socialism as its greatest threat. While this did not mean that Jews suddenly disappeared from BVP criticism, it implied a shift in emphasis in that the *völkisch* Right was now seen as the greater danger.[66]

Following the Rathenau murder, for example, the BVP argued that 'the German Nationals aren't a whit better than the Communists', and at a district meeting of the party in late June 1922 one speaker insisted that the BVP distance itself from the radicalism of the DNVP and other *völkisch* groups.[67] Similarly, an article of 26 April 1923 attacked Streicher for his virulent anti-Semitism: 'Our approach to the "Jewish question" is clearly defined by the principle of Christian justice. Therefore we have nothing in common with any form of *Radau-* and *Rucksackantisemitismus*.'[68]

This approach was further demonstrated after the Hitler Putsch, when the BVP warned of *völkisch* harmfulness (*Gemeinschädlichkeit*) and praised Cardinal Faulhaber's rejection of the anti-Semitic hate campaigns, 'which—in their pogrom-like character—threaten to become a cultural disgrace [*Kulturschande*]'.[69] Remarkably, however, this stance changed following the arrests of Hitler and his cronies. Now the party suddenly blamed the Jews for supporting the *völkisch* cause and the right-wing movement for accepting such help. The *Sonntags-Friede*, moreover, emphasized again the differences between Catholics and Jews, who were racially alien and therefore dangerous. In two articles of late December

---

[66] W. Hannot, *Die Judenfrage in der Katholischen Tagespresse Deutschlands und Österreichs 1923–1933* (Mainz, 1990), 107.

[67] Ibid., 27.6.1922.   [68] Ibid., 26.4.1923 'Pressebanditen'.

[69] Ibid., 10.11.1923 'Die nationale Revolution'; 14.11.1923 'Kulturkampf oder Vaterland?' See also Nuremberg's Catholic weekly, *Sonntags-Friede*, 25.11.1923. In 1922 Faulhaber repeatedly denounced the 'Jewish press'. It is also unclear whether or not his opposition to Judeophobia 'persisted through the Weimar Republic into the dark years beyond'. D. L. Niewyk, *The Jews in Weimar Germany* (Manchester, 1980), 60; see Cardinal Faulhaber, *Judaism, Christianity and Germany. Advent Sermons in St Michaels, Munich, in 1933* (London, 1934), 4–19.

1923 entitled 'Judaism and Catholicism' the Catholic weekly had the following to say on the modern 'Jewish question':

Owing to their adroitness and single-mindedness, both being inherent in their race, they attained economic, political, and cultural supremacy . . . As leaders of the proletariat they turned large parts of the working class into a Jewish defence force [*Judenschutzgruppe*] . . . It is typical of certain *völkisch* circles to accuse the Catholic Church of philo-Semitism [*Judenfreundschaft*] when they themselves permitted the Jewification [*Verjudung*] of our people or even wittingly or unwittingly promoted just that . . . And the Catholic Church! . . . it fought the rampant [*alles überwuchernden*] Jewish spirit . . . If they [the *völkisch*] only learned from history they could see that the Catholic Church—unlike them—always took the selfsame view on the matter.[70]

Similarly, the *Bayerische Volkszeitung* asked Streicher how he financed 'the Jewish-American style völkisch propaganda', only to answer the question itself by hinting that wealthy Jews supplied a 'Judas reward (*Judaslohn*) for the staging of the infernal hate campaign against the Catholic Church [*Inszenierung der infernalen Kulturkampfhetze*]'.[71] In another article of this kind a few weeks later, the BVP organ linked the Jews with Freemasonry and then asserted that a number of *völkisch* leaders were members of Masonic lodges. This led the paper to the far-fetched but tempting conclusion that Jews and Nazis were uniting in an effort to damage the prospects for a Christian state: 'It is all but certain that the anti-Semitic campaign was also paid for with Jewish moneys . . . Jewish Freemasons enlisted the help of the Nazis in order to avert the imminent danger of Jewish-Marxist liberalism being overcome by the towering ideals of the Christian state.'[72]

In other words, the period of opposition to Nazi anti-Semitism was rather short-lived, since the BVP soon realized that the failed coup of November 1923 did very little to discredit the *völkisch* movement. Although the party was aware of the hazards involved in even partially accepting the racist message, its use of such language reveals the prejudices found not only among the groups of the extreme Right. Given the BVP's post-war policies on the subject, however, it seems likely that its approach in 1922–4 reflected more than just a reaction to the dangers of National Socialism or to the popularity of *völkisch* ideology. Thus, however much Jews may have welcomed BVP resistance to the radical Right, they were mistaken in identifying this with a sudden wave of sympathy for

---

[70] *SF*, 2.12.1923 and 9.12.1923. See also 20.1.1924 'Aus Welt und Kirche'.

[71] *BV*, 23.4.1923 'Größenwahn oder Blasphemie'.

[72] Ibid., 2.5.1924 'Der Freimaurer im Kampf gegen den christlichen Staat. Jüdisch-freimauerische Hintergründe der Völkischen'. See also 5.4.1924 'Was ist Wahrheit?'

a downtrodden minority. If the Jews voted for the Catholic Party in Nuremberg, which they probably did not do in great numbers,[73] they did so because in Bavaria the BVP was the only reliable force that could challenge the Nazi movement. Therefore circumstances particular to Bavaria enabled the BVP to appeal to anti-Semitic tendencies without being identified with the right-wing *Radauantisemiten*.

THE LEFT

The Left during this period continued to underestimate *völkisch* racism and at times even showed sympathy for anti-Jewish feelings. Although the sources are very limited—the KPD, for example, had no local newspaper—the existing material suggests that the socialist parties largely ignored the 'Jewish question'.

Rathenau's death in June 1922 was the first incident requiring comment. Whereas the SPD accused 'reactionary forces' of the murder,[74] the USPD paper examined the causes of political anti-Semitism in some detail. In general, the party argued, the 'socialism of fools' benefited high capitalism and the agrarian élites, both of whom were 'far more capitalistic than Jewish capitalists'. The paper then went on to describe how the Jews—but not only the Jews—had developed 'usury and capitalism', how they had emerged as both the 'masters of haggling' (*Schachers*) and capitalism's most trenchant critics. Finally, the USPD maintained that the disappearance of exploitation would logically entail the end of 'Jewish exploitation'.[75] On the whole, then, the USPD tended to ignore ways of solving the current problem of anti-Semitism by alluding to its abolition in some future socialist state. Moreover, using words like haggling (*Schacher*) and usury (*Wucher*) in connection with 'Jewish business practices' hardly sensitized the party's supporters against discrimination.

This is not being too critical of the Left. For example, when a Jewish SPD member proposed to visit Streicher rallies in late 1922 in order to counter Nazi propaganda, the main party speaker replied: 'If you

---

[73] In Nuremberg the BVP won only 6 per cent of the vote in May 1924 and 7.5 per cent in December 1924. Reiche, *Development*, 84. On the whole, traditional and rural Jews were more likely to vote for the BVP. See P. Pulzer, *Jews and the German State. The Political History of a Minority, 1848–1933* (Oxford, 1992), 245: 'The anti-Semitic tendencies of the BVP did not stop Jewish citizens from voting for it. Among them were rabbis in Munich and Regensburg, . . . members of the Schweinfurt branch of the *Bund gesetzestreuer jüdischer Gemeinden*, as well as other Orthodox and Conservative Jews, who were more numerous in Bavaria than in other parts of Germany.'

[74] *FT*, 26.6.1922 'Der schwarz-weiß-rote Meuchelmord'; 29.6.1922 'Der Rathenau-Platz in Nürnberg'.

[75] *Sozialdemokrat*, 5.7.1922 'Der Sozialismus des dummen Kerls'.

believe that we accept money from Jews so that our workers may have their backs [*Buckel*] thrashed, you are wrong! There are many Jews whose behaviour provokes feelings of misgiving!'[76] Similarly, a report on the German Day in the SPD's *Tagespost* indicated how easy it was for the enemies of Nazism to appropriate *völkisch* language. Before we quote the entire passage it is worth noting that the following article was the only discussion of anti-Semitism in the first two weeks of September 1923:

> On Sunday, at around 9 a.m., I walked along the Vestnertorgraben. Ahead of me a family. Elegant appearance. Easy to ascertain non-aryan descent, judging from their faces. Great surprise, then, to witness the following dialogue: Son: 'In Schweinfurt they . . . [the socialists] want to hold up a train . . .' Father: 'Yes, but in Saxony they have already held up a few trains, the rogues. Well, Saxony is today nothing but a bolshevist enclave.' I walked on, not trusting my ears, and soon passed them . . . But they were really Jews, as one short glance at them revealed. I continued, involuntarily recalling the last sentence on Nazi posters: 'Jews not welcome' [*Juden haben keinen Zutritt*].[77]

Like the KPD in the following years, the Social Democrats ridiculed or belittled right-wing anti-Semitism in 1924. Prior to the Bavarian state and Reichstag elections, for example, the party tried to prove that Jews and nationalists cooperated on a number of occasions. 'The Fascist Leader—A Jew'[78] still made fun of the idea that Mussolini was really a Jew, but this did not prevent the SPD from establishing a relationship between the DNVP and its alleged enemy, world Jewry.[79] Moreover, the *Tagespost* doubted the sincerity of General Ludendorff's anti-Semitism, since the latter had allegedly supplied the Jews with flour for their 'ritual pastries'

---

[76] BStAN Rep. 218/1 I Nr 339 Polizeibericht Nr 4650. See also the police report of 21.3.1924 on a *Deutsche Arbeiterpartei* meeting in: NSDAP Hauptarchiv Reel 17a: 'A Communist . . . supported Streicher's words, to the effect that Communists were also "national". One had to respect men like Schlageter, Hitler, and Ludendorff . . . The KPD was ready to march hand in hand with the *völkisch*.' After the Bavarian state elections in April 1924 the Nuremberg police confiscated 70 KPD leaflets entitled 'Down with the Jew Republic'. H.-H. Knütter, *Die Juden und die deutsche Linke in der Weimarer Republik 1918–1933* (Düsseldorf, 1971), 186.

[77] *FT*, 6.9.1923 'Momentbild vom "Deutschen Tag"'.

[78] Ibid., 5.4.1924. For an attempt to place Marx outside the Jewish tradition, see 31.1.1924 'Sozialdemokratie und Nationalismus':

The Jew Marx from the Rhein province, who in early years had already transcended Judaism and who had received his entire education, as well as the impressions of his youth from Christian families, and Friedrich Engels, whose background was Protestant-Pietistic, were twins [Zwillingspaar], so that to speak of a Marxist view is inaccurate; at most one could call it Marxist-Engelsian.

[79] Ibid., 17.4.1924 'Von Juden begründet—von Juden geführt!'

(?) during the war.[80] The only article attacking Jew-hatred in this period was one listing nine prominent enemies of the *völkisch* creed.[81] And even in that case the paper referred to historical persons instead of commenting itself on the dangers of racism.

Although the party took anti-Semitism somewhat more seriously towards the end of the year, the terms of the debate changed very little. Nazis like Anton Drexler 'sang the old song of the Jews being responsible for everything',[82] *völkisch* leaders were 'hysterical fools, unscrupulous careerists, and ruthless demagogues',[83] and 'political children were scolding the Jews'.[84] The SPD paper also disproved claims that past governments were overwhelmingly Jewish by noting the actual number of Jews in former cabinets.[85] Finally, the party's *Wahlzeitung*, the *Nürnberger Abendpost*, attacked Streicher's propaganda against the municipal *Milchzentrale*. Contrary to the Nazi leaders' assertions, the city did not provide for the distribution of kosher milk. This was handled by the 'middle-class, anti-Jewish *Zentralmolkerei*', and it was clear that the paper wished to embarrass right-wing anti-Semitism by showing that Nazis and Jews frequently worked together.[86] The attempt to deride *völkisch* racism was further evident in an article questioning the record of Fritz Ertl, a well-known local Nazi: 'During the period of inflation he opened an account in a Jewish bank and asked the owner to give him tips on how to speculate. Beyond that, he frequented a Jewish teacher, whom he also asked for similar tips. That's what the Jew-baiter [*Judenfresser*] Ertl looks like.'[87]

If these examples seem unduly critical, it is because the 'other side of the coin' did not exist, at least not in the socialist press between 1922 and 1924. Since our sample concentrated on the crucial periods before elections or during times of crisis, it is possible that other, more sensitive articles did appear, or that left-wing leaders did condemn anti-Semitism in private. On the other hand, if we consider the immediate post-war years, when the approach to the 'Jewish question' was marked by similar signs of indifference and opportunism, we find nothing unusual in the above findings. It seems quite likely, furthermore, that socialists felt compelled to comment on anti-Semitism after such events as the Rathenau

---

[80] *FT*, 3.4.1924 'Ludendorff in seinem eigenen Spiegel'. See also 16.4.1924 'Geld stinkt nicht'.
[81] Ibid., 5.4.1924 'Urteile über die Völkischen'.
[82] Ibid., 14.11.1924 'Hoffnungslos!'
[83] Ibid., 27.11.1924 'Schwarz-weiß-roter Konflikt'.
[84] Ibid., 3.12.1924 'Die "Judenregierungen"'.   [85] Ibid.
[86] Stadtbibliothek Nürnberg Nor. 547 2 o, 6.12.1924.
[87] Ibid., 'Die völkischen Stinkbomben'.

murder or the German Day, but that this was not necessarily the case in times of relative peace, even if Streicher repeatedly tried to isolate the Jewish community with his slanderous propaganda. Finally, working-class anti-Semitism should not be discounted: at least until 1924, Jews remained the target of right-wing attacks, and the Left may have realized how inexpedient a defence of the Jews would be.

Perhaps the most striking development of these years was the general swing to the right by the moderate 'bourgeoisie'. Political parties and their respective newspapers not only understood the reasons for the *völkisch* vogue, they perceived them as fully justfied; and if these groups some-times criticized the means pursued by Hitler or Streicher, they agreed that something had to be done against the debilitating influences of democracy and Marxism. The formely liberal *Fränkischer Kurier*, for example, ex-tolled the virtues of the National Socialist movement, and all parties to the right of the DDP ascribed great importance to the *völkisch* cause. All this, of course, implied racist thinking, but although most opinion-forming bodies employed anti-Semitic language, doing so was no longer consid-ered necessary. The period 1922–4, in other words, saw the internaliza-tion of exclusionist thinking; many Germans now viewed Jew-hatred in politics as a given; and they accepted this either as a necessary evil or as a necessary consequence of the events surrounding Germany's defeat and humiliation.

If we look at the BVP, for instance, we find that the party only briefly condemned anti-Semitism, namely at a time when its own position in Bavarian politics was threatened by a right-wing coup. After the failure of the Hitler Putsch, however, Catholic newspapers returned to a policy of vilification in which Jews were seen as conspiring with their alleged enemies. Social Democrats, on the other hand, hoped to check the right-wing groups by denying their *völkisch* credibility. Both the BVP and the SPD, then, questioned the anti-Semitic motives of right-wing extremists.

The only party concerned with the rise of political anti-Semitism also had the highest number of Jewish supporters. The DDP, it can be argued, became Nuremberg's *Judenschutztruppe* precisely because no other party was willing to take Jew-hatred seriously. Perhaps most striking of all, therefore, was the absence of open opposition in this period, the general silence which revealed the damage that had been done between 1918 and 1921. From now on it was what the press and the parties did not say that formed the basis of Jewish–Gentile relations and eventually led to the 'social dissociation' found in the early years of the Third Reich.

DÜSSELDORF

Rathenau's death in June 1922 gave rise to serious divisions within the city. As elsewhere, workers took to the streets, but in Düsseldorf, perhaps more so than in other cities, left-wing organizations decided to move beyond mere verbal protestations. In the aftermath of the murder, left-wing agitators closed municipal offices, halted work at factories, and insulted pedestrians. Vandalism was widespread, as were strikes and traffic jams. While a majority of citizens condemned Rathenau's murder, many were equally appalled by the ensuing violence. In their view, the socialist parties had acted irresponsibly and had used the general anti-*völkisch* sentiment for their own purposes.[88] As a result, the moderate *Deutscher Gewerkschaftsbund* as well as the Catholic unions refused to participate in the demonstrations for the 'protection of the Republic'.[89]

If the events surrounding the murder of Rathenau reminded many of the revolutionary period in 1918/19, the Ruhr invasion in January 1923 did nothing to dissipate the charged atmosphere in Düsseldorf. Although French and Belgian troops had occupied parts of the city in 1921, taking quarters in schools and private houses, the Rhenish population at the time grew more or less accustomed to foreign control.[90] This changed, however, in 1923. The French now began to seize offices, factories, and communication lines, forced civil servants to leave the city, and expelled both the mayor, Emil Köttgen, and the provincial governor, Walter Grützner. Financial difficulties, especially in the area of taxation, as well as high unemployment, made matters worse.[91]

Moreover, the trial and subsequent shooting of Leo Schlageter in May 1923 further exacerbated existing tensions. Schlageter, a former officer and member of the Free Corps Löwenfeld, had blown up a railway line near Düsseldorf. Although other acts of terror had been common, the harsh sentence, as well as the fact that the French had dismissed various appeals for clemency, encouraged right-wing groups to idealize Schlageter and make him into a national hero. These circles were also worried about rumours of separatist uprisings in the area.

Yet Düsseldorf was little affected by secessionist tendencies at the time. Even though demonstrations for a Rhenish Republic took place in late September, all parties except the KPD opposed such measures. In addi-

---

[88] HStAD Reg. Düss. 16047, 16893, 16894.   [89] StAD XXI 49.

[90] P. Hüttenberger, *Düsseldorf. Geschichte von den Anfängen bis ins 20. Jahrhundert*. Band 3: *Die Industrie- und Verwaltungsstadt (20. Jahrhundert)* (Düsseldorf, 1989), 326–7.

[91] Ibid., pp. 343–5. In October 1923, there were 63 applicants for every job opening; the city had to support 80,000 unemployed men, including their families; and many of the sick and elderly could no longer afford medical treatment.

tion, most of the instigators were outsiders, so that further attempts to rally the population behind their cause became increasingly difficult.[92] Finally, because the September protests ended in violence, resulting in a number of deaths, Düsseldorf's citizens were even less inclined to support the separatists after 1923.[93]

Unlike Nuremberg, Düsseldorf was home to a relatively weak Nazi party in this period.[94] Sometime after the war, the engineer Alfred Brunner had founded a local chapter of his *Deutsche Sozialistische Partei*. Yet the *DSP* never gained much backing, depite positive coverage in the *Freie Meinung*, the main organ of the Düsseldorf *Schutz- und Trutz-Bund*. (The latter organization had around 1000 members; it was outlawed after the Rathenau murder.) As early as March 1921 Brunner's party appears to have dissolved, a development attributable to two main factors: first, socialist organizations repeatedly disturbed right-wing meetings; and second, the French strictly enforced laws against the dissemination of nationalistic propaganda.

Brunner eventually cooperated with the Düsseldorf NSDAP, which was established in December 1922. Yet the local Nazi Party was more a creation of the Munich executive than that of a group representing Düsseldorf's *völkisch* constituency. This was reflected in the low number of active members (approximately 150), many of whom were former supporters of the *Organisation Consul*, as well as by the fact that, after the NSDAP was banned in Prussia, the Munich organization officially took over the local party. Not surprisingly, the *Völkisch-Sozialer Block* received only 2.1 per cent in the May 1924 Reichstag elections, a rather poor performance compared to its national average.

In this period anti-Semitic incidents were rare. In July 1922 a group of *völkisch* youths insulted and bullied the Jewish newspaper editor M. Löwenstein in the neighbouring town of Elberfeld, but otherwise no serious attacks on Jews were reported.[95]

[92] Attempts to implicate the Jews in the separatist movement also originated elsewhere. See, for example, the letter by the provincial governor to the Düsseldorf Jewish community, printed in the *CV-Zeitung* of 31 May 1923: 'I won't fail to point out whenever possible, and in particular during lectures in unoccupied Germany, that the accusations made against the Jewish population in the occupied territories by the *Gollnower Anzeiger* and the *Deutsche Zeitung* are completely made up.'

[93] G. J. Gemein, *Die Deutschnationale Volkspartei in Düsseldorf 1918–1933*, unpublished Ph.D. thesis (Cologne, 1968), 33; W. Matull, *Der Freiheit eine Gasse. Geschichte der Düsseldorfer Arbeiterbewegung* (Bonn, 1980), 128.

[94] The following is based on V. Franke, *Der Aufstieg der NSDAP in Düsseldorf. Die nationalsozialistische Basis in einer katholischen Großstadt* (Essen, 1987), 89–99. According to the police in Elberfeld, the *Schutz- und Trutz-Bund* had 1000–1200 members in that city: HStAD Reg. Düss. 16012, 421.

[95] HStAD Reg. Düss. 17054.

'PROTESTANT BOURGEOISIE'

As we may recall, the DDP in Düsseldorf was relatively weak and dependent on a hard core of supporters. This did not change after 1922, for left liberals in the Rhenish city continued to suffer defeat after defeat at the polls. This meant that the party became more homogeneous, and thus potentially more favourable to Jewish concerns. On the other hand, the DDP might have resorted to anti-Semitism as a means to improve its electoral chances. However, given its constituency as well as the existence of other, more reliable parties in this respect, such behaviour seemed all but futile. Finally, the Democratic Party rejected Jew-baiting on ideological grounds, a fact that should also be kept in mind.

Unfortunately, little material exists on the DDP. The party had to rely on a weekly (and sometimes bi-monthly) newspaper, the *Düsseldorfer Beobachter*, and could expect to receive positive coverage from the *Lokalzeitung*, which was owned by Isaak Thalheimer, a progressive Jew. Still, we may come to some understanding of the left liberal position on the 'Jewish question' in this period by studying how these papers reacted to the events of the day.

The *Lokalzeitung* was often apologetic in its approach. At the same time, it viewed anti-Semitism as a tactical device to divert attention from the real culprits. *Völkisch* pamphlets calling on the people to purge themselves of the 'Jewish menace', for example, were inspired 'in order to divert the people's wrath from Ludendorff and his cronies and from the billionaires . . . to the 600,000 Jews, 90 per cent of whom belong to the middle classes [*Mittelstand*], while the other 10 per cent together own less than Krupp, Stinnes, Stumm, and Tyssen'.[96] The paper also linked Jew-baiting with economic disorder. After the Hitler Putsch, for instance, Thalheimer commented that ruthless politicians were using the unemployed for their dangerous game.[97] As both articles suggest, anti-Semitism was taken seriously, even though the explanations for its success were not always accurate.

Düsseldorf's left liberals were particularly concerned with the outcome of the Hitler–Ludendorff trial. The *Beobachter*, for example, was very surprised at Ludendorff's malicious attacks on the Jews, given that so many of them had served in the army and died for Germany.[98] The paper

---

[96] *LZ*, 1.7.1922 'Lokalpolitischer Brief'.   [97] Ibid., 17.11.1923.

[98] *Beobachter*, 5.4.1924 'Ludendorff und die Juden'. This did not stop the DDP from opposing an SPD motion in the municipal council to repeal Ludendorff's honorary citizenship and change the names of Ludendorff Street and Ludendorff School. See *Stenographische Berichte der Stadtverordnetenversammlung*, 24.3.1924, Bloem (DDP): 'a city council meeting [is] not the place to judge historical figures.'

also carried a leader by the chairman of the party, Erich Koch-Weser, in which the latter condemned the National Socialists not only for their anti-Semitic platform, but equally for their dangerous 'political and economic obessesiveness [*Verranntheit*] and irresponsibility'.[99]

Prior to the May 1924 Reichstag elections, the DDP was forced to deal with anti-Semitism on a number of occasions. Although the party tried to appeal to patriotic sentiments when it contrasted its programme with that of the Left,[100] the Democratic Party time and again condemned the Jew-baiting of the *völkisch* movement. In an article on National Socialism, for example, the *Beobachter* pointed out the inconsistencies of right-wing anti-Semitism, which blamed the Jews for having caused the war on the one hand, and for having undermined the German war effort on the other.[101] Yet a few days later the DDP organ dismissed the racist creed in unequivocal terms: 'And it is therefore reprehensible, nay, a downright crime against the fatherland, if Germans deny other Germans their patriotism or their "Germanness", only because they supposedly belong to a different "race". How many Germans actually exist today who can say of themselves that they are of pure German blood?'[102]

This reasoning was used in the paper's articles in November and December of that year, when Germans were asked to go to the polls for the second time in six months. While the *Lokalzeitung* tried to ridicule the nationalism of the DNVP,[103] the *Beobachter* persisted in its opposition to *völkisch* anti-Semitism. In an article on 'The duty of mothers', the paper called into question the validity of racial differences, arguing that in Franconia Gentiles were often mistaken for Jews. The article also mentioned how anti-Semitism disrupted Jewish–Gentile relations in schools, and concluded with a warning not to ignore the dangers of racism: 'It is the most important duty of women and mothers . . . not . . . to regard the wearing of swastikas as a trivial game, but to brand the harmfullness of the anti-Semitic cause everywhere.'[104]

[99] *Beobachter*, 5.4.1924 'Demokratie und Judentum'. See also 22.3.1924 'Politische Umschau': 'One may speak ill of individual German Jews, just as one may speak ill of individual German Christians. In their entirety Germany's Jews are just as good Germans as Germany's Christians.'
[100] StAD XXI 331 DDP election newspaper 'Der Reichstagswähler am Niederrhein': 'It [the SPD] still has not found the proper approach to the great German past and to national feelings [*nationalen Gefühlswelt*].'
[101] *Beobachter*, 26.4.1924 'Wie herrlich leuchtet das Hakenkreuz!'
[102] Ibid., 3.5.1924 'Seid einig, einig, einig!'
[103] Ibid., 6.12.1924 'Lokalpolitischer Brief'. See also 29.11. 1924 'Lokalpolitischer Brief', where Thalheimer admits that he will vote Democratic but insists that his paper will remain neutral.
[104] *Beobachter*, 7.12.1924 'Die Pflicht der Mütter'.

We see again that the DDP was adamant in its rejection of anti-Semitism. More important still, the party never failed to comment on the spurious claims made by racists that the Jews were foreign bodies in the German polity, who were unable to assimilate because of their supposedly alien blood. This was all the more remarkable, given its poor showing in both elections. In May the DDP received 4.5 per cent, in December 4.1. Its 'bourgeois' rivals to the right, by contrast, won 26.8 and 24.9 per cent respectively.[105] Protecting or defending the Jews was hardly popular in 1924, but the DDP in Düsseldorf remained convinced that *völkisch* anti-Semitism was an evil that had to be destroyed.

This was certainly not the case for the German People's Party, which continued to espouse conservative if not 'reactionary' policies, as the following description indicates: 'It [the DVP] fights under the old colours of black-white-red. It hopes for the re-emergence of German power and greatness under a German *Volkskaisertum* . . . Our battle cry remains the same: First the fatherland, then the party.'[106] Because the DVP felt compelled to support the nationalist cause whenever necessary, it often excused right-wing terrorism, like Rathenau's murder, as an understandable outcome of Germany's dismal state.

The city council member Kempes, for example, remarked that it was too early to say whether 'right-wing elements' were responsible for Rathenau's murder,[107] while the *Düsseldorfer Zeitung* condemned the 'wicked act' but intimated that others had more to gain from it than the *völkische Mordbuben* 'in their youthful immaturity':[108] 'One ought to be doubly careful with suspicions in these excited times so as not to stir up class hatred. After all it is possible that certain foreigners have acted as agitators in order to provoke disorder and confusion in Germany and then to fish in troubled waters.'[109]

Against this, the *Düsseldorfer Nachrichten* admitted that anti-Semitism had played at least some part in the assassination of Rathenau. The paper,

---

[105] B. Brücher et al., *Dokumentation zur Geschichte der Stadt Düsseldorf. Düsseldorf während der Weimarer Republik 1919–1933. Quellensammlung* (Düsseldorf, 1985), 194. The DVP gained around 11 per cent in both elections, the DNVP 16 in May and 14 per cent in December.

[106] StAD XXI 311 election leaflet May 1924. A police report on right-wing groups in Elberfeld included the DVP: HStAD Reg. Düss. 16765, p. 446. In Essen former DVP members were behind attempts to form a local NSDAP organization: HStAD Reg. Düss. 15717 Polizeipräsident Essen, 14.6.1922.

[107] HStAD Reg. Düss. 16894, *Düsseldorfer Zeitung* of 26.6.1922.

[108] *DZ*, 2.7.1922 editorial.

[109] Ibid., 25.6.1922. An editorial on the following day put this in similar terms: 'Both the policy of fullfilment and democracy will regain the initiative as a result of this crazy act . . . while the right-wing cause will suffer irreparable damage.'

which was supportive of the 'national Right' (DVP, DNVP), mentioned how the foreign minister's 'selflessness and personal inviolability' had been depreciated by anti-Semitic politicians;[110] the paper also argued that the main motive for Rathenau's murder was the belief that the latter had done too little to reverse the effects of the Versailles Treaty.[111]

On the whole, the DVP expressed considerable sympathy for the *völkisch* movement. As was the case with the *Fränkischer Kurier* in Nuremberg, the press highlighted the patriotism of the Nazis, and ignored other aspects of National Socialism which were hardly appealing to respectable burghers fearful of violence and radicalism. This was especially true during the Hitler–Ludendorff trial. The *Düsseldorfer Zeitung*, for example, judged that only the enemies of Germany would benefit from such acts of *Selbstzerfleischung*: 'The demolition of a number of public figures; the destruction of the valuable fruits of national recruitment; hatred between German people, who belong together for good or ill; smirking *Schadenfreude* by all our socialist enemies.'[112] The *Düsseldorfer Nachrichten*, moreover, compared the attempted coup with the revolutionary upheaval of 1918/19, and conceded that at least Hitler was of German stock, whereas his critics, 'those literary figures who emigrated from Austria',[113] were wrong to assume that they had the right to discuss matters dear to most Germans. The paper also described the advocates of a harsh sentence as guardians of Zion (*Zionswächter*),[114] who lacked

empathy for the national and patriotic convictions of the so-called 'traitors', who have become guilty because they loved their fatherland perhaps too much with their hearts . . . There may be groups who, like Shylock, prefer to maintain appearances, but they are advised to be cautious and to quietly respect German sensibilities [*das deutsche Gefühl*].[115]

This anti-Semitic bias, although veiled and indirect, was repeated in the run-up to the May Reichstag elections. As so often before, the SPD was the party of Sklarz und Parvus-Helphand, 'the party's nouveaux riches',[116] but the DVP also professed to be 'the truly *völkisch* party',[117] and concluded that Germany belonged to the Germans: 'No flooding through

---

[110] *DN*, 25.6.1922.   [111] Ibid., 27.6.1922 editorial.
[112] *DZ*, 6.4.1924 'Der Prüfstein'. See also 11.4.1924 'Die Quittung'. Unfortunately, the *Düsseldorfer Zeitung* did not appear during and immediately after the Hitler Putsch.
[113] *DN*, 2.3.1924 'Ein Rückblick'. See also 24.4.1924 'Schuld und Sühne'.
[114] Ibid., 30.3.1924 'Ein Rückblick'.
[115] Ibid., 1.4.1924 'Das Urteil des Volksgerichts'.
[116] *DZ*, 2.4.1924 'Zwei Garnituren'.
[117] StAD XX 311 election leaflet May 1924 'Wer ist völkisch?'

aliens [*Ueberflutung durch Fremde*]. Borders closed to Eastern Jews.'[118] In addition, the People's Party hoped for a coalition with the DNVP in the new government,[119] a stand that was further underpinned by a truce between the two parties in Düsseldorf.[120] Although the DVP used anti-Semitic imagery less frequently in this period than in the immediate post-war years, it still found such language helpful, especially before elections, and in its nationalist pathos wished to see all forces expelled from the country which belittled the extent of German suffering. Although the DVP did not have to compete with the DNVP, therefore, it believed that 'the Jews' remained hostile to the spiritual recovery of the nation.[121]

Unfortunately, little material exists on the Düsseldorf *Wirtschaftsbund* (*Wirtschaftspartei*), which received 8.4 per cent of the vote in the May 1924 municipal elections.[122] Hüttenberger has described the party as 'a party political lobby of the *Haus- und Grundbesitzervereins* as well as of the hotel and restaurant trade',[123] and most evidence in the city archive suggests that the 'middle-class interest group' was more concerned with schools, streets, and sewers than with the intricacies of party politics.[124] Anti-Semitism, though perhaps not absent,[125] was never an important weapon in the arsenal of the movement.[126] Finally, the *WB* occasionally received favourable coverage from the *Lokalzeitung*; the Nuremberg *Wirtschaftspartei*, on the other hand, would have neither received nor wanted such coverage from a paper owned by a progressive Jew.[127] In short, while hardly any documents survive to elucidate the approach to the 'Jewish question', we may safely conclude that the issue was of minor concern to the party in Düsseldorf.

---

[118] StAD XX 311 DVP pamphlet attacking the *völkisch* parties. Another passage read: 'The anti-Semitic *Semiimperator* (1919) tried to prove that the Hohenzollern were contaminated with Jewish blood [*verjudet*]. The German People's Party rejects with much indignation such a mean disparagement of the House of Hohenzollern by the *völkisch*.'

[119] *DZ*, 28.4.1924 'Der Sinn der Reichstagswahl'.   [120] Gemein, *DNVP*, 37.

[121] See *DN*, 23.11.1924 (Morgen) 'Ein Rückblick'.

[122] Brücher, *Dokumentation*, 194.   [123] Hüttenberger, *Düsseldorf*, 362–3.

[124] StAD XXIV 1117. See also Franke, *NSDAP*, 33.

[125] StAD XXI 231 election leaflet December 1924: 'Do everything to destroy the DDP, the party of international capital, and its deadly influence.' See also StAD Plakatsammlung Mappe 16 'Drei peinliche Fragen', where the *WB* calls the DDP 'the party of international bank capital'. Still, these are the only examples among nearly forty leaflets and eight posters.

[126] See StAD Plakatsammlung 16 'Mit Hitler und Mussolini?': 'The National Socialists continue to fight the department stores, so far as they are in Jewish hands, while Christian department stores like Peters in Cologne enjoy their sympathy. An economic analysis, however, must apply the same standards to all large-scale enterprises of the retail trade.' For the *Wirtschaftspartei* and anti-Semitism, see Martin Schumacher, *Mittelstandsfront und Republik. Die Wirtschaftspartei—Reichspartei des deutschen Mittelstandes 1919–1933* (Düsseldorf, 1972), 21, 48–9, 55; Pulzer, *State*, 247.

[127] Hüttenberger, *Düsseldorf*, 363.

The DNVP, of course, believed the 'Jewish question' to be no small matter, but a central problem to be solved if Germany was to regain her lost pride. Following the Rathenau murder, for example, the DNVP tried to distance itself from the *Mordbuben*, but maintained that it was just as bad 'how this crime . . . was exploited by political agitators'.[128] In the aftermath of Rathenau's death the party continued to call for the purging of Jews from influential positions,[129] but following the Ruhr occupation nationalist organizations were severely restricted.[130] What is more, the Düsseldorf DNVP seems to have rejected the extremism of *völkisch* radicals like von Graefe and Wulle, as a letter by its leader, Dr H. Ellenbeck, to Kuno Graf von Westarp suggests: 'This boastful nationalism is the superficial bawl which has caused our demise . . . We have here in the occupied western border areas [*Grenzmark*] a strong awareness of national feeling [*Nationalgefühl*]. However, we reject its exaggerated and boorish manifestations, of which Mr Wulle is the prototype.'[131]

Finally, the DNVP decided to concentrate more on questions of education in this period, partly because it felt obliged to assist the Protestant Church, and partly because of the danger involved in keeping too high a profile at a time when other *völkisch* groups were being dissolved.

Prior to the May 1924 Reichstag elections, however, the party recaptured the initiative, focusing on the *Wirtschaftsbund*,[132] but also giving prominence to the racist agenda: the struggle for the DNVP was still one against 'the corrosive spirit of Jewry in all areas'.[133] Moreover, a few months later the party turned against the SPD, a move intended to 'unite the middle classes behind it';[134] this was also one reason for reasserting the party's *völkisch* credentials.[135] In short, between 1922 and 1924 the right-wing nationalists upheld their racist message, although in comparison to earlier periods the DNVP was more interested in combating 'Jewish influence' than creating a purely 'German' society.

[128] *Niederrheinische Bote*, 26.6.1922 'Wer hat Schuld'.

[129] Ibid., 14.10.1922 'Deutschnationale Wege'.

[130] Gemein, *DNVP*, 30. The French disbanded the *Stahlhelm*, the *Deutscher Offiziersbund*, and the *Reichskriegerbund Kyffhäuser*. The DNVP had already suffered in the autumn of 1922. See the letter by Ellenbeck to Westarp in StAD XXI 339: 'For three months now we German Nationals haven't been allowed to hold a meeting. Our newspapers are forbidden, including the *Kreuzzeitung*.'

[131] StAD XXI 339, 14.11.1922. Von Westarp became leader of the DNVP in March 1926; he was generally considered a 'moderate' in his party.

[132] Gemein, *DNVP*, 35.

[133] *Niederrheinische Bote*, 5.4.1924 Advertisement 'Deutsche Männer und Frauen!' See also StAD XX 331 Handbill 'Mit echtem deutschen Volkstum gegen Judentum und jüdischem Parlamentarismus!'

[134] Gemein, *DNVP*, 37.   [135] Ibid.

To end our brief survey of the 'Protestant bourgeoisie' in Düsseldorf, we need to look at the reaction of the Church to the above events in this period.

Interestingly enough, the *Sonntagsblatt* was now much more cautious than after the war, when racism was a predominant aspect of its stance on the 'Jewish question'. In the years 1922–4, only five articles touched on the issue, most of which revealed a slight shift in perception on part of the Protestant weekly. The Rathenau murder, for example, was a vile act, since the foreign minister 'was . . . the most able member in the current government'.[136] During the trial of the suspected assassins, the paper commented 'that it is right of the supreme court to warn against a certain kind of anti-Semitism. We can only hope that people will soon differentiate between German-*völkisch* and anti-Semitic'.[137] To be sure, the paper had nothing against other kinds of anti-Semitism, as long as they did not threaten the peace of Düsseldorf's respectable citizens. Thus, in the annual report of the district synod Jews were blamed for socialism's hatred of religion,[138] and a few months later Pastor Harney welcomed Gustav von Kahr's expulsion of *Ostjuden* from Bavaria, 'who have implanted themselves to everyone's detriment'.[139]

This approach was further evident in the main article on the Hitler Putsch. Like the *Düsseldorfer Nachrichten*, the *Sonntagsblatt* declared Hitler and Ludendorff true patriots, 'who could have performed great deeds, if they had had patience and had shown discipline. We sincerely regret the loss of these men'.[140] What we have, in short, is an acceptance of *völkisch* values without its ugly concomitants (i.e. radicalism): by embracing everything *völkisch*, the Church took Jew-hatred for granted. When the *Sonntagsblatt* distinguished between anti-Semitism and 'Germandom', therefore, it implied that Jews should keep to themselves so that the Nazis would not feel provoked into acts of violence and bloodshed.

CATHOLICISM

Before 1922 the Centre Party in Düsseldorf complained of racism within the ranks of the far Right, but also let it be known that Jews were involved

---

[136] *SB*, 2.7.1922 'Zeitschau'.   [137] Ibid., 22.10.1922 'Zeitschau'.
[138] Ibid., 17.6.1923 'Jahresbericht.'
[139] Ibid., 11.11.1923 'Zeitschau'. Throughout the early 1920s Bavaria attempted, usually in vain, to expel Eastern Jews from its territory. See, for example, S. Adler-Rudel, *Ostjuden in Deutschland. 1880–1940. Zugleich eine Geschichte der Organisationen, die sie betreuten* (Tübingen, 1959), 115 and S. E. Aschheim, *Brothers and Strangers. The East European Jew in German and German Jewish Consciousness, 1800–1923* (Madison, Wis., 1982), 242–3.
[140] Ibid., 18.11.1923 'Zeitschau'.

in revolutionary activities which harmed the moral fibre of the nation. As early as April 1922, however, a growing number of Düsseldorf's Catholics stood more firmly in the Republican camp, fully supporting the policies of the Reich government under Joseph Wirth.[141]

Rathenau's murder caused anger and outrage among Centre supporters. A protest march attracted many thousands of demonstrators, and the speakers showed how much the party had learned in the aftermath of Erzberger's violent death.[142] At one such event, the secretary of the workers' union, Theodor Drösser, explained that 'the Jew was more Christian than many a Christian', while the party leader and former member of the Pan-German League, Clemens Adams, opined: 'he was a Jew, but we Centre people have never disparaged a noble and able person because he was a Jew. This kind of foolish anti-Semitism we have never supported.'[143]

Although Adams's words entailed the assumption that Jews who displayed contemptible behaviour were even more vulnerable because they were Jews than their equally 'criminal' Gentile neighbours (this, indeed, was the crux of Centre attacks on the revolutionaries of 1918/19), his message was quite clear: Catholics condemned recent manifestations of *völkisch* hysteria and defended the accomplishments of the Republic.[144] In particular, working-class groups within the Centre condemned the anti-Semitism of those who had had nothing in common with the murderers:

Rathenau also died as a Jew, although he was a better German than many a bawler, although he acted more Christian than many a Christian. Only too many may feel guilty in their hearts for having contributed to the stupid [*blöden*] Jew-baiting, without realizing that every mean word intensified the atmosphere of hatred, until it culminated in this terrible murder.[145]

The Hitler Putsch occasioned ridicule and bitterness, but on the whole the Centre Party was more concerned with the Ruhr crisis than with the events in Munich. The *Tageblatt*, for example, commented that it was

---

[141] StAD XXI 9 General meeting of 22.4.1922. Also W. Stump, *Geschichte und Organisation der Zentrumspartei in Düsseldorf 1917–1933* (Düsseldorf, 1971), 47: 'A majority in the Düsseldorf Centre approved of . . . Wirth's course.' The Centre politician Wirth had reacted to the Rathenau murder by proclaiming: 'There stands the enemy, where Mephisto drips his poison into a people's wounds . . . That enemy stands on the Right.' Pulzer, *State*, 242.

[142] StAD XXI 9. Erzberger was killed by members of the *Organisation Consul* in August 1921. He had been exposed to virulent attacks by the far Right for his role in the Reichstag Peace Resolution of 1917 and his later tax reforms as Finance Minister of an SPD–Centre coalition.

[143] Ibid.   [144] See Stump, *Geschichte*, 48 n. 183.   [145] *Aufwärts*, 30.6.1922.

typical of Bavarian politics, 'that the Munich *Spießer*, who earlier tolerated the *Matthäser-Bierkeller-Revolution* of the Galician Kurt Eisner, now
fell for the braggart Hitler and General Ludendorff'.[146] In this article,
Eisner is portrayed as a comical figure rather than as a threat, and the
reference to his background, though reminiscent of earlier anti-Semitic
assaults, suggests that the Centre paper was deriding the political instincts
of the Munich populace.

This changed during and after the trial of Hitler and Ludendorff.
Although the Centre fraction in the city council refused to support the
SPD motion against the general, it abstained from voting on the matter,
thereby guaranteeing its passing.[147] Moreover, in a number of highly
publicized meetings the party attacked Ludendorff's anti-Catholicism,[148]
and sharply criticized the court's final verdict.[149]

Even if the Centre Party remained divided on such matters as the
Republican defence organization, *Reichsbanner*, and in spite of existing
differences between Catholic youth and workers' groups with more conservative Centre officials,[150] the party continued to reject *völkisch* extremism. For example, it denounced the *Jungdeutscher Orden* for its links with
the Nazis,[151] and warned Catholics prior to the May 1924 Reichstag
elections of the right-wing extremists. The *Aufwärts*, moreover, explained
that 'our modern state is no racial community, and in particular no racial
breeding cooperative [*Rassenzuchtgenossenschaft*], but rather a cultural
community to which everyone may belong who accepts and serves it'.[152] In
a meeting of the local CV, Clemens Adams spoke out against anti-
Semitism: 'The Catholic Party rejects making Israelites into second-class
citizens . . . The Centre shall support Jewry.'[153]

While the *Düsseldorfer Tageblatt* condemned *völkisch* assertions that
Jews had suffered little during the previous war,[154] Centre leaflets tried

---

[146] *DT*, 14.11.1923. See also *Aufwärts*, 12.11.1923 'Revolverkomödie und Volksschicksal'
and 13.11.1923 'Die Diktatur'.

[147] *Stenographische Verhandlungsberichte der Stadtverordnetenversammlung*, 25.3.1924. As
with the DDP, the Centre Party rejected the motion on 'legalistic' grounds.

[148] *DT*, 26.3.1924 'Katholiken Düsseldorfs!'; 7.4.1924 'Katholizismus und Vaterland';
7.3.1924 'Katholiken heraus!'

[149] Ibid., 2.4.1924 'Das Münchener Urteil': 'The political trials of the past weeks belong
to the darkest chapters in Germany history.'

[150] Stump, *Geschichte*, 51–5.

[151] StAD XXI 194 'Rheinisches Jungzentrum—Monatsblätter für die Windhorstbunde',
January 1924: 'The Jungdo is anti-Semitic and anti-Catholic.'

[152] *Aufwärts*, 2.4.1924 'Wahrer und falscher Patriotismus'. See also 2.5.1924 'Volk, Nation und Staat'.

[153] *DT*, 2.5.1924 'Christentum und Antisemitismus'.

[154] Ibid.: 'The fallen are silent, but the living should shrink from dishonouring their
memory. Such behaviour . . . is disgraceful.'

to undermine such racist tenets. In one such piece, for example, a fictitious *Stammtischbruder* commented: 'And to persecute the Jew simply because he is a Jew is nonsense!'[155] Various issues of the *Jungzentrum*, although often nationalistic, distanced the party from the *völkisch* movement and its 'worship and glorification of German ways [*deutscher Art*]'.[156]

It needs to be said, however, that anti-Semitism was frequently regarded as a veiled attack on the Catholic Church, so that the critique of National Socialism was always also a defence of Christian values. In November and December 1924, for example, much of the propaganda was directed against the 'new German paganism' of the Right.[157] By and large, however, the Centre moved away from earlier forms of anti-Semitism, concentrating instead on Nazism's denial of one of the 'basic tenets of the Christian *Heilsgeschichte*, the eschatological hope (in theory) and missionary zeal (in practice) . . . according to which the Jews are still eligible for salvation and election.'[158] Düsseldorf's Catholics, in short, feared that Hitler, Rosenberg, and Ludendorff were undermining, if not destroying, the basic values of Christianity.

THE LEFT

Following the Rathenau murder, the parties of the Left demanded sweeping reforms of the political system. The USPD called on the government to purge the police and judiciary, to proceed against DNVP newspapers, and to bar nationalists from the civil service and army.[159] The party also questioned whether the anti-Semitic tone of the right-wing press was not in large part responsible for the brutal murder.[160] This line of argument was equally prominent in the SPD's *Freie Presse*. Many of the articles were concerned with 'reactionary politics' and Republican unity, but the paper realized that the Jews remained a primary target of *völkisch* propaganda. One headline, for example, reminded all workers, employees, and civil servants that the struggle against racism was necessary in order to protect the Republic of Weimar. Unfortunately Rathenau had underestimated this threat: 'He didn't defend himself against the *völkisch* agitators

[155] StAD XXI 21 'Das Zentrum'.
[156] StAD XXI 194 April issue 'Stellung zum Völkischen'. See also the June 1924 issue.
[157] *Aufwärts*, 16.11.1924 'Eltern, bewahret eure Kinder vor den völkischen Lockungen!'; 5.12.1924 'Der deutschvölkische Wolf im Schafspelz'; *DT*, 5.12.1924 'Wir klagen an . . .'
[158] U. Tal, *Christians and Jews in Germany. Religion, Politics and Ideology in the Second Reich* (Ithaca, 1975), 225.
[159] *VZ*, 26.6.1922.
[160] Ibid., 30.6.1922 'Mitteldeutsche Presse'. See also the issue of 27.6.1922.

and Jew-baiters who, because of his Jewish descent, disgraced him over and over again.'[161]

The basic tenor of KPD pronouncements, by contrast, was intended to champion working-class consciousness. The leading article in the *Freiheit*, for example, mentioned Rathenau only in passing, while 'labour's terrible predicament' was repeatedly underlined. Rathenau's death 'is unconnected to the person, but is aimed at the achievements of the Revolution',[162] and it was therefore necessary to remember the hundreds of workers still languishing 'in the dungeons of this Republic'.[163]

This approach re-emerged in the run-up to the May 1924 Reichstag elections, only now Jews were considered to be involved in the financial support of the Right. The DNVP's plan to eliminate Jewish influence, for instance, was ridiculed: 'Everything which is even remotely Jewish [*jüdisch angetippt*] is supposed to be destroyed. That means a lot of work. There is a rumour that Wulle contains a splash or two of Semitic blood and that the Pope too may be infected with Jewry [*jüdisch infiziert*].[164] Most of the time, however, the KPD wanted to show that capitalists, including Jewish ones, were responsible for *völkisch* successes. 'Jew-money doesn't stink!' one caption read, and the article went on to describe how Jewish and Christian capitalists had paid Austria's fascists billions under the condition 'that the movement oppose the working class rather than Jewish capital'. The article then ended with a warning to all those who ignored the unity and power of the working class: 'The circumcised and uncircumcised German money-bags, the native [*bodenständigen*] and international exploiters know very well what is at stake for them when the German working class awakens and calls them to account.'[165]

Occasionally KPD polemics against the SPD involved similar 'accusations',[166] but generally the Communist Party tried to question the sincerity of Nazi anti-Semitism. Whereas in 1923 the party had engaged in nationalist propaganda in order to resist the demands of Western capitalist

---

[161] *Freie Presse*, 26.6.1922 'Arbeiter, Angestellte, Beamte!—Schützt die Republik!'

[162] HStAD Reg. Düss. 16893, Nr 15. This argument was also evident in a later commentary on the disruption by Nazis of a 'Heine meeting': 'On the bourgeoisie's instructions the Nazis tried to get the revolutionary poet, not the Jew.' *Freiheit*, 16.12.1930 'Vernichtet die faschistische Brut'.

[163] *Freiheit*, 26.6.1922.

[164] Ibid., 11.4.1924 'Das Gesicht und das Wesen der Wahlparteien'. See also 21.3.1924 'Kampf der sozialen Demagogie der Deutschvölkischen'.

[165] Ibid., 30.4.1924, See also 2.5.1924 'Kämpft mit den Kommunisten': 'The *völkisch* attack Jewish capital—and take money from Jewish and Christian capitalists to fight the workers.'

[166] HStAD Reg. Düss. 16870 (I), Nr 153 'Bezirksleitung des Roten Frontkämpfer-bundes', 31.12.1924.

powers (the Soviet Union had realized then that the latter was a greater threat to the country's survival than the German 'bourgeoisie'), the KPD now hoped to discredit the far Right without displaying too pronounced a nationalistic platform.[167] Whatever the nature of these moves, then, and we may assume that they were largely opportunistic, it is more than likely that they eventually became 'integral to the party's ethos'.[168]

Surprisingly, the SPD in Düsseldorf employed a similar tactic prior to the May elections. On the one hand, the party attacked the KPD for cooperating with the Nazis;[169] on the other hand it argued that the DNVP took money from Jewish financiers. A number of articles in the *Volkszeitung*, which was again in the hands of the SPD, pointed out that the DNVP was hardly the right party to pursue an anti-Semitic pro- gramme: 'The party founded by von Stahl isn't doing too well in this area . . . as news from Silesia indicates. According to latest reports, Frhr v. Richthofen, the German-National's top candidate, has a Jewish grand- mother, thus being able to shake hands with Wulle.'[170] Still, even though the SPD organ maintained that the supposedly anti-Semitic conservatives received help from wealthy Jews,[171] it never implied that the latter were just as bad as the right-wing agitators. Unlike the KPD, Social Democrats continued to protest against assaults on Jews like Albert Einstein,[172] and unlike the Communists they allowed the Zionist workers' organization, *Poale Zion*, to publish an appeal in their newspaper.[173]

This was also the case towards the end of that year. At a socialist meeting on 29 November, for example, the DDP member Grünewald thanked the SPD for its criticism of Jew-hatred.[174] A few days later, the *Volkszeitung* observed with dismay that at a rally of the *Völkisch-Sozialer Block* a Communist member had agreed with *völkisch* statements on the 'Jewish question'.[175] Finally, one day before the voters went to the polls, the SPD once again warned against the right-wing menace: 'Reject the

---

[167] StAD XII 1579 Leaflet 'Nieder mit den Faszisten (sic) und Separatisten!' Also H.-H. Knütter, *Die Juden und die deutsche Linke in der Weimarer Republik 1918–1933* (Düsseldorf, 1971), 180 and E. Silberner, *Kommunisten zur Judenfrage. Zur Geschichte von Theorie und Praxis des Kommunismus* (Opladen, 1983), 180. On Soviet influence in this regard, see C. Fischer, *The German Communists and the Rise of Nazism* (London, 1991), 52 and H. A. Winkler, *Von der Revolution zur Stabilisierung. Arbeiter und Arbeiterbewegung in der Weimarer Republik 1918 bis 1924* (Berlin and Bonn, 1984), 579.

[168] Fischer, *Communists*, 61.   [169] *VZ*, 8.4.1924 'Die Avantgarde der Reaktion!'

[170] Ibid., 17.4.1924 'Das Antisemitenpech'.

[171] Ibid., 19.4.1924 'Wer sind die Deutschnationalen'; 26.4. 1924 'Deutschnational- Deutschvölkisch'.

[172] Ibid., 3.5.1924 'Das Hakenkreuz Deutschlands Untergang'.

[173] Ibid., 'An die jüdischen Wähler!'

[174] Ibid., 29.11.1924 'Unsere zweite Massenkundgebung'.

[175] Ibid., 3.12.1924 'Düsseldorfer Angelegenheiten'. See also 29.11.1924 'Plauderei'.

völkisch . . . who . . . have neither economic nor political principles and only excel in complaining about Jews and Social Democrats.'[176]

Perhaps the picture of the SPD in this period was less clear-cut as a result of pressure put on the party following the socialist union in September 1922. Most of the USPD voters had joined the KPD,[177] a fact that was especially painful to the Düsseldorf SPD, given its already poor performances in 1919 and 1920. As could be expected, the party's showing in 1924 was not much better.[178] In May it won 9 per cent, as opposed to 24 per cent for the KPD, and in December it increased its share by only 3 per cent, while the Communists secured over 22 per cent of the vote. In other words, the SPD's precarious position may have led some officials to employ methods that showed very little respect for the fears of the Jewish community, but which were considered helpful in the party's agitation against its political adversaries.

As in Nuremberg, separatist thinking in this period was accepted by a number of political parties in Düsseldorf. Both the DVP and DNVP, for example, realized that nationalistic propaganda would not be tolerated by the French; both parties also assumed that the electorate was adequately informed about their stance on the 'Jewish question'. Similarly, the Protestant Church altered its approach by scaling down its racism and concentrating more on the positive elements of the *völkisch* movement. By accepting the Nazi Party as a valuable ally in the fight for Germany's renewal, both the DVP and DNVP, as well as the Protestant Church, implicitly excluded the Jewish community from this struggle against the country's so-called enemies.

The Centre Party, by contrast, understood that the *völkisch* movement, although insignificant in Düsseldorf itself, was a serious threat to the Catholic Church. This threat, moreover, was not limited to party political struggles, but involved the entire *Weltanschauung* of a great number of German Christians. The Centre Party therefore turned against anti-Semitism for two reasons: first, because the Düsseldorf chapter supported the Republic and opposed those groups who challenged the achievements of the 1918/19 Revolution; and second, because *völkisch* beliefs undermined the party's values and were seen as equally damaging for both Catholics and Jews. In short, as long as attacks on Jews were linked with attacks on Christianity or the Republic, the Centre was obliged to ward off

---

[176] Ibid., 6.12.1924 'Und nun wählen!'

[177] W. Matull, *Der Freiheit eine Gasse. Geschichte der Düsseldorfer Arbeiterbewegung* (Bonn, 1980), 114.

[178] Brücher, *Dokumentation*, 194.

racist propaganda. However, since the Republic was never sacrosanct and political survival always vital, the Centre Party was prone to ignore the problem of anti-Semitism without necessarily succumbing to it.

This was already evident in the treatment of the 'Jewish question' by the SPD for, although the party consistently rejected Jew-baiting in this period, it occasionally questioned the integrity of right-wing anti-Semitism. Clearly a tactical device, this policy of discrediting one's political opponent was made at the expense of the Jewish community. Nevertheless, despite the party's weakness in Düsseldorf, the SPD still managed to concentrate on the dangers of racism. As yet convinced that Republican values could hold or even attract voters, Social Democrats continued to fight anti-Semitism, even if this was hardly conducive to political survival.

Political survival was certainly foremost in the minds of the Communist leadership. The KPD associated Jews with the DNVP, maintained that the *völkisch* movement received financial aid from wealthy Jewish capitalists, and explained right-wing successes in terms of Jewish assistance. Since the party was very powerful in the Düsseldorf area, these attempts to place the Jews in the Nazi camp and the Nazis in the Jewish camp cannot be seen as simple acts of desperation. Here tactics became all important because the success of the movement meant everything, and the consequences of right-wing anti-Semitism were accordingly ignored.

SUMMARY

The most obvious difference in the political landscape between Nuremberg and Düsseldorf in this period was the much greater success of the Nazi Party in Nuremberg. By the end of 1924, moreover, the entire right-of-centre vote in the Franconian city was substantially higher (10 per cent) than in Düsseldorf. Many factors may have contributed to this development, but as we can see from the above discussion of the 'Jewish question', the political climate in Nuremberg also allowed other parties to employ anti-Semitic imagery with impunity.

This was so above all in the case of the BVP and SPD. Whereas in Düsseldorf the Centre Party condemned the excesses of *völkisch* propaganda throughout the years 1922–4, the BVP in Nuremberg continued to stress the insurmountable gap between Catholicism and Judaism during these same years. Only briefly did the Bavarian People's Party repudiate anti-Semitism—namely at a time when its position in the Bavarian state was threatened by a right-wing coup. The Centre Party in Düsseldorf, on the other hand, which had no reason to fear a Nazi onslaught in the

Rhineland, recognized that Jew-hatred was part of a larger attack on Christian values.

Similarly, while the SPD in Düsseldorf at one point implied that right-wing organizations were receiving money from wealthy Jews, Social Democrats in Nuremberg went even further: they borrowed language from *völkisch* sources and made accusations of intimate ties between Nazis and Jews. While their attacks on anti-Semitism were half-hearted at best, the SPD in Düsseldorf usually went out of its way to criticize the bases of right-wing Jew-hatred.

Perhaps the 'Jewish question' explains the success of the NSDAP in Nuremberg. Unlike in Düsseldorf, for example, the parties most inclined to reject *völkisch* propaganda were not really interested in doing so; for they both realized that defending the Jews was unpopular and appropriated the ideas and values of the far Right when dealing with the problem of anti-Semitism. In the Rhenish city, by contrast, where the combined support of the Centre and SPD amounted to over 40 per cent of the vote in December 1924, the opposition to Jew-baiting was more pronounced and widespread. Düsseldorf's Jews could rely on these parties as well as the DDP, while their Nuremberg counterparts could only assume that the SPD was not hostile—even if this did not entail sympathy, as was the case with the Democratic Party.

Although right-wing anti-Semitism continued unabated, both the DVP and DNVP were less concerned with it than in the immediate post-war era. What emerged instead was a cross-party consensus over the benefits and importance of *völkisch* ideals. In Nuremberg this consensus possibly included groups to the left of the DVP, where the fear of losing valuable support led to indifference and cynicism. In Düsseldorf, exclusionist thinking was largely confined to the far Right, even though the KPD displayed very little concern for the anxieties of the Jewish populace. Finally, the differences between the two cities can be inferred from the distinct approaches to the 'Jewish question' by the 'middle-class interest groups'. Whereas in Düsseldorf, the *Wirtschaftsbund* seemed to ignore the matter altogether, its Nuremberg parallel attacked the Jews in the most nefarious language imaginable. It seems that this difference indicates anti-Semitism's appeal in both cities: in Nuremberg, only the DDP refrained from racist language, in Düsseldorf everyone except the extreme Right (including the DVP) and extreme Left agreed that Jew-baiting was a dangerous affair.

5

Dormancy and difference
1925–1929

Perhaps the world would have been turned completely upside down
had not, in the very last minute, stiff laundry [*steife Wäsche*] been
invented for civilians, transforming a shirt into a white board [*Brett*]
and thus making it unlike underwear.

Hermann Broch, *Die Schlafwandler* (1931–2)

Prior to the onset of the depression, Germany witnessed a period of
relative stability. The Dawes Plan had given the country breathing-space
to raise the required funds to cover her financial obligations, economic
production roughly recovered its pre-war levels by 1928, and the extremists at both ends of the political spectrum remained weak and paralysed.
Nevertheless, there were signs which pointed to continued divisions
within the population: on the economic side, the government's stabilization policy of 1924 'provoked the most persistent and programmatic
political response of the pre-depression period',[1] forcing those of its citizens who held liquid assets in the form of savings, pensions, and bonds to
look for political alternatives. The government's deflationary measures
also meant the de facto abrogation of the eight-hour work-day, a massive
and unprecedented dismissal of civil servants and public employees, a
severe restriction of credit, and a strong rise in unemployment.

On the political side, all the parties which had participated in government coalitions after 1924 fared worse in the May 1928 Reichstag
elections than they had in either May or December of 1924. While the
DNVP eventually came under the influence of the right-wing anti-
parliamentarism of Alfred Hugenberg, the Centre drifted towards a more
authoritarian line under Ludwig Kaas. During the mid-1920s, therefore,
when the Republic appeared quite successful, 'there was a conspicous

---

[1] T. Childers, 'Inflation, Stabilization, and Political Realignment in Germany 1919–
1928', in: G. Feldmann et al., *Die Deutsche Inflation. Eine Zwischenbilanz* (Berlin and New
York, 1982), 414. For a succint discussion of the stabilization crisis and its effects, see T.
Childers, *The Nazi Voter. The Social Foundations of Fascism in Germany, 1919–1933* (Chapel
Hill, NC, 1983), 52–3, 65, 73, 93.

failure of both conservative and "middle" political parties effectively to integrate their supporters (and themselves) into the Weimar system'.[2]

On the other hand, it must be said that many perceived the years 1925–9 to be less divisive than any other period during the brief existence of the Weimar Republic. Although this undoubtedly raised expectations that could not be met at a later stage—and thereby may have contributed to a further crisis of confidence in the system—the so-called 'Golden Twenties' was a period of fewer tensions of the kind experienced after the Revolution or during the Ruhr occupation. This was reflected in both domestic and foreign affairs: in the former area, housing programmes and unemployment insurance benefited millions of German workers; in the latter domain Stresemann led the country back into the international community.

The 'Jewish question' was also not as hotly debated as in previous years. Two instances, however, deserve special attention. In 1925 Julius Barmat, a Russian Jew with close connections to Social Democracy, was arrested when it became known that his company had been receiving loans from the Bank of Prussia and the German Postal System without sufficient information regarding his financial credibility. Despite rumours that high-ranking officials in the SPD had been implicated, including the Jewish leader of the party's delegation in the Prussian Landtag, Ernst Heilmann, the final verdict of March 1927 dismissed these claims; Barmat was found guilty of bribery and sentenced to eleven months' imprisonment.[3] For many onlookers, however, the 'scandal' surrounding Barmat disclosed the moral corruptibility of the 'system', and reminded them of the early months after the war, when such shady business deals had been common practice.

A potentially more damaging case was one involving the Sklarek brothers in 1929. The owners of a clothing factory in Berlin, the Sklareks had managed to secure a contract for the various types of uniforms required by the city. More important, the brothers had also devised a method for receiving payments from the city treasury for deliveries which were never made. Two of the brothers had joined the SPD to further their ends, and it eventually came to light that a number of city officials had received

[2] R. Bessel, 'Why did the Weimar Republic Collapse?', in: I. Kershaw (ed.), *Weimar: Why did German Democracy Fail?* (London, 1990), 133. On the difficulties of finding common ground among liberals, who were often dependent on special interest groups, see D. Langewiesche, *Liberalismus in Deutschland* (Frankfurt, 1988), 249. For a similar argument emphasizing the contradiction between the 'demands of democracy and the needs of capitalism', see D. Abraham, *The Collapse of the Weimar Republic. Political Economy and Crisis* (New York, 1986), XV. For a more general work, see E. Kolb, *The Weimar Republic* (London, 1988), 66–7.

[3] E. Eyck, *A History of the Weimar Republic. Volume I. From the Collapse of the Empire to Hindenburg's Election* (Cambridge, Mass., 1962), 329.

bribes from them. In particular, the fact that Mayor Böss had bought a coat from one of the Sklareks 'for a price which even a rank amateur would have recognized as unrealistically low',[4] hurt the reputation of municipal politics. Again Jews were involved, and although the public was more concerned with the reliability of state employees, right-wing parties used the scandal to highlight Jewish 'infiltration' of Germany's social and political life.

While it seems doubtful that these affairs could have substantially strengthened the prospects of National Socialism,[5] they do allow us to examine the course of the 'Jewish question' in these years. What will emerge in this chapter, then, is a rather mixed picture, one which illustrates both the continuity of Weimar history and the varieties of local and regional experience. By and large, anti-Semitic activities were suspended in this period, when the economy showed signs of recovery and ideology was replaced with pragmatism in local politics. However, there remained, especially in Nuremberg, an undercurrent of hostility to Jewry which was the result of previous efforts to isolate the Jews and which could erupt at any moment.

Hermann Broch's image of 'starched shirts', quoted at the beginning of this chapter, was the sense of bourgeois tranquillity and repose that came with improvement of the economy and greater domestic peace. These 'starched shirts', however, were not enough to hold back the forces that had been unleashed after the war, even where dormancy (as in Düsseldorf) seemed to be pronounced enough to make a difference. What was missing was a democratic consensus independent of temporary recuperation. What was missing was the equality of the Jewish citizen.

NUREMBERG

The municipal elections of 7 December 1924 once again revealed the strength of Nuremberg's far Right. Streicher's list won six seats, the *Volksgemeinschaft Schwarz-Weiß-Rot*, which consisted of the *Völkischer Block*, the DNVP, and the National Liberals (DVP), received nine, and the *Wirtschaftspartei* (*Bayerischer Mittelstandsbund*) four. While the SPD gained twenty seats, the combined vote for the DDP, *Christlicher Volksdienst*, BVP, and KPD amounted to just eleven.[6] At first it seemed unlikely that Luppe could muster the necessary support for the smooth

---

[4] E. Eyck, *A History of the Weimar Republic*. Volume II. *From the Locarno Conference to Hitler's Seizure of Power* (Cambridge, Mass., 1963), 251.

[5] H. Luppe, *Mein Leben* (Nuremberg, 1977), 180.

[6] H. Hanschel, *Oberbürgermeister Hermann Luppe. Nürnberger Kommunalpolitik in der Weimarer Republik* (Nuremberg, 1977), 231.

128   *Dormancy and difference, 1925–1929*

running of the city's affairs, as the BVP and *Christlicher Volksdienst* obstructed his work and supported Streicher's policy of vilification. But in April 1925, when the BVP's Anton Braun resigned, his party rivals in the municipal council decided to pursue a more conciliatory approach towards the mayor. Moreover, in early 1926 two Communists joined the SPD fraction, so that Luppe now no longer had to rely on the cooperation of the Bavarian People's Party.

Until 1929 Nuremberg's mayor was able to ignore his enemies in the city council, while confronting the *völkisch* movement in Middle Franconia. Hitler had refounded the NSDAP in February 1925, and a month later had already attended a rally in Nuremberg which attracted a crowd of over 4500.[7] According to Munich headquarters, Nuremberg soon emerged as the 'centre of the movement', an assessment fully in line with an official report of 1927.[8]

Throughout the twenties, Nuremberg firms suffered from a lack of operating capital and foreign orders resulting in numerous business failures, reduced working hours or total layoffs, and a high rate of unemployment. As Martha Moore-Ziegler has argued, the post-war increase in protectionist tariffs adversely affected Nuremberg's trade: 'For Nuremberg, the depression began in the mid-1920s and the effects of the Great Depression at the end of the decade were only compounded by the economic malaise of the previous five years.'[9]

Meanwhile, the Nazi Party benefited from a number of other factors in the run-up to the December 1929 municipal elections. First, the campaign against the Young Plan provided the movement with an aura of respectability. Second, the division within the nationalist camp, which had contested in 1924 the elections as part of a single bloc, caused the electorate to turn to the better organized National Socialists. Third, the NSDAP drew some support from first-time voters.[10] While the parties that had made up the *Volksgemeinschaft Schwarz-Weiß-Rot* in 1924 lost six seats, Streicher's list improved its vote by nearly 4 per cent, to 15.6, taking eight seats in the municipal council, second only to the SPD. Among right-wing parties, only the *Christlicher Volksdienst* and the *Wirtschaftspartei* managed to score comparable successes: the former gained three seats, the latter five.

[7] R. Hambrecht, *Der Aufstieg der NSDAP in Mittel- und Oberfranken (1925–1933)* (Nuremberg, 1976), 87.
[8] Ibid., 96.
[9] M. Moore-Ziegler, *The Socio-Economic and Demographic Bases of Political Behavior in Nuremberg during the Weimar Republic 1919–1933*, unpublished Ph.D. thesis (Virginia, 1976), 87.
[10] E. Reiche, *The Development of the SA in Nürnberg, 1922–1934* (Cambridge, 1986), 91.

If support for the *völkisch* movement proved unabated in this period, so did the appeal of anti-Semitism. Reports of racist incidents in schools,[11] veterans' associations,[12] gymnastic clubs,[13] and cultural centres abounded,[14] and the judiciary more often than not dismissed Jewish pleas for help.[15] By 1929 it became increasingly difficult for Jewish families to find housing in Nuremberg.[16]

The municipal council, on the other hand, failed to respond to Nazi Jew-baiting.[17] One reason for this may have been the unwillingness of many to take Streicher seriously, but at the same time it also reflected milder and more widespread forms of prejudice and fears that the Nazis could capitalize on a treatment of the issue. Thus, in a city council meeting of 13 May 1925, Mayor Luppe replied to Streicher's demand to discuss the 'Jewish question' by noting that 'no one would want to prohibit Mr Streicher and his friends from touching on the "Jewish question". But to say, as council member Holz did today, that in every Jew there was also a sadist is too much.'[18] All this led the local Jewish newspaper to the following bitter remark on the state of Jewish–Gentile relations in Nuremberg:

When talking about the external conditions, we must unfortunately acknowledge the historical fact that Nuremberg has preserved and retained its unique [*eigen-und einzigartiges*] brand [*Gewächs*] of anti-Semitism . . . The voice of public opinion and conscience was hardly audible, and both the preachers and representatives of religion and humanity have up till now failed to protest against the injustice and heartlessness which their fellow citizens and fellow human beings had had to endure and still have to endure.[19]

Even though the situation for most Jews did not improve in this period, the 'Jewish question' itself was mentioned less frequently between 1925

[11] See, for example, *NFM*, 14.4.1927 'Antisemitismus an Mittelschulen': 'It is difficult for an outsider to appreciate how strong anti-Semitism is at this school . . . But this is the case at other high schools too, and last year the conditions weren't better either.'

[12] *Abwehrblätter*, 20.5.1925, 42; *Im Deutschen Reich*, 7.5.1926.

[13] *NIG*, 1.1.1925 'Aus der Abwehrbewegung'.

[14] *Protokollbuch der israelitischen Gemeinde*, V, 19.8.1929, 364.

[15] NSDAP Hauptarchiv Reel 91, Police report of 9.7.1926 on 'Ritualmord' articles in the *Stürmer*: 'Incidentally, it was also established that the article did not cause a great stir.' See also the State Attorney's report of 5.11.1928 and Hambrecht, *Aufstieg*, 265–6, 282–4. For the way in which the judiciary responded to accusations of 'Jewish predominance' in Nuremberg's social life, see StAN *Stadtchronik* 1925, 638. For a general discussion, see C. Levitt, 'The Prosection of Antisemites by the Courts in the Weimar Republic—Was Justice Served?' in: *LBIY* (1991).

[16] StAN F5 QNG 404a B. Kolb, *Die Juden in Nürnberg. Tausendjährige Geschichte einer Judengemeinde von ihren Anfängen bis zum Einmarsch der amerikanischen Truppen am 20. April 1945* (Nuremberg, 1946), 45.

[17] See StAN C7/IX Stadtratsprotokolle (SRP) 364, 396, 458.

[18] StAN C7/IX SRP 358.   [19] *NIG*, 1.1.1927 'Rückblick auf das Jahr 1926'.

and 1929 than after the war or during the period of inflation. For one thing, fewer elections meant fewer occasions for conflict. For another, there was the belief in the need for constructive politics, especially on the local level. This in turn was related to the development described in Chapter 4: anti-Semitism was an accepted fact of life, and therefore no longer had to be promoted or defended. Whereas the enemies of *völkisch* racism remained quiet in order to avoid confrontation, the supporters of the extreme Right felt confident enough to trust the effects of previous propaganda efforts.

'PROTESTANT BOURGEOISIE'

The DDP, for example, had very little to say on the subject. Both the *Nürnberger Zeitung* and the *Nürnberg-Fürther Morgenpresse* failed to comment on the anti-Semitic implications of the Barmat and Sklarek affairs, the former because it was taking a more neutral stance on many issues since 1924, the latter because of DDP involvement in the scandals. However, in the run-up to the presidential elections of 1925 and the Reichstag elections of 1928, the Democratic Party did confront the problem of Jew-hatred, even if the instances in which it did so were few and far between. One such piece supported the Marx candidacy in the spring of 1925, and compared modern anti-Semitism to the persecution of the Christians under Nero: 'Then it was the Christians who were responsible for all troubles—today it is the Jews.'[20] In May 1928, moreover, the main party organ carried a number of articles faulting different parties for their anti-Semitic platform. These included the BVP,[21] the DVP,[22] and of course the DNVP.[23] The paper also argued that Nazi support was solely due to the party's 'furious anti-Semitism', an indication of how much of an electoral asset Jew-baiting was perceived to be.[24] Finally, the *Morgenpresse* urged its readers to avoid the *völkisch* parties: 'Don't vote for any of the numerous *völkisch* groups, for they favour violence over the law, fight a single segment of the population, the Jews, and employ brutish methods in their struggle.'[25] Despite scant documentary evidence, therefore, we may con-

[20] Stadtbibliothek Nürnberg Nor. 2258 2 o 'Wahlzeitung des Deutschen Volksblocks' (DDP, *Bauernbund*).
[21] *NFM*, 24.4.1928 'Die Partei der Eigenstaatlichkeit'.
[22] Ibid., 19.5.1928 'Deutsches-Volkspartei-Theater': 'Their anti-Semitism? With their *Stahlhelm* people! Their Jewish friendships? Where Jewish votes are expected, as in Bavaria!'
[23] Ibid., 10.5.1928 'Die Deutschnationalen in der Agitation'.
[24] Ibid., 16.5.1928 'Noch wenige Tage.'
[25] Ibid., 14.5.1928 'Wählen ist Bürgerpflicht!' The above examples suggest that anti-Semitism was still used as a propaganda device, even though most contemporary sources have not survived.

clude that the DDP continued to reject all forms of anti-Semitism for reasons having to do with its ideology and clientele.

The lack of documentary evidence is also a problem in evaluating the parties of the Right. The *Fränkischer Kurier*, for example, refrained from overt Jew-baiting, and we must rely on information from the DDP organ to discover whether the DNVP employed racism in its election material of 1928. The Barmat and Sklarek scandals are another case in point. While the *Kurier* mentioned the Jewish background of some of the defendants,[26] it concentrated more on the involvement of high-ranking SPD and DDP officials in the affair.[27] This did not mean that Nuremberg's main 'bourgeois' newspaper failed to see the connection between 'Jewish finance' and Social Democratic politics. In a piece on 'Loeb' Sonnemann's support of Bebel's business endeavours, the paper argued that the same practices were common in the Weimar Republic: 'This connection has ever since remained exemplary of the relationship between capitalist democracy and Social Democracy.'[28] But by and large, the *Kurier* displayed little interest in the 'Jewish question'; nationalism was expressed in other terms.

Thus, prior to the May 1928 Reichstag elections, the paper called on its readers to vote either DNVP or DVP, both of which stood firmly in the nationalist camp.[29] The *Kurier* also maintained that the Sklarek scandal was not just an example of corruption in local politics but an illustration of Germany's terrible state of mind: 'It is no longer a case of "Sklarek" . . . it has become a case of "Germany". An honest, poverty-stricken, and steadfast . . . people is being led to the edge of the abyss by the unscrupulousness of a leadership devoid of any tradition and therefore of any inhibitions.'[30]

It was hardly surprising, given the paper's well-documented nationalism, that the NSDAP on the whole received favourable coverage. This was especially the case during Nazi rallies in Nuremberg. For instance, in August 1929 the *Kurier* heartily welcomed the participants at such a meeting, even though it did not agree with each and every aspect of National Socialism. When violence erupted between supporters of the

[26] *FK*, 8.1.1925 'Holländische Enthüllungen des Korruptionssystems der deutschen Sozialdemokratie'; 15.1.1925 'Neue Belastungen im Barmat Skandal'.

[27] Ibid., 6.1.1925 'Die Katastrophe der Sozialdemokratie im Barmat-Kutisker Skandal'; 28.9.1929 'Die Riesen-Betrugsaffäre Sklarek. Wurmstichigkeit sozialistischer Kommunalpolitik'.

[28] Ibid., 28.1.1925 'Ausreden'. The paper used such expressions as 'the red Schmocks'. The banker and industrialist Leopold Sonnemann founded the *Frankfurter Zeitung* in 1856.

[29] Ibid., 9.5.1928 'Nationales Deutschtum, an die Front'; 15.5.1928 'Die Frauen am 20. Mai'.

[30] Ibid., 10.10.1929 'Der Fall Sklarek'.

rally and the KPD, only the Communists were made responsible for the disturbances.[31]

Moreover, Richard Hamilton's thesis that the position of the *Fränkischer Kurier* was a possible cause of upper-class voting patterns is confirmed by the election results.[32] In 1928 those city districts which contained the highest number of *Kurier* readers voted heavily in favour of the DNVP (*Mittelpartei*)—in the Stadtpark area nearly 25 per cent, in Luitpoldhein 19.5 per cent—while the city average for the party amounted to only 11.6 per cent.[33] In later elections these disparities were not quite as glaring, for the nationalist camp now decided to back the NSDAP, but there still remained a correlation between the paper's readership, its support for the DNVP, and the actual results of Hugenberg's party.

The DNVP also had to face opposition from the *Christlich-sozialer Volksdienst*. Originally founded in Württemberg in 1924, the *Volksdienst* became a national force when a group of disaffected Nationalists refused to cooperate with Hugenberg concerning the conduct of the anti-Young campaign and the relationship with the white-collar unions.[34] In Nuremberg, the *Volksdienst* had already competed in the 1924 municipal elections, claiming 2.4 per cent of the vote; in 1929 it increased its share by nearly 4 per cent, thus seriously damaging DNVP prospects.

The *Christlich-sozialer Volksdienst* defined itself as 'an extension of missionary work into the field of politics'.[35] Far from being committed to occupational sectors or special interest groups, it wanted the state to conform to the rule of God. The party therefore rejected everything that conflicted with Protestant ethics, including 'rendering absolute such relative values as the state, race, economy, and culture'.[36] Equally important, however, was the struggle against 'damage to the people' such as the *Schund* and *Schmutz* which threatened to engulf the nation's youth.

The 'Jewish question', it seems, was seldom discussed. While on the one hand the *Volksdienst* acknowleged its Christian Social origins, on the other it refused to support the radicalism of Streicher and his cronies. This approach was clearly evident in an article of October 1925: 'Until

---

[31] Reiche, *Development*, 74–5.

[32] R. Hamilton, *Who Voted for Hitler?* (Princeton, 1982), 214.

[33] StAN F5 QNG 421: R. Gömmel/G. Haertel, *Arbeitslosigkeit und Wählerentscheidungen in Nürnberg von 1928 bis 1933*, Seminararbeit (Nuremberg, 1968), 39 ff.

[34] Childers, *Nazi Voter*, 133.

[35] G. Opitz, *Der Christlich-soziale Volksdienst. Versuch einer protestantischen Partei in der Weimarer Republik* (Düsseldorf, 1969), 86.

[36] Ibid., 96.

now we have deliberately refused to comment on the Streicher movement, as we did not wish to give the impression that we lacked an appreciation for the claims of *völkisch* ideology.'[37] Similarly, when the National Socialists disrupted a *Volksdienst* conference that same month, Pastor Stählin condemned 'this kind of Jew-baiting' as a disgrace to the German people. At the same time, however, he conceded that the anti-Semites had been instrumental in altering the terms of the debate: 'one has rightly begun to speak of Jews and Germans instead of Jews and Christians; one recognizes how misleading is the . . . talk of "German citizens of a Jewish persuasion"; one has come to see that the Jew and the German constitute two different types of human existence.'[38]

In later years the party retreated somewhat on this issue. To be sure, its newspaper still attacked Hugenberg's publishing house and film company for having failed to eliminate Jewish influence; it still spoke of 'Hebrews' in the Reichstag and of 'Jewish-legalistic business practice' by the Nazis.[39] But on the whole, these charges became less prominent as the *Volksdienst* distanced itself from the extremism of the far Right. Having said that, between 1925 and 1929/30 the party showed no sympathy towards the Jews, and even less towards radicals of all stripes, and wholeheartedly welcomed the *völkisch* cause as valuable and important to the spiritual rejuvenation of Germany.

The *Wirtschaftspartei* was never particularly friendly to the Jews, and there was no reason for this to change after 1924. What did change, however, was the overall importance of the question in these years; whereas in 1925 the party still employed the language of extreme hatred, this was no longer true in 1929.

During the Barmat scandal, for example, the party portrayed Eastern Jews as 'scum',[40] while chiding the Centre Party for its close contacts with the Barmat family.[41] In a lead article of 13 February 1925, moreover, the *WP* paper used the images of rot and decay to describe the impact of the *Ostjuden* on the nation:

It is the revolting maggots who force their way into the open flesh and who fatten themselves up until they buzz away like blowflies. Vile worms, created by God in anger, loathed by the living, a burden, a harm . . . A tenacious, a dangerous

---

[37] *Der Christliche Volksdienst* (Nuremberg), No. 10/1925.   [38] Ibid.

[39] *Der Volksdienst* (Nuremberg), 13.9.1930 'Deutschnat. Partei u. Christlich-sozialer Volksdienst'; 6.9.1930 'Der 14. September'; Stadtbibliothek Nürnberg Nor. 1362 2 0 'Hitler-Bibel Reformation'.

[40] *Nürnberger Bürgerzeitung*, 6.1.1925 'Das Hougout der Hochfinanz'. The German term is *Auswurf*.

[41] Ibid., 2.2.1925 'Kreditnot und Barmatschwindel'.

race . . . They all became fat and round in front with bent horns . . . Kill the blowflies, slaughter the worms, if recovery, if strength, if freedom is to return.[42]

Four years later, the Sklarek scandal once again occasioned bitter attacks,[43] but this time politics itself was blamed for the malaise. Since even DNVP officials were implicated in the affair, the *Wirtschaftspartei* spoke of an epidemic which was eating away the last remnants of decency in the country. This idea was also put forward in the run-up to the 1928 Reichstag elections. Now the party's diagnosis sounded like pre-war complaints about the dangers of socialism and democracy: 'That is the crucial question [*Schicksalfrage*] of our day, when socialism and alien [*landfremde*] capitalist ideas are gaining ground in order to detroy the remains of German *Wesen*, German *Art*, and German *Sitte*.'[44]

It seems likely, therefore, that anti-Semitism was no longer regarded as a means to attract voters: no one could outperform the Nazis at their own game, and the *WP* understood quite well that any attempt at doing so was doomed from the start. What is more, after 1925 the 'Jewish question' itself became less of an issue because it was generally recognized that everyone to the right of the DDP accepted (or at least pretended to accept) *völkisch* ideals. From the *Fränkischer Kurier* to the *Christlich-sozialer Volksdienst*, there was no mention of the fact that the Jews were being excluded from this consensus, and in the light of earlier pronouncements, no one ever expected the *Wirtschaftspartei* to turn philo-Semitic in the foreseeable future.

The Protestant Church in Nuremberg likewise treated the subject with greater circumspection after 1924. This had already been the case earlier, when the clergy relied on the political parties to take up the question, but now it involved deeper problems concerning Christianity and the *völkisch* cause. What we therefore encounter in the years 1925–9 is a strange mixture of racism and Christian ethics, an unsuccessful attempt to combine the two and yet to preserve their distinctness.

On the one hand, then, we have articles condemning the influence of Eastern Jewry and the 'Jewish press',[45] while on the other we are confronted with references to Christ's Jewish background, the sacredness of

[42] *Nürnberger Bürgerzeitung*, 13.2.1925 'Schmeißfliegen!'

[43] See, for example, the issues of 26.10.1929 'Wochenschau'; 30.10.1929 'Wieder ein Galizier'; and 1.11.1929 'Der Aufstieg der Sklareks'.

[44] Ibid., 21.4.1928 WP appeal. See also numerous other articles in the *Bürgerzeitung* of April and May 1928. The 5.5.1928 issue 'reminded' its readers that Bela Kuhn [*sic*] was originally Bela Kohn.

[45] *EvGN*, 9.8.1925 'Aus Kirche und Welt'; 4.7.1926 'Rundschau'; 27.3.1927 'Aus Welt und Leben'.

the Old Testament, and God's eternal mercy.[46] This ambivalence was particularly apparent in a series of 'programmatic' essays on the 'Jewish question'. Arguing that the Nuremberg community was especially keen on the matter, the *Evangelisches Gemeindeblatt* offered a comprehensive discussion of the problem of anti-Semitism from an 'official point of view'.[47]

In all three articles we find numerous accusations against the Jews, most of which were widely believed at the time. Jews were alleged to be creative only when it was to their advantage; their influence extended to all areas of social and political power; and they held Germany hostage to views and ideas which corrupted the moral fabric of the nation. Jewish ideas contained 'something corrosive [*Zerfressendes*], biting [*Aetzendes*], caustic [*Auflösendes*]', but were never contemplative, constructive, productive. It was therefore absolutely essential to bring about 'the inner immunization of our people against all corrosive and destructive, un-German and un-Christian influences'.

The articles also dealt with the racial aspect of the 'Jewish question'. According to the Protestant weekly, the real problem facing Germany was the 'racial difference between the Jews and other peoples', and in spite of statements to the contrary, nothing could change this fact of life. Thus mixed marriages were to be avoided, as were attempts at an *Eindeutschung des Judentums*. But the emphasis on racial differences, the paper continued, should not lead to a crude 'race materialism', for the aim of all Christians was still the 'racial improvement' of the Jews through conversion. The fight, in other words, was to be a noble one, free from inflammatory talk, and worthy of a Christian people:

But he [the Wandering Jew] should not be able to say, once he reaches his final destination, that he hasn't passed through Christian countries. We shall behave in such a way that, when God lifts the curse from him and he may rest in peace, he will want to seek his home among those who greeted him with kindness, bore him with self-denial, strengthened him through hopeful patience, gladdened him through true love, and saved him through constant intercession.

The Protestant Church in this period displayed both a sense of concern about the implications of racist thought (which in many ways was a

---

[46] Ibid., 9.8.1928 'Altes Testament—Gottes Wort??!'; 21.8.1927 'Zum Sonntag Israels'. God's mercy was primarily there to redeem the 'Jewish race': 'God reveals his glory in an obstinate people, the most resistant matter [*widerstrebendsten Stoff*], the Jewish race. The less valuable the earthly matter, the greater God's magnificent power.'

[47] The articles were printed in nos 33–35/1926 of the Protestant weekly. The author was the director of the local seminary.

theologically motivated distaste of right-wing extremism) and a predilection for *völkisch* doctrines. To square the two remained an impossible task, and we are left with the awkward impression that the layman had to hate and love the Jews at the same time. With all the propaganda against them, however, the latter were well advised not to rely too heavily on the benign nature of Christianity's missionary zeal.

CATHOLICISM

Political Catholicism, by contrast, was more cynical in its treatment of the 'Jewish question'. As in the years 1922–5, the BVP refused to commit itself to a specific line of argument, so that we come across various responses to the problem of anti-Semitism. On the whole, however, the People's Party showed little in the way of sympathy for the Jews.

The *Bayerische Volkszeitung*, for example, reported very sparingly on the Barmat scandal; in those rare instances when it did, Eastern Jews figured as the main villains.[48] During the Sklarek scandal, moreover, which again involved Centre politicians, the paper ridiculed Nazi connections with the baptized 'Jew' Dr Frenzel in order to contrast Streicher's accusations of other parties with his own behaviour.[49] But the BVP also supported appeals that contained anti-Semitic undertones. Thus a leaflet opposing the expropriation of the dynasties, which was co-signed by the BVP, included the following statement: 'The planned expropriation law is called for by the following un-German persons: Ruczinski, Levi, Landsberger, Nathan, Katzenstein, Rosenfeld.'[50]

In the run-up to elections, the People's Party was equally opportunistic. In May 1928 the SPD was castigated for its support of non-denominational schools and the NSDAP for its irresponsible tactics, but the party never reproached the latter for its anti-Semitic platform. The *Bauernbund*, on the other hand, was unelectable because it had cooperated with the 'Jew' Eisner in 1918.[51] One year later, however, in a session of the city council, the BVP's Nikolaus Sommer condemned Karl Holz of the NSDAP for his constant racist remarks, 'since during the war members

[48] *BV*, 22.1.1925 'Der Sumpf' speaks of 'Eastern Galicians'.... (*Ostgalizier*) and 'immigrated Eastern money-makers'.

[49] Ibid., 10.10.1929 'Vom Hitlerfreunde Dr. Frenzel-Fränkel. Der ehemals mosaische Parteibeamte der Deutschen Volkspartei beführwortete den Erzbergermord und verherrlichte den Rathenaumord'.

[50] *CV-Zeitung*, 23.7.1926, 397 'Unlauteres Kampfmittel'.

[51] See, for, example, *BV*, 19.5.1928 'Vor der großen Entscheidung!' BHStA Abt. V FlgSg 58 20.5.1928 'Der Bauernbund als Totengräber eines freien Bauernstandes!'

of all denominations sacrificed their blood and life for the German fatherland'.[52]

Prior to the December 1929 municipal elections, the party took yet another approach. This time it rejected all forms of electoral alliances against Marxism or the Jews, but insisted that it could do so only on the grounds that it had always fought both groups. The National Socialists, the BVP continued, had achieved nothing with their provocations and fanaticism: 'The lord mayor, whom one wanted to "eliminate", is more firmly in control than before, the department stores haven't disappeared, and the influence of Jewry . . . has surely not diminished.'[53]

If the People's Party had little positive to say about the Jews, the Catholic weekly, *Sonntags-Friede*, was even less forthcoming. In all eight articles touching on the problem of anti-Semitism, the paper was outspoken in its opposition to everything 'Jewish'. In February 1925 it compared the Spanish Inquisition to the extermination of workers, peasants, and the bourgeoisie under 'Sinowjew-Apfelbaum, Radek-Sobelsohn, Litwinoff-Karfunkelstein, Joffe-Moses, and the other Jewish *Sowjethäuptlinge*'.[54] In October and December of that year the paper warned all workers that only Jews gained from revolutionary upheaval, while they ended up being 'the Jews' vassals' (*Judenknechte*): 'No, you aren't the priests' vassals [*Pfaffenknechte*], but . . .'[55] It was the Jews' own fault, moreover, that the Nazis were attacking them during the campaign against the expropriation of the dynasties, for 'among the six signatories of the proposal . . . are no fewer than four Jews: Nathan, Levy, Katzenstein und Dr Kuczinsky'.[56] Finally, the Catholic weekly asked its readers to consider the likely outcome of continued squabbles within Christian society: 'Someone once made a joke about Meyerbeer's opera *The Huguenots*: "Catholics and Protestants beat each other while the Jew [*der Jud*] sets it to music [*macht die Musik dazu*]." Isn't it sad how Christians are at loggerheads—to the enjoyment of everyone else?'[57]

Whereas the BVP acted opportunistically, revealing its deep-seated antipathies towards the Jews, the Catholic Church in Nuremberg was even more hostile. All this, however, was unrelated to the party's position in Nuremberg politics, where the BVP cooperated with Mayor Luppe

[52] StAN C7/IX SRP 450, 12.6.1929.
[53] Staatsbibliothek München 4 o Bavar. 3157 v8 'Bayerische Volkspartei und Gemeindepolitik. Ein Appell zu den Nürnberger Stadtratswahlen am 8. Dezember 1929'.
[54] *SF*, 22.2.1925 'Schlagworte'.
[55] Ibid., 11.10.1925 'In Rußland.'; 24.12.1925 'Die Kirche.'
[56] Ibid., 28.3.1926 'Politische Wochenschau'.
[57] Ibid., 13.3.1927 'Vom Kampffeld der Kirche'. For 'Jewish-socialist' school teachers in Vienna, see the 7.10.1928 issue under the heading 'Vom Erntefeld der Kirche'.

after 1925 and where its share of the vote hovered at around 8 per cent from late 1924 to March 1933. In Bavaria too, support for the People's Party remained fairly stable, as the NSDAP benefited primarily from the poor showing of the Protestant 'middle' parties.

In other words, anti-Semitism was still taken seriously by BVP supporters and Catholic officials. We find little evidence to the contrary, which is surprising, given the implications of racism for Christian theology. Deeply embedded in the city's culture, anti-Semitism was recognized as a powerful force in Nuremberg politics. There was no sense in disputing that fact, and for most Catholics there was even less need to resist the consequences.

THE LEFT

The Left, by contrast, acted cynically without necessarily opposing the Jews as such. As in earlier periods, both the SPD and KPD questioned the sincerity of right-wing anti-Semitism, arguing instead that Jews and Nazis made up the strangest of bedfellows.

For example, in an SPD meeting in January 1925, the party's speaker claimed that Streicher's anti-Semitism was so vicious only because the Nazis hoped to conceal Jewish support for their movement: 'If the National Socialists swing the censer, then only to drive out money's scent of garlic [*Knoblauchduft der Gelder*].'[58] Moreover, when the NSDAP fraction, newly constituted in September 1925, was introduced to the public, the *Tagespost* was quick to point out that one of its members had a suspiciously 'Jewish' name.[59] Similarly, in September 1925 the SPD's Martin Treu inquired into the basis of rumours suggesting connections between Fritz Ertl of the NSDAP and Jewish families in Nuremberg;[60] and in 1929 Treu asked Streicher for his opinion on the baptized Jews in the NSDAP.[61]

Prior to the May 1928 Reichstag elections, the *Tagespost* again confronted right-wing racism, but at the same time condemned an appeal by the Jewish community to vote for the DDP's Julie Meyer. In the former case, the paper dealt with the 'racial' background of the famous pilot von Hünefeld, whose monarchism and anti-Semitism stood in stark contrast to his mother's Jewish ancestry: 'In itself the family tree of an ocean flyer

[58] *FT*, 28.1.1925 'Der Rechtskurs in Deutschland'. See also 4.2.1925 'General v. Lüttwitz erteilte die Erlaubnis. Der Träger eines alten Adelsgeschlechts läßt sich vom Juden Barmat 'Mittel' geben!'

[59] Ibid., 23.9.1925 'Die Mitglieder dieser Fraktion sind Holzwarth, Streicher, Löw (!!!), Buttmann, Wagner und Zipferl.'

[60] StAN C7/SRP 366, 30.9.1925.   [61] StAN C7/SRP 458, 27.11.1929.

[*Ozeanflieger*] is unimportant. In the case of Hünefeld, however, it has to be mentioned in order to disclose the background of *völkisch* hysteria.'[62]

In the case of the Meyer candidacy, the *Tagespost* censored a leaflet signed by prominent members of the Nuremberg community in support of 'the first Jew to be nominated by a party since the Revolution . . . well, should the Democratic candidate Meyer represent the interests of her constituency or the interests of the synagogue?' the paper asked, and although the party may have felt passed over by this appeal, it nevertheless ignored the simple fact that only the DDP had been courageous enough to have put forward a Jewish candidate.[63] This was also ignored by the Communists, who went even further, alleging that the DDP was the party of Jewish business interests:

Apart from the banker, the hop merchant, and the lawyer, one of the signatories, namely Rosenzweig, is president of the Jewish community. Nothing but genuine [*waschechte*] capitalists as financial supporters of the Democrats. The working-class thus appreciates that the Democrats, despite all calls for a *Volksgemeinschaft*, serve the interests of capitalism.[64]

Finally, at the time of the Sklarek scandal Social Democrats often tried to divert attention from their own involvement in the affair, either by referring to corruption under the Empire or by reminding the far Right of its close relationship with prominent Jews.[65] The Sklareks, for instance, were used by Hindenburg's journalists as 'lightning-rods', even though they too belonged 'to the Old Testament'.[66] The German nationalist Bruhn, moreover, was 'a *Duzfreund* of the Jewish racing stable owner [*Rennstallbesitzer*] Sklarek, and this friendship even allowed for Mr Bruhn to get his ears boxed by Max Slarek'.[67] All this led the SPD's Vogel to the following observation in a meeting of his party in late October 1929: 'Why does the Nazi hate campaign against bank capital stop short of these

---

[62] *FT*, 29.4.1928 'Ozeanflug und Antisemitismus'. See also the 9.7.1928 commentary on another Streicher scandal: 'But if Streicher even sits at one table with his sworn enemies, *the Jews*, . . . if one speaks of Jewish contributions to the National Socialist party chest, then it is difficult to conclude that Streicher's behaviour has been impeccable.' Also, 20.11.1929 'Ein sauberer Spitzenkandidat'.

[63] Ibid., 5.5.1928 'Demokratische oder jüdische Kandidatur?'

[64] *Nordbayerische Volkszeitung*, 9.5.1928 'Die Geldgeber der Demokraten'. See also the article entitled 'Adolf Hitler und seine Canaille', where the KPD organ notes that the former propaganda chief of the *Völkischer Beobachter*, Otto May, finds Hitler too 'Jew-friendly [*judenfreundlich*]': 'Pretty Adolf has become too Jew-friendly for his former propaganda chief. Between the lines of his brochure one can read that Hitler is . . . totally dependent on the Jews, just as all the other *völkisch* leaders are.'

[65] See, for example, *FT*, 14.10.1929 'Korruption unter dem Kaiserreich'.

[66] Ibid., 29.9.1929 'Sklarek als Blitzableiter'.

[67] Ibid., 15.10.1929 'Sklarekerei unterm Hakenkreuz'.

people [Jewish capitalists and people like Klöckner, Hatzfeld, and Cuno]?'[68] The answer, presumably, was that Nazi anti-Semitism never affected wealthy Jews, whose money the party required in order to finance its election campaigns.

The combined vote for the Left between December 1924 and September 1930 never fell below 45 per cent and never exceeded 50 per cent. It seems likely, therefore, that both parties' approach to the 'Jewish question' had little to do with declining fortunes or desperate moves, but rather reflected the need to account for the cultural climate in Nuremberg. While we can safely conclude that neither the SPD nor the KPD intended to provide alternative anti-Semitic platforms, both parties knew there was nothing to win from taking a philo-Semitic position, as there was also nothing to lose from challenging the sincerity of Nazi Jew-baiting. Thus, if the Left consciously applied anti-Semitic stereotypes, it did so without really wishing to discriminate or persecute. The consequences of this behaviour, however, were unpredictable and fraught with danger.

Although the 'Jewish question' appeared less important in Nuremberg in the mid-1920s, the Jewish population was still strongly threatened by the hostile atmosphere which existed between Gentiles and Jews. This was only partly due to the continued influence of Streicher and the NSDAP, for many other sectors in society either ignored or exploited the subject, and a great many agreed with the Nazis that 'Jewish' influence was a great evil which had to be eradicated if Germany was to regain her lost pride.

With the exception of the DDP, the 'Protestant bourgeoisie' tried to combine *völkisch* dogma with respectable politics. The *Wirtschaftspartei*, for example, dropped its racist language without discarding its anti-Semitic bias; the Church hoped to redefine conversion as the need for racial improvement; and the *Volksdienst* appreciated both the greatness of Germany and the madness of Streicher's methods. All this went hand in hand with the recognition that the Jews remained outside the wider national community. Moreover, the relative mildness of attacks on the 'Jewish spirit' cannot be seen as a hopeful sign for growing tolerance, but must be taken instead as the outcome of political expediency and the widespread internalization of the cultural code of exclusion.

Against this, high growth rates and the absence of social turmoil might have weakened the immediate appeal of anti-Semitism, but in Nuremberg, as well as in the country at large, economic stability never materialized. In its absence, therefore, any improvement in the relationship

---

[68] See, for example, *FT*, 23.10.1929 'Nicht mit dem Rüstzeug der Barbaren'.

between Jews and Gentiles depended on a liberal consensus, not a nationalist *völkisch* one. This liberal consensus, however, did not exist, and it was therefore hardly surprising that so few resisted the initial anti-Semitic legislation introduced by the Nazis in 1933.

The two parties least prone to support the *völkisch* consensus, the Catholic BVP and the socialist SPD, proved equally culpable: the former because it never took a firm stand on the issue, knowing full well that its own anti-Semitism undermined Christian tenets; and the latter because it never recognized the effects of its policy of ridicule. It is difficult, moreover, to determine whether the BVP's ideological and tactical anti-Semitism was more damaging than Social Democracy's cynical approach to the 'Jewish question', for the latter reached a far wider audience, while the impact of the former on its constituency was far from decisive. Thus, whatever the result of their respective outlooks on the subject, both parties failed to address the potential danger of anti-Semitism, leaving the DDP as the only party willing to take the problem seriously.

DÜSSELDORF

In June 1924, Robert Lehr became Düsseldorf's Lord Mayor, ushering in a new era of cooperation between the Centre Party and the DVP/DNVP. Although Hüttenberger has compared this development to the 'old war coalition which comprised the Vaterlandspartei',[69] the agreement between the two groups did not overcome many differences that still remained. In addition, Lehr's pragmatic course, which manifested itself in his refusal to support the planned erection of a Schlageter monument in 1929, occasioned resentment among members of his own party, the DNVP.[70] The appointment of the new mayor, in other words, did not mean that nationalism was on the rise, but rather reflected the growing willingness of most parties to compromise on issues that ignored matters of principle.

This was also evident during the presidential elections in April 1925. Marx's victory in Düsseldorf, for example, was offset by the fact that many Catholics had voted for Hindenburg, who received 38.7 per cent in Düsseldorf, 8.5 per cent more than the combined vote for the DNVP, DVP, *Wirtschaftspartei*, and National Socialists in December 1924.[71] Equally revealing were the results of the May 1928 Reichstag elections,

---

[69] P. Hüttenberger, *Düsseldorf. Geschichte von den Ursprüngen bis in 20. Jahrhundert.* Band 3: *Die Industrie- und Verwaltungsstadt (20. Jahrhundert)* (Düsseldorf, 1989), 362.

[70] W. Först, *Robert Lehr als Oberbürgermeister. Ein Kapitel deutscher Kommunalpolitik* (Düsseldorf, 1962), 228.

[71] V. Franke, *Der Aufstieg der NSDAP in Düsseldorf. Die nationalsozialistische Basis in einer katholischen Großstadt* (Essen, 1987), 36–7.

which saw an increase in the support for the SPD and *Wirtschaftspartei*, but a 6 per cent decline for the Centre Party.[72] According to the local civil servants' association, the self-employed now turned increasingly toward the *Wirtschaftspartei*, while many state employees chose the SPD for its welfare programme.[73]

In 1929 both the anti-Young campaign and the municipal elections indicated how little the far Right could rely on radical nationalism to attract support. In the former case, only 2.8 per cent voted for the freedom law, a result well below the national average of 13.8 per cent.[74] In the case of the municipal elections, the *Wirtschaftspartei* gained at the expense of the DNVP, DVP, and DDP, receiving a remarkable 13.4 per cent of the vote. The Centre Party, by contrast, managed to improve its share by 4 per cent compared to 1928.[75] Even if we consider the more authoritarian lines taken by Kaas and Hugenberg in this period, it seems likely that nationalism as such played only a small part in the decision-making process of the electorate. One possible reason for this may be seen in the French withdrawal from Düsseldorf late in 1925, which denied the far Right one of their most effective propaganda campaigns.

A brief look at the NSDAP underlines this assessment. The newly founded party—it had reconstituted itself in August 1925—failed to make an impact on local politics in the period under review. Elberfeld remained the Nazi stronghold until 1928, when Hitler decided to end the quarrels in the *Gau* leadership by transferring power to the Düsseldorf branch.[76] A party office was set up in the working-class neighbourhood of Gerresheim, but this move proved just as ineffectual as the opening of a 'German Bookshop' in September 1928, which closed three months later because of financial problems. Most meetings, moreover, were held on an irregular basis, and by April 1929 the Düsseldorf NSDAP counted only 160 active members.[77] Only in early 1930 did the party emerge as a local force, a development we shall turn to in the next chapter.

As in Nuremberg, unemployment never disappeared from the city, and throughout the 1920s Düsseldorf continued to have one of the highest jobless rates of any major German town. In 1927, for example, 15,655 were on the dole, a figure that rose to 25,412 in 1929 and 42,933 in 1930.[78] Listing these numbers has a twofold purpose: first, we need to keep in mind that the 'golden years' in Düsseldorf consisted not only of the

---

[72] B. Brücher et al., *Dokumentation zur Geschichte der Stadt Düsseldorf. Düsseldorf während der Weimarer Republik 1919–1933. Quellensammlung* (Düsseldorf, 1985), 199.

[73] Franke, *NSDAP*, 45.   [74] Ibid., 47.

[75] Brücher, *Dokumentation*, 197.   [76] Franke, *NSDAP*, 118–19.

[77] Ibid., 128–30. The NSDAP won 2.4 per cent of the vote in the 1929 municipal elections.

[78] Brücher, *Dokumentation*, 375.

construction of new bridges, a new airport and stadium, and of the successful 'Gesolei' fair,[79] but also saw structural problems which brought hardship to many people; and second, we need to show that Düsseldorf's economy was hardly better off than its Nuremberg counterpart, where unemployment played an equally disturbing role for numerous citizens.

Thus, if both cities suffered from the effects of war, revolution, inflation, and, in the case of Düsseldorf, occupation, the 'Jewish question' was still treated differently by important sections of society in each town. In Düsseldorf we find only a few reported incidents of a serious nature in these years, all of which found coverage in the press. In Nuremberg, by contrast, only the Jews (and sometimes the DDP) complained about frequent assaults and ongoing discrimination.

In June 1925 the *CV-Zeitung* and local papers commented on the anti-Semitic tirades of the Mayor of Benrath, Melies. His remarks, made during a theatre performance in Düsseldorf and overheard by the Jewish Democrat Manes, forced various groups to take sides on the 'Jewish question'.[80] Three years later, the city's synagogue was desecrated by Nazi youths on the eve of Constitution Day.[81] Unlike similar events in Nuremberg, however, both episodes gave rise to heated exchanges, suggesting in effect that the 'Jewish question' was still a contentious issue and not simply a synonym for political and social racialism. It was therefore not very surprising that Rabbi Eschelbacher's history of the Düsseldorf community, published in 1929, could speak of the 'good relationship between Jews and Gentiles', and note that many non-Jews showed great interest in everything 'Jewish', as was the case during meetings organized by the Jewish community in the weeks and months leading up to local and national elections.[82]

'PROTESTANT BOURGEOISIE'

There are few signs that the DDP changed its course over the years. This was due in part to the overall absence of the 'Jewish question' in the political debate after 1925, to the homogeneous character of the party, which received even fewer votes in 1928 and 1929 (3.5 and 2.4 per cent respectively), and to the DDP's low profile on the matter. For example, in the propaganda material for the 1928 Reichstag elections, the problem of

---

[79] 'Gesolei' stood for 'Gesundheitspflege, soziale Fürsorge und Leibesübungen'.
[80] *CV-Zeitung*, 5.6.1925, 417 'Die gestörte Festvorstellung'.
[81] Ibid., 17.8.1928, 456 'Synagogenschändung in Düsseldorf'.
[82] M. Eschelbacher, *Festschrift zur Feier des 25 jährigen Bestehens der Synagoge* (Düsseldorf, 1929), 52–3.

anti-Semitism was mentioned nowhere,[83] and in the party press the question was seldom if ever discussed.[84] What we encounter instead, however, is an attempt to defend the Democratic Party from outside attacks, regardless of whether these were directed against Jews or Gentiles.

This was clearly visible in an article on the 'Melies affair'. Responding to anti-Semitic accusations that in the course of the exchange Manes had provoked the Mayor of Benrath into his anti-Semitic utterances, the *Beobachter* remarked that Manes was a respected member of the Düsseldorf community, both as head of the chamber of commerce, the commercial court, and the association of retailers, and as a city council member for the Democratic party.[85] Thus the paper did not so much defend his Jewishness as his stature in the community as a successful and distinguished businessman and politician. Although the mere fact that the DDP continued to put forward a Jewish candidate was impressive, and although the party never displayed any shift in policy on the 'Jewish question', we may assume that the Democrats tried to avoid the topic at a time when it received little coverage in the country at large.

The *Lokalzeitung*, on the other hand, whose Jewish owner, Isaak Thalheimer, was a well-known progressive, often combined condemnation with the nonchalance of a detached observer. This was the case during the Barmat scandal—'Only that which Hugo Stinnes spurns is left over for Kutisker and comrades'[86]—as well as during the 'Melies affair':

If he [Melies] had merely called Mr Manes a lout things could have been settled by the court, but why a Jewish lout? . . . But the Jews can demand security—just as all other decent persons can—and expect to enjoy at least the primitive protection offered by a box attendant in a theatre . . . If Mr Manes appeals to his co-religionists in this matter, he may count on their full support.[87]

When Nazi youths smeared paint on the walls of the local synagogue and destroyed some of its windows, the *Lokalzeitung* wrote about 'the modern propaganda for the dissemination of patriotism [*Vaterlandsliebe*]', whose effects appealed to those 'staid [*gesetzten*] gentlemen with a gentle smile for every disgraceful deed'.[88] When, prior to the May 1928

---

[83] StAD Plakatsammlung Mappe 1.

[84] See, for example, the issues of the *Beobachter* during the Barmat scandal, as well as the papers' account of the desecration of the synagogue, 25.8.1928 'Aus dem Verbreitungsgebiet'. To add to our problems, the *Beobachter* went defunct in 1928, so that we must rely on the left liberal but independent *Lokalzeitung* instead.

[85] *Beobachter*, 6.6.1925 'Aus dem Verbreitungsgebiet'.

[86] *LZ*, 3.1.1925 'Wirtschaftliche Wochenschau': 'The first question concerns Christian or Jew, the next nationalist or socialist. If it's a republican, then the system is blamed for the morass.'

[87] Ibid., 6.6.1925 'Lokalpolitischer Brief'.

[88] Ibid., 18.8.1928 'Lokalpolitischer Brief'.

Reichstag elections, Thalheimer discovered an advertisement in a provincial paper, in which a local firm was looking for an intelligent, young, and Protestant secretary, the *Lokalzeitung* noted that the company no doubt followed discriminatory practices, given the unlikelihood of its searching for a Protestant secretary with democratic or even Communist leanings.[89] What we have here, then, is a more relaxed attitude towards the whole question, as is evident from the non-ideological and sometimes cheeky repudiation of anti-Semitism, as well as from the general absence of more programmatic essays dealing with the subject. Between 1925 and 1929, left liberals decided to take advantage of this convenient silence, which did not mean that they suddenly ignored the wider dangers of Jew-baiting.

The main 'liberal' paper to the right of the DDP, the *Düsseldorfer Zeitung* (renamed *Stadt-Anzeiger* in 1928), whose previous position included strong nationalism and frequent racialism, now put on a neutral guise. This entailed both a continued emphasis on patriotism and the rejection of violent anti-Semitism. For example, the Melies–Manes dispute was recounted objectively, but when the mayor's lawyers claimed their client had been misquoted, the paper retorted: 'We heard . . . with our own ears that the said expressions . . . were used by Mr Melies, and see no reason to take back what we reported in yesterday's edition.'[90] The DVP organ also had little to say on the Barmat scandal, even though an editorial of 5 January 1925 expressed the hope that sooner or later Germans could feel safe from 'a group of speculators and spongers, who had made themselves comfortable at the moment of our collapse'.[91] Still, the 'villainous immigrants', as the paper called them, were relatively unimportant in comparison to the 'high and highest state officials', who repeatedly abetted the shady business deals of Barmat and his cronies.[92]

Similarly, the DVP condemned the desecration of the synagogue, and described the perpetrators as brutalized youths lacking all scruples and honour.[93] At the same time, the *Stadt-Anzeiger* attacked 'Polish swindlers' and 'Polish philistines' (in reference to the rather unphilistine lifestyle of the accused) during the Sklarek scandal, but refrained from employing anti-Semitic imagery in the further course of the affair.[94] On the whole, then, we find that the DVP displayed little concern for the 'Jewish question' in this period; as elsewhere, the formerly hostile People's Party decided to ignore the question at a time when other issues preoccupied the political parties in Düsseldorf.

[89] Ibid., 5.5.1928 'Lokalpolitischer Brief'.   [90] *DZ*, 4.6.1925 'Gegendarstellung'.
[91] Ibid., 4.1.1925 'Korruption'.   [92] Ibid., 14.1.1925 'Barmat'.
[93] *Stadt-Anzeiger*, 12.8.1928 'Unerhörte Ausschreitungen'.
[94] Ibid., 29.9.1929 'Streiflichter' and 1.10.1929 'Nachlese'.

This was true even for the DNVP. According to Gisbert Gemein, party meetings after 1925 became less aggressive and demagogic, instead focusing on such 'non-ideological' matters as taxation and the budget.[95] Thus the DNVP scaled down its agitation against the Republic, leaving this to other right-wing organizations such as the *Stahlhelm*, which gradually emerged as mobilizing forces suffusing the country's nationalists with a new sense of confidence and hope.[96] In the person of Field-Marshal Hindenburg, moreover, the party found a substitute for the exiled emperor, and in the remaining years of the Republic staged a number of celebrations in honour of the ageing president.[97]

In January 1928 Dr Willfried Kossmann took over the DNVP leadership in Düsseldorf. Although this involved a shift in policy towards the Republic—the new chairman supported Hugenberg's radical course—the Düsseldorf branch continued to cooperate with the Centre in municipal affairs. Future conflicts were thus foreseeable, and by late 1929, following the dismal failure of the anti-Young campaign and the party's poor performances in the Reichstag and municipal elections (where the DNVP received 8 and 11.4 per cent respectively), a split between the warring factions seemed all but inevitable.[98]

Turning to the 'Jewish question' in these years, we find that the DNVP, while not shelving the issue altogether, paid less attention to it than in earlier periods. For example, the official party organ, *Der Führer*, contained no anti-Semitic statements during the Sklarek scandal, and avoided Jew-baiting prior to the May 1928 Reichstag elections. Instead, the DNVP relied on the *Düsseldorfer Nachrichten*, whose coverage often comprised anti-Semitic stereotypes reminiscent of the years 1918–24. According to the *Nachrichten*, the Barmat scandal, or 'the Galician morass [*Sumpf*]', showed how the 'oriental protégés [*Schützlinge*]' had benefited from the friendly assistance of their 'compatriots' after the Revolution.[99] The same was true for the Sklareks: 'German youth and manhood bled in the trenches, the people [*Volk*] in the *Heimat* hoped and worried, the Sklareks delivered boots, tents, blankets, war matériel—of course in return for a share in the war profits.'[100]

In the run-up to the May 1928 elections, the *Nachrichten* carried a number of DNVP ads, many of which stressed national and Christian

[95] G. J. Gemein, *Die Deutschnationale Volkspartei in Düsseldorf 1918–1933*, unpublished Ph.D. thesis (Cologne, 1969), 40–1.

[96] P. Fritzsche, *Rehearsals for Fascism. Populism and Political Mobilization in Weimar Germany* (Oxford, 1990), 189.

[97] Gemein, *DNVP*, 42; Fritzsche, *Rehearsals*, 159.   [98] Gemein, *DNVP*, 51, 59.

[99] *DN*, 8.2.1925 'Ein Rückblick'. See also 4.1.1925 (Morgen) 'Ein Rückblick'.

[100] Ibid., 28.9.1929 'Gebrüder Sklarek'.

values.[101] Two posters, moreover, indicated that, at least on a national level, anti-Semitism remained an important electoral device. The first, entitled 'Front-line soldiers! *Stahlhelm* comrades!', warned against the surrender of German interests to 'alien [*land- und volksfremde*] elements'. The second one, which also originated outside Düsseldorf, went beyond that, and portrayed twelve prominent Jews, including Arthur Rosenberg, Georg Bernhard, and Rudolf Hilferding. Directed in particular at the voters of the SPD and KPD, the picture denoted that any further support for either party would lead to 'Jewish' predominance. It was therefore up to the electorate to answer the question: 'German people! Shall these be your leaders?' with an emphatic but definite 'no'.[102]

We must remember, however, that in Düsseldorf itself the DNVP refrained from outright Jew-baiting. Neither in party meetings nor in propaganda material do we find the kind of anti-Semitism common in the immediate postwar era. One party advertisement even went so far as to chide the *Völkisch-Nationaler Block* in 1928 for dismissing the Old Testament as Jewish and attempting to establish a 'Wotan cult'.[103] Thus, if the party continued to reject 'Jewish' influence and power, it did so with less enthusiasm: since everyone knew its position on the question, and since everyone was busy with other matters, anti-Semitism for the time being played only a small part in the deliberations of the local DNVP.

The Protestant Church took a more cautious line after 1922 by embracing everything *völkisch* and at the same time criticizing radicalism and violence. From 1925 to 1929 the *Evangelisches Sonntagsblatt* only occasionally dealt with the issue, but on the whole its position changed very little. Again, 'modern-Jewish men of letters' and 'Jewish pamphleteers [*Pamphletisten*]' were insulting William II and Protestant priests, Jewish high finance was enslaving the nation, and German theatre-goers demanded protection from the destructive 'Jewish-international taste'.[104] On the other hand, the Düsseldorf weekly condemned the desecration of numerous synagogues, 'reports of which unfortunately surface from time to time'.[105] The approach taken, in other words, resembled that of the *Christlich-sozialer Volksdienst* and the Protestant Church in Nuremberg,

[101] The *Rheinische Landeszeitung*, which was DNVP-friendly, wrote the following on the DDP (10.5.1928 'Wahlkampf-Wahlkrampf'): 'Another Democratic poster depicts a blond Brünnhilde with a blond boy, and announces the party's goal as the provision for accommodation, prosperity, and knowledge [*Wohnungen, Wohlstand und Wissen*]. All that's really missing is the caption: Vote blond—and so democratic!'

[102] StAD Plakatsammlung Mappe 4. [103] *DN*, 19.5.1928.

[104] *SB*, 5.4.1925 'Kleine Pfeile'; 31.1.1926 'Mehr Würde'; 7.3.1926 'Pflichterfüllung' in the 'Soziale Beilage'.

[105] Ibid., 24.3.1929 'Zeitschau'.

where Christian love and racial exclusiveness formed part of a strange dialectic:

> Just as one is demanding a German God and a German faith, so wide circles are yearning for an image of Jesus equal to the spirit of our race and untainted by alien and Semitic influences. But does not the history of Christian piety prove that the power of the Christian faith . . . prevails over every race, every nation, every individual, character, and temperament?[106]

CATHOLICISM

The Centre Party in Düsseldorf, which after 1922 had moved into the Republican camp, now confronted a number of problems often directly related to its understanding of the nature of the state. This was evident, for example, during the presidential elections of 1925, when a substantial percentage of Catholics voted for Hindenburg on the grounds that he represented order and discipline, while his Roman Catholic opponent, Wilhelm Marx, stood for the present system and, perhaps even worse, received support from Social Democracy. Thus Hindenburg's victory and the temporary retirement of Wirth from national politics can be interpreted as just as much of a turning-point as the subsequent election of Kaas to the leadership of the party and the shift towards a more authoritarian approach within the Centre.[107] A further sign of growing tensions within the party was the debate over the expropriation of the dynasties, which saw one side arguing that such a measure was un-Christian, and another contending that the dynasties had to 'share the burdens of Germany's state'.[108] Finally, a conflict emerged on the issue of whether or not to support the *Reichsbanner*, the Republican defence organization largely in the hands of Social Democracy. In Düsseldorf only the youth organizations of the Centre fully endorsed the groups' activities, although it has been estimated that a quarter of its members belonged to the Centre Party.[109] The *Reichsbanner* question, however, was only part of the wider issue of how to reconcile the party's cooperation with the far Right in the Reichstag (until 1928) and the municipal council with Republican ideals and loyalty to the state.

This was also reflected in the Centre's approach to the problem of anti-Semitism. For instance, during the Barmat scandal, which the Tageblatt called 'an unholy alliance between politics and business, which enabled

---

[106] *SB*, 31.1.1926 'Das Christentum und die völkische Frage'.
[107] W. Stump, *Geschichte und Organisation der Zentrumspartei in Düsseldorf 1917–1933* (Düsseldorf, 1971), 63.
[108] Ibid., 65.   [109] Ibid., 144.

the alien [*Fremdling*] Barmat, while the German people lay dying, to amass millions,'[110] the party again employed language evoking images of the sly and devious *Ostjude*:

Mr Issak Barmat, a Lithiuanian citizen, "immigrated" to Berlin in July 1922 without the necessary documents, and has since traded in everything that can be bought . . . and today owns, among other things, a castle in Schwanenwerder. Display no envy, fellow citizens! Especially the hundred thousand of you who, while the *Ostjude* was purchasing a castle, couldn't even purchase a one-room apartment![111]

By contrast, in the first round of the presidential elections, the Düsseldorf Centre Party distributed a leaflet against the candidate of the national Right, Karl Jarres, claiming he represented 'intolerant, anti-Semitic, and anti-Catholic forces'.[112] What is more, the *Tageblatt* printed an appeal by the *Reichsbanner* in August 1925 which described the dangers of Jew-baiting for Germany's domestic and international well-being.[113]

A few years later, however, we come across two articles which suggest that the Centre Party remained uncomfortable with the entire subject. In the first piece, a book review of *The German Jew and Anti-Semitism* by Max Hachenberg, long passages were quoted in which the author asked his co-religionists to maintain a low profile—'I demand of you . . . to exercise restraint'—so as to ensure their gradual and smooth assimilation.[114] The second article, however, went much further. This time the party organ attacked the *Lokalzeitung*, whose style of reporting ('gossip [*Klatsch*] from the Scheunenviertel') did not follow the 'Talmudic maxim' of spreading good among one's neighbours. As long as Germany was still a Christian state, the paper continued, all minorities and 'alien elements' had to respect the laws and traditions of the nation. In other words, as long as this consensus prevailed, it was up to the majority population to guarantee 'that no alien [*den Sittengesetzen gesinnungsfremde*] agitators travelled around the country to undermine the age-old moral [*sittlichen*] values of this Christian-Germanic land and to cultivate [*den Boden zu beackern*] other, oriental moral laws [*Sittengesetze*].'[115]

When the *Lokalzeitung* responded to this article by accusing the Centre organ of anti-Semitism, the latter replied that, first, no other factor had contributed more to the spread of Jew-hatred in Düsseldorf than Thalheimer's *Lokalzeitung*, and that, second, the *Tageblatt* had always rejected anti-Semitism, which was 'crude, mindless, untruthful, and

---

[110] *DT*, 15.2.1925.
[111] Ibid., 1.2.1925 'Mitbürger!' See also 4.1.1925 'Staatskredite'.
[112] StAD XXI 22 'Jarres?' [113] *DT*, 16.8.1925 'An alle Republikaner'.
[114] Ibid., 30.10.1927. [115] Ibid., 6.11.1927.

un-Christian'.[116] This, together with the party's emphasis on 'brotherly love which knows nothing of class and racial hatred' and the fact that its propaganda material contained no signs of anti-Semitism, might suggest vigorous opposition to all forms of Jew-baiting on part of the Centre Party.[117] Yet we must also keep in mind that the above statements on the Christian state and its enemies revealed deep misgivings about the role of. 'Jewish' individuals and institutions in Germany's political life. While the party usually avoided anti-Semitic polemics in its treatment of the question, memories of war and revolution led to attacks on those Jews who failed to recognize the limits of their freedom. In short, while the Centre Party continued to dismiss racism, it retained a distinct aversion to 'Jewish proclivities' for criticism and subversion.

THE LEFT

As was the case with most other parties in this period, both the SPD and KPD seldom discussed the 'Jewish question' in public. When it did intrude on them, however, they took similar views to the ones examined in Chapters 3 and 4. Thus, Social Democrats still castigated anti-Semitism, while their Communist opponents exhibited cynicism whenever they dealt with the subject.

The SPD often went out of its way to express disapproval over racist Jew-baiting. In March 1925, for example, it associated the political murders of post-war Germany with rabid anti-Semitism ('the gospel of political criminals'), which poisoned the hearts of young children.[118] During the 'Gesolei' fair, moreover, the party noted that brochures advertising the event abroad included references to Düsseldorf as the birthplace of the poet Heine, whereas the same pamphlets designed for a German audience omitted this fact, 'for otherwise right-wing organizations wouldn't have come to the birthplace of the prince-hater and prince-mocker [*Fürtsenhassers- und Verspotters*]'.[119] The Manes–Melies confrontation, on the other hand, was portrayed as the reaction of a die-hard anti-Semite to Offenbach's play *La Belle Hélène*, in which the appearance of a 'typical' Jewish character had given rise to the embarrassing comments by Melies.[120] Interestingly enough, the *Volkszeitung* remarked that such outbreaks of hatred were normally confined to *völkisch* rallies in the unoccu-

---

[116] *DT*, 20.11.1928 'Die Giftspritze'.
[117] Ibid., 19.5.1928 Front-page article; see the dozen or so leaflets for the 1929 municipal elections in StAD XXı 26.
[118] *VZ*, 2.3.1926 'Gedächtnisfeier für Reichspräsident Ebert'.
[119] Ibid., 18.5.1926 Report on Stahlhelm visit to the 'Gesolei'.
[120] Ibid., 8.6.1925. The 'play' was originally written as an operetta.

pied areas of Germany, an indication perhaps of the limited impact of radical anti-Semitism in Düsseldorf.

Predictably, the SPD touched on the Barmat and Sklarek scandals with great care, for in both 1925 and 1929 Social Democrats faced charges of bribery and embezzlement as part of the investigations into the affairs. Barmat, for example, was either defended by the *Volkszeitung* or linked to certain conservative politicians just as 'crafty as the craftiest *Ostjuden*'.[121] The Sklarek brothers, of course, were members of the SPD, and the only excuse the party organ could offer was that even the anti-Semite Bruhn had enjoyed intimate contacts with these Jewish crooks.[122] The KPD, by contrast, exploited the news of SPD involvement in the Barmat case, but tended to ignore the background of the accused. Four years later, however, the *Freiheit* opined that 'money stinks as little for the Social Democrats as it does for the German Nationals—also if it comes from Jews,'[123] and carried a front-page cartoon depicting a number of 'Jewish-looking' men about to escape the country with heavy bags while the public prosecuter turned a blind eye to the scene.[124] What is more, the KPD intimated that Social Democracy was wholly or in part under the influence of Jewry, as the following piece prior to the 1928 Reichstag elections seems to suggest: 'Monk and rabbi—both stink! Therefore the worker can neither choose the Centre nor the SPD, but must give his vote to the Communist Party, which alone has fought all these reactionary and anti-proletarian measures!'[125]

If we compare the approach of both parties in these years with the one taken in earlier periods, we must conclude that very little had changed. The SPD remained clearly opposed to anti-Semitism; the KPD remained clearly indifferent to the matter. The SPD continued to attack Jew-baiters; the KPD continued to belittle them. The SPD refused to employ anti-Semitism; the KPD employed it whenever it proved expedient.

The mid-1920s in Düsseldorf were marked by pragmatism, so that ideological issues, although not completely missing, remained largely subdued. This was most evident in the cases of the DVP and DNVP, who in the past had viciously attacked the Jews, but it was also characteristic of the DDP, which surmised that silence was most opportune in the absence of debate. The Protestant Church, on the other hand, pursued a policy

---

[121] Ibid., 30.1.1925 'Ein weiterer Kredit-Skandal'. See also 18.1.1925 'Ein Bankrott altpreußischen Beamtentums'.

[122] Ibid., 27.9.1929 '10 Millionen!'

[123] *Freiheit*, 10.10.1929 'Schwarz-weiß-rot-goldener Sklarek-Sumpf'. See also 9.10.1929 'Die Duzfreunde der Sklareks'.

[124] Ibid., 15.10.1929.   [125] Ibid., 16.5.1928 'Der Rabbi und der Mönch.'

combining racism with Christian love, thereby testifying to continued doubts as to how the 'Jewish question' was best confronted.

On the whole, then, Düsseldorf's Jews must have felt relatively secure in this period. With the termination of French rule, moreover, as well as the consistently poor performance of the NSDAP, there seemed to be no basis for extreme nationalism in the Rhenish city. Even if this did not lead to a liberal consensus, it created an atmosphere of general tolerance at a time when other, more pressing needs were on the agenda.

While the Jews could again rely on the SPD and DDP, the Centre Party retained traditional anti-Jewish prejudices, which were put to use once the party believed itself to be encountering 'alien' ways of life. Although this occurred rather infrequently, it pointed to the strength of anti-Jewish feelings among Catholics after 1918. The Jews, in other words, might rely on the Centre for an uncompromising stance against the far Right, but they were expected to keep quiet on a variety of sensitive issues which called for restraint.

Compared to Nuremberg, then, the 'Jewish question' in Düsseldorf remained a matter of controversy, and saw few parties trying to combine *völkisch* dogma with responsible politics. As in Nuremberg, however, economic 'stability' in Düsseldorf could not last forever, so that those parties which accepted compromise now were not necessarily inclined to accept it later. Nevertheless, the difference between the two cities was one of consensus: not between liberal values on the one hand and *völkisch-*nationalist ones on the other, but between the presence of debate in Düsseldorf and a 'harmony of conviction' in Nuremberg.

6

In Hitler's shadow
1930–1933

In the Empire, Social Democrats followed anti-Semites from village to village in hope of a confrontation. In the Republic, the Social Democrats were victims of this provocative strategy. Not the lack of resources but limits on their use in the specific conditions of the late 1920s shaped the SPD response to nazism in Marburg.

Rudy Koshar, *Social Life, Local Politics, and Nazism: Marburg, 1880–1935* (1986)

Two crucial events in the autumn of 1929 marked the beginning of Weimar's final years. The Wall Street crash of October, which destroyed confidence in the domestic American economy, reverberated across Europe, depriving many countries, and in particular Germany, of vital foreign loans. The death of Gustav Stresemann, moreover, meant that from now on moderate politics was even less likely, both at home and abroad. Future diplomacy would rely on coercion rather than compromise, and the realignment of the 'middle' in Germany proved a near-impossible task.

The fall of the last Weimar coalition government with a parliamentary majority in early 1930 was the inevitable outcome of this failure to adapt successfully to democratic politics and to accept responsibility. While the SPD refused to support an increase in employee contributions (which would have cost the party votes in a future election), the DVP, now under the growing influence of big business, wanted substantial cuts in benefits. The end of the Müller cabinet thus saw the apogee of political discord, and the subsequent dependence on Hindenburg's emergency decrees revealed once again how fragile the democratic basis of Weimar politics had been.

Whereas left liberalism slowly but surely whithered away, first as a result of continued electoral setbacks and then through an ill-fated marriage with the *Jungdeutscher Orden*, the SPD's situation deteriorated due to the party's toleration of a Brüning government bent on dismantling all

those social welfare advances for which Social Democrats had previously
fought. The Centre Party, meanwhile, welcomed the advent of Brüning's
more authoritarian regime and, although deciding to remain in the SPD-
led coalition of Prussia, also favoured cooperation with the NSDAP in
1932 in the hope of discrediting Hitler and the Nazi Party. Thus, within
the context of deepening economic troubles, increasingly bitter distribu-
tional disputes, and enduring political strife, there existed little interest in
coming to terms with such issues as the 'Jewish question', which on the
whole seemed less threatening to the well-being of the Republic than
Hindenburg's emergency legislation or the violent street brawls between
Nazis and Communists. Finally, since the Left often mistook *völkisch*
anti-Semitism for opportunism, while the Centre viewed it as a veiled
attack on the Catholic Church, the Jews expected more from both parties'
political opposition to Nazism than from their refusal to accept anti-
Semitism as a permanent aspect of Germany's social life. Hitler, in other
words, determined the agenda of the debate.

NUREMBERG

As had been the case in the late 1920s, Nuremberg suffered from a
disproportionately high level of unemployment in the last years of the
Weimar Republic. By the end of 1930 nearly 40,000 city residents, or 18.1
per cent of the 1925 workforce, were without a job. Of these, 14,500
people, or 38.2 per cent of the unemployed, received insurance benefits
and a further 7166, or 18.9 per cent of the unemployed, emergency
unemployment benefits. Two years later, the number of jobless citizens
reached 57,000, or 27.2 per cent of the workforce. Many of these, however, were no longer eligible for any form of support, and only one-third
of them received some assistance, if very little. At the same time, the steep
rise in welfare costs forced Nuremberg, like other municipalities, to abandon various projects and to reduce its staff.[1] Yet most parties, including
those who made up the *Bürgerliche Arbeitsgemeinschaft* (DVP, DNVP,
Wirtschaftspartei), agreed that Nuremberg's administration was doing its
best to alleviate the worst effects of the depression and that Luppe was not
to blame for the current malaise.[2]

The NSDAP, on the other hand, demoted municipal politics to 'a small
battlefield of agitation' by attacking department stores and denouncing

[1] M. Moore-Ziegler, *The Socio-Economic and Demographic Bases of Political Behavior in
Nuremberg during the Weimar Republic, 1919–1933*, unpublished Ph.D. thesis (Virginia,
1976), 87–8.
[2] H. Hanschel, *Oberbürgermeister Hermann Luppe. Nürnberger Kommunalpolitik in der
Weimarer Republik* (Nuremberg, 1977), 365.

numerous forms of advertisement, as well as the production of supposedly un-Christian plays.[3] Most disturbing of all, however, was the growing appeal of the party at the polls. In September 1930, the Nazis won 24 per cent of the vote in Nuremberg, compared to 18.2 per cent in Germany as a whole. While the DNVP was relegated to the role of a minor party, receiving only 6500 votes, the *Christlich-sozialer Volksdienst* managed to secure nearly twice that number. Still, neither the gains of the *Volksdienst* nor the more modest advances of the *Wirtschaftspartei* could disguise the fact that the conservative-nationalist camp lost thousands of votes to the extreme Right.[4] Nazi successes were also gained at the expense of the DVP and DDP/*Staatspartei*, both of which were reduced to insignificant splinter parties.

The Bavarian state elections of April 1932 saw a further dramatic increase for the NDSAP in Nuremberg. Taking 37.6 per cent of the vote, the party now emerged as the strongest political force in the city, over-taking the SPD by nearly 20,000 votes. Three months later, the Nazi Party hoped to improve on this result by holding dozens of meetings and staging well-attended rallies in and around Nuremberg. Nevertheless, the July 1932 Reichstag elections proved to be a turning-point: for the first time in the Weimar Republic, the local NSDAP received roughly the same amount of support from the electorate as in the nation at large (37.8 and 37.3 per cent respectively). Even more disconcerting for Streicher and his supporters, the party was now plagued by financial troubles and personal rivalries, which seriously damaged its position in the final weeks of 1932. In November, for example, the NSDAP accounted for 'only' 32.8 per cent of the Reichstag vote in Nuremberg; and in December, as well as in early 1933, the Stegmann revolt, which involved a power struggle between members of the Franconian SA and the *Gau* leadership under Streicher, revealed how difficult it was to maintain party discipline when frustration was growing over the fact that Hitler still had not attained power.[5]

Although the depression contributed to the rise of National Socialism, it would be wrong to view the relationship between the two as straightfor-ward. Thus the NSDAP scored best in areas where there was relatively little unemployment (the agrarian regions of Middle Franconia), while in Nuremberg the party gained most in districts with a high number of civil servants and professionals, both of whom suffered less from the effects

---

[3] Ibid., 370.

[4] E. C. Reiche, *The Development of the SA in Nürnberg, 1922–1934* (Cambridge, 1986), 94–5.

[5] For the Stegmann Revolt, see Reiche, *Development*, 146–72.

of the slump than, say, small shopkeepers or unskilled workers.[6] In *Luitpoldhein*, for example, which was a 'typical mansion district' full of independent businessmen, lawyers, and doctors, the Nazi vote increased to 55.8 per cent in November 1932, at a time when the NSDAP declined virtually everywhere else in Germany.[7] Most important in this connection was the ideological predisposition of many who had lived through both war and revolution, and who were constantly reminded by such papers as the *Fränkischer Kurier* that the 'system' was responsible for their current miseries.[8]

This was also reflected in the way Gentiles confronted the problem of anti-Semitism. Not only did attacks on Jewish schoolchildren or Zionist organizations receive little coverage in the press,[9] but when Streicher was sued for libel his 'fanatical conviction' more often than not proved a mitigating circumstance.[10] The CV, meanwhile, acknowledged the good-will of the 'authorities', but complained about indifference among the lower echelons of the police and judiciary.[11] In short, while the 'Jewish question' no longer commanded the attention it received in the early twenties, there were no signs pointing to an improvement in relations between Nuremberg's Gentiles and Jews. On the contrary, little if anything was done to show solidarity with the much-maligned minority.

'PROTESTANT BOURGEOISIE'

In fact, if we take the DDP, which changed its name to *Deutsche Staatspartei* in the summer of 1930, we find that its marriage with the *Jungdeutscher Orden* brought to light differences which in the past had been obscured. On the one hand, a number of dedicated Democrats under Otto Stündt refused to join the new party (his old companion-in-arms, Julie Meyer, became a member of the SPD), while on the other, men like city council Eickemeyer moved more and more to the right. Mayor Luppe described this development vividly in his memoirs: 'Regrettably the Democratic Party also dwindled in Nuremberg. The conversion into the

---

[6] R. Hambrecht, *Der Aufstieg der NSDAP in Mittel-and Oberfranken (1925–1933)* (Nuremberg, 1977), 188–9; StAN F5 QNG 421: R. Gömmel and G. Haertel, *Arbeitslosigkeit und Wählerentscheidungen in Nürnberg von 1928 bis 1933*, Seminararbeit (Nuremberg, 1968), 38 ff.

[7] StAN F5 QNG 421: Gömmel and Haertel, *Arbeitslosigkeit*, 38 ff.

[8] Reiche, *Development*, 131; R. Hamilton, *Who Voted for Hitler?* (Princeton, 1982), 214.

[9] *Protokollbuch der israelitischen Gemeinde*, V, 467–8, 471.

[10] Hambrecht, *Aufstieg*, 266–7, 278, 284.

[11] Ibid., 275. Unlike other areas of Germany, the depression did not occasion a 'new wave of anti-Semitism' in Nuremberg. A. Paucker, *Der jüdische Abwehrkampf gegen Antisemitismus und Nationalsozialismus in den letzten Jahren der Weimarer Republik* (Hamburg, 1969), 16.

State Party led the radical wing (Tempel, Stündt, and so on) to leave and join the Democratic Association [*Demokratische Vereinigung*]; some Jews now preferred the Bavarian People's [Party], where their votes were at least not wasted.'[12]

This did not mean, however, that most left liberals changed their views on the 'Jewish question'. Luppe, for example, condemned Nazi attacks on the Jews in Nuremberg's welfare committees, claiming that the latter had 'always cooperated in an exemplary manner'.[13] Prior to the September 1930 elections, moreover, the *Nürnberg-Fürther Morgenpresse* warned of the dangers inherent in *völkisch* anti-Semitism: 'It is complete madness, nay criminal, to say such stuff to the uncritical people, to incite them to pogroms and civil war.'[14]

Nevertheless, when the party organ collapsed a few months later, and when the *Staatspartei*'s electoral fortunes declined ever more, the problem of anti-Semitism became less acute. Only once do we encounter a brief dicussion of the matter by left liberals in the municipal council. In April 1931, city councillor Walter Eickemeyer defended a new tax proposal by showing that those having to pay over 500 marks were mainly Jews. This caused his party colleague, city councillor Geppert, to criticize him for currying favour with the National Socialists.[15]

Since we lack material which might touch on further conflicts of such a nature in the *Staatspartei*, we must rely on the above recollections by Luppe, as well as on scattered remarks by others, to assess the gradual erosion of left liberalism in Nuremberg. Otto Stündt's comments at a meeting (possibly the only official one in Bavaria) commemorating the death of Walther Rathenau, for example, seem to confirm Luppe's words:

Rathenau was a German Jew . . . It is significant . . . that even in the Democratic Party during the time of its first flourishing [*Blüte*] a district conference rejected his candidature for the National Assembly Elections with reference to his denomination. Looking back at this episode it is perhaps easier to understand why such a Democratic Party had to fail.[16]

With the demise of the DDP/*Staatspartei*, in other words, the Jews lost their most vocal supporters. What remained of the old liberal party was a small group fighting for survival, whose followers were unlikely to defend

[12] H. Luppe, *Mein Leben* (Nuremberg, 1977), 283.
[13] StAN C7/IX Stadtratsprotokoll (SRP) 364, 9.4.1930.
[14] *NFM*, 13./14.9.1930 'Freie Bahn der Vernunft'.
[15] StAN C7/IX SRP 489, 22.4.1931. Eickemeyer left the *Staatspartei* in 1932, and became second mayor in the aftermath of Hitler's '*Machtergreifung*'. Hanschel, *Luppe*, 361.
[16] *Echo*, May/June 1932, 41.

minority rights at a time when they themselves were under threat of extinction.

Nuremberg's conservative forces also faced the possibility of extinction. In fact, the outcome of the July 1932 elections gave the 'traditional' Right little cause for self-congratulation. Although the DNVP recovered some of its losses, standing now at 3 per cent of the popular vote, the various groups that had broken away from the DNVP in 1930 were practically defunct. And although the Nationalists increased their share to 6.4 per cent in November, capitalizing on, among other things, Hitler's insistence that he be given the chancellorship in a coalition government, there is little indication that the DNVP could have regained a commanding position in Nuremberg's political life. Whatever can be gleaned from the sources, moreover, suggests that the 'Jewish question' was either ignored or interpreted to the effect that mutual exclusion was in the best interest of Jews and Gentiles alike.

The *Fränkischer Kurier*, for example, carried a special issue of the *Süddeutsche Monatshefte*, with contributions from both anti- and philo-Semites on the question. While the *Kurier* remained impartial throughout, it asked its readers to consider all arguments in the 'debate', given the significance of 'one of the most decisive but also one of the most complicated problems that has faced the German people in the post-war years'.[17] Otherwise Nuremberg's main 'bourgeois' newspaper had little to say, although it continued to espouse a fierce nationalism, defamed parliamentary democracy, and prior to elections supported those parties which upheld the old colours of black, white, and red.[18]

The *Christlich-sozialer Volksdienst* took the view that '*völkisch* awareness' was good as long as it did not degenerate into '*völkisch* extremism'. According to the left liberal *Nürnberg-Fürther Morgenpresse*, the *Volksdienst* refrained from Jew-baiting up until 1930,[19] a judgement we cannot fully support in light of earlier pronouncements to the contrary.[20] However, what the *Morgenpresse* probably did want to say was that the *Volksdienst* showed relatively little hostility towards the Jews compared to the other 'Christian' parties in Nuremberg.

On the other hand, we must remember that stressing *völkisch* values while condemning racist fanaticism usually caused confusion rather than clarity. This is borne out by two articles in the *Volksdienst*. The first, of

[17] *FK*, 9.9.1930 'Die Judenfrage'.

[18] See, for example, 11.7.1932 'Ringendes Deutschtum ringsum', where the paper praised the ethnic Germans of Romania for their 'racial-*völkisch* fanaticism'. See also 19.7.1932 'Blut und Verantwortungslosigkeit', 30.7.1932 'Wie wähle ich am Sonntag?' and 5.11.1932 'Bleibt der schwarz-weiß-roten Fahne treu!'

[19] *NFM*, 25.8.1930 'Ist eine evangelische Partei nötig?'   [20] See Chapter 5.

early 1931, admitted that the 'aryan *Völkerfamilie*' was far superior to other groups or nations, and argued against any concept of 'equality' between the races. At the same time, however, the article dismissed attempts on part of the *Deutschchristen* to turn the Protestant Church into a rallying ground for racial intolerance.[21] The second piece, appearing over a year later, reminded all 'earnest' Christians in the NSDAP that God had created Jews and Gentiles equal: 'We demand that those earnest Christians who believe to have found their political home [*Heimat*] in the National Socialist Party emphasize with the utmost vigour that before God all races are equal, including the Jews. The Jews are condemned by God because they crucified Jesus, not because they are a Jewish race.'[22] Similarly, the Protestant Church in Nuremberg warned against elevating '*völkisch* awareness' to the status of religious dogma:

It is certainly right to say that a people ought to preserve its racial purity; it is also the right [*Lebensrecht*] of the German nation to protect itself against domination [*Überfremdung*] by other races and to stem the influx of Slavs and Eastern Jews. But . . . we equally object to hatred of other races or to the fight against the highest good [*das Höchste*], namely belief in Christ, under the pretext of maintaining the race [*Rassenpflege*].[23]

What we have here, then, is a combination of arrogance and humility, a respect for the nation as well as for God's commandments. Hatred was to be avoided, as was racial supremacy. But contradictions emerged, and it became increasingly difficult to insist on equality when one's own people was so obviously superior. If both the *Volksdienst* and the Protestant Church rejected Nazi anti-Semitism, they did so because it threatened certain key Christian convictions, not because the Jews themselves were seen as equal members of the German polity. Finally, most 'Christian' parties in Nuremberg realized that Jew-baiting was no longer an electoral asset, following the phenomenal rise of a movement which could claim an intellectual heritage of radical *völkisch* anti-Semitism.

This was also true for the *Wirtschaftspartei*. Having been one of the worst enemies of the Jews in the past, the 'middle-class' interest group now decided to concentrate on its main *political* enemy in Nuremberg, the NSDAP. Thus, prior to the September 1930 Reichstag elections, the party organ claimed that the far Right's 'mendacious hate propaganda'

---

[21] *Volksdienst*, 31.1.1931 'Rassekultus und Christentum'.
[22] Ibid., 8.10.1932 'Volk Gottes'.
[23] *EvGN*, 7.8.1932 'Jesus und das Volkstum'. This was the only article in the Protestant weekly touching on the 'Jewish question' in this period.

was just as dangerous as left-wing agitation.[24] To be sure, the SPD and KPD, 'who had celebrated feasts . . . with Barmat and Kutisker and Sklarek,' remained prime targets,[25] but on the whole the *Wirtschaftspartei* felt more inclined to respond to the Nazi threat than to socialist activities. We need to keep in mind, however, that this opposition was based mainly on the fear that Hitler would establish a party dictatorship, eliminating all dissenting voices and stifling free competition—and not so much on specific differences with National Socialist ideology.[26] The *Wirtschaftspartei* therefore continued its struggle against 'all socialist and anti-Christian efforts aimed at destroying the economy and culture',[27] all of which amounted to a spiritual curse on the German nation.

CATHOLICISM

The BVP, by contrast, pursued a policy which comprised a number of different and often contradictory messages. Largely on the defensive in Bavaria, the party recognized for the first time that too little had been done to check the growing influence of National Socialism. In particular, the Ministry of the Interior complained about the lenient approach taken by the Nürnberg-Fürth police under its notorious leader, Heinrich Gareis.[28] Although the BVP managed to receive aproximately one-third of the vote in Bavaria throughout the early 1930s, it faced considerable opposition at the hands of the Nazis, who scored their greatest victory in July 1932, when they emerged as the largest political force in the state.[29]

As far as the 'Jewish question' was concerned, Nuremberg's Catholics continued to hold conflicting views, even though sympathy was rarely expressed. Thus the BVP announced that Nazi anti-Semitism was often nothing else but fraud, while at the same time it provided space for CV appeals in the local party organ.[30] On the one hand, then, we find cynical utterances linking Nazis with Jews, while on the other we find responsible commentaries on the dangers of racial hatred.

[24] *Nürnberger Bürgerzeitung*, 2.9.1930 'Lokale Nachrichten'; 11.9.1930 'Ihr wahres Gesicht'.
[25] Ibid., 11.9.1930 WP appeal 'Mittelstand in Stadt und Land!'
[26] Ibid., 20.7.1932 WP appeal 'An das freiheitlich-nationale Bürgertum.'
[27] Ibid., 27.7.1932 'Das Gebot der Stunde.'   [28] Hanschel, *Luppe*, 376.
[29] In Nuremberg, the BVP hovered at around 8 per cent between 1930 and 1933. In 1930 the BVP/DNVP/*Bauernbund* coalition, which had ruled Bavaria since the mid-twenties, collapsed. The BVP now relied on the goodwill of Bavaria's Social Democrats, who tolerated the minority government in order to prevent a Nazi takeover. See F. Wiesemann, *Die Vorgeschichte der nationalsozialistischen Machtübernahme in Bayern 1932/1933* (Berlin, 1975), 111 ff.
[30] *BV*, 6.7.1932. See Paucker, *Abwehrkampf*, 58–9.

In the run-up to the 1930 Reichstag elections, the former approach seemed to prevail. In an article entitled 'Jew-hatred and National Socialists', for instance, the *Bayerische Volkszeitung* claimed that a *völkisch* cartoonist had offered his services to Jewish defence organizations. After having given a few other pertinent examples, the paper concluded with a quote by Hitler in which the Nazi leader confessed that his movement retained an anti-Semitic plank in order to appease its constituency: 'Hitler, it follows, can betray his anti-Semitic principles just as easily as the above-mentioned National Socialist subordinates [*Unterführer*].'[31]

In April 1931, moreover, the BVP's Emmanuel Deggendorfer advised his National Socialist colleagues in the municipal council to back Eickemeyer's tax proposal, 'since this tax would above all hurt Jews'.[32] In short, political Catholicism at times pandered to the prejudices of the electorate by alluding to Hitler's 'bogus' Judeophobia, or by intimating that anti-Semitism was a justified and therefore widespread phenomenon.

In July 1932, however, the Bavarian People's Party alternated between straightforward opposition to anti-Semitism and unyielding cynicism. In a piece on 'Mussolini against Hitler', for example, the party organ highlighted the Duce's rejection of racism ('Patriotism [*Nationalstolz*] didn't require racial deleriums [*Delirien der Rasse*]'), which had no place in Italian culture:

Mussolini also rejects anti-Semitism with a disparaging gesture. Anti-Semitism didn't exist in Italy. Jewish Italians [note: 'Jewish Italians', not 'Italian Jews'!] have always proved themselves both as citizens and soldiers . . . The Duce's only response to the current lot of the Jews is summed up in three words of disdain: Oh, the scapegoat![33]

Similarly, the *Bayerische Volkszeitung* printed a BVP appeal to all German Christians reminding them of their duty to place supernatural revelation above 'blood kinship to the German race'.[34]

Yet at the same time, the party continued to make disparaging remarks about Jews in avowedly Christian parties. Thus the *Evangelischer Bund* in Nuremberg, which criticized the Pope for insisting that Germany pay her reparations, included a member by the name of Frenkel ('called Fränkel when he was still Jewish'). Even more revealing, in the view of the BVP, was a report in the *Abend* which suggested that a Nazi parliamentarian in Saxony was really a Jew.[35] In addition, the *Volkszeitung* exploited the news

[31] Ibid., 30.8.1930; 4.9.1930 'Hitlers kaufen beim Juden'.
[32] StAN C7/IX SRP 489, 22.4.1931.   [33] *BV*, 6.7.1932.
[34] Ibid., 15.7.1932 'Deutsche Christen! Katholiken und Protestanten'.
[35] Ibid., 15.7.1932 'Glossen vom Tage' and 'Ein Jude als Naziabgeordneter?'

of an unusual archaeological discovery in Rome: to the surprise of the scientists, a swastika had been found on the remains of an ancient Jewish burial sight. This, 'one of history's cruel ironies [*Treppenwitz der Weltgeschichte*],' according to the paper, had embarrassing consequences for the 'worship of the racially pure and racially holy swastika'. Hence the article ended with a sigh of pity for the followers of a now lost cause: 'Poor Aryan brothers, what fine prospects await you!'[36]

Finally, a piece in the Catholic weekly, *Sonntags-Friede*, disclosed how difficult it was for the Church to square its traditional dislike of 'Jewish materialism' with its 'newer' awareness of the dangers involved in any form of anti-Semitism. We shall quote from this article (which described Christian persecution under the Communists) at length in order to illustrate the aforementioned dichotomy:

If one knows that a large part of widely circulated newspapers is in the hands of free-thinkers and Jews . . . then one is of course not surprised about this conspicuous silence; even more so, if one considers that a substantial number of Bolsheviks have adopted their current Russian-sounding names for their earlier Jewish ones. Dog does not eat dog. (This observation has nothing at all to do with anti-Semitism.) . . . Just as devout Jewry found words of outrage over Christian persecution in Mexico, so now a number of devout Israelites have joined Catholics and Protestants in a protest against the dreadful policies of the Soviets.[37]

In so far as the Jews kept their distance from sensitive areas reserved for the majority population, they were welcomed and respected. But once they moved beyond these confines they were subjected to harsh criticism. True, official Catholicism reverted to its former practice of cultural discrimination, thus shedding most racial connotations found in statements of the postwar era; true too, some Jews may have decided to vote for the BVP in light of the miserable performance by the *Staatspartei* and the ever-growing threat posed by National Socialism. But by and large, Nuremberg's People's Party offered little resistance to the verbal and sometimes physical onslaught directed against the city's Jewish minority.

THE LEFT

Nor did the SPD prove more helpful. Even if cooperation between Social Democrats and Jewish organizations took place behind the scenes, the picture obtained from public pronouncements tells a very different story. Both in the city council and the party press the SPD exploited the 'Jewish

---

[36] StAN C7/IX SRP 489, 19.7.1932 'Das Hakenkreuz ein jüdisches Symbol.'
[37] *SF*, 2.3.1930 'Im Reiche des Antichrist'. See also 11.9.1932 'Ausflug in die Zeit', where the paper linked the *Frankfurter Zeitung* to 'powerful Jewish circles'.

question', and only rarely do we come across more sympathetic treatments of the issue.

In April 1930, for example, council member Nikolaus Eichenmüller defended a 'Jewish presence' in the city's welfare committees by noting 'rabbis were not called in on my suggestion, but because this accorded with legal requirements. Besides, Rabbi Freudental [*sic*] was only represented in the main committee and not in any of the sub-committess.'[38] Three months later, the Social Democrat Behnschnitt responded to anti-Semitic slurs by questioning the 'Aryan' background of some of Nuremberg's leading Nazis: 'If ever a racial test using Dinter's theory . . . were to be employed, it could mean an unpleasant surprise for some of these gentlemen.' Moreover, when Karl Holz (NSDAP) advised the SPD to expel all 'flat-footed' members [*Plattfüßler*] from the party, Nuremberg's second mayor, Martin Treu, retorted in a rather childish fashion: 'You also have Jews [*Bei Euch sind ja auch Juden*]'.[39] Finally, in a reference to possible Nazi–Jewish connections, the SPD's Georg Lowig compared Willy Liebel's (NSDAP) personal attacks on Social Democratic members of the council with his allegedly more refined behaviour towards wealthy Jews: 'He doesn't address Schocken like that.'[40]

The *Fränkische Tagespost* employed similar language in its coverage of *völkisch* anti-Semitism. Prior to the September 1930 Reichstag elections, for example, the paper expressed its doubts on a number of occasions as to whether Nazi Jew-baiting was in fact 'genuine'. Thus Hitler's Jew-hatred was contrasted with National Socialist activities in Plauen, where 'the swastika is a shield for Jewish capitalists to exploit poor workers and women even more'. In the party's *Wahlzeitung*, furthermore, we find appeals to the unemployed which dismissed Nazi racism as a sham since Hitler favoured 'the admittance of Polish reapers [*Schnitter*]'.[41] We also encounter the by now familiar accusation of National Socialist collusion with Jewish capital. 'Although the Nazi can't stand the Jew, *his money doesn't stink*', one caption read,[42] and it was clear that such headlines undermined the effects of a few other, more critical articles dealing with National Socialist racism.[43]

---

[38] StAN C7/IX SRP 468, 9.4.1930.

[39] StAN C7/IX SRP 472, 25.6.1930. Martin Treu was a member of the *Abwehrverein*. Whatever his accomplishments in that organization, public statements such as the one above qualified his role as an opponent of racism.

[40] StAN C7/IX SRP 478, 8.10.1930.   [41] Ibid., 'Erwerbslosentribüne'.

[42] Ibid., 12.9.1930: 'In reality, however, Mr Liebel takes money from the Jews whom he daily abuses and devours [*frißt*], and whose orders he receives with delight.'

[43] Ibid., 10.9.1930 'Mehr Macht der Sozialdemokratie!': 'The National Socialists incite the saddest and most despicable racial hatred!' It must be said, however, that this, with the exception of an appeal by the *Menschenliga* (ibid., 'Gegen die Kulturschande des Antisemitismus'), was the only article of its kind.

Finally, this approach persisted two years later, when the SPD again sought to damage the right-wing cause. In July the *Tagespost* wrote a sarcastic piece on a report that models of Hitler had been on order from a Jewish firm: 'The great Adolf, made in this factory—at a Jewish company! Hard to believe: Adolf—Jewified [*verjudet*].'[44] In November the SPD organ provided one more example of how the party viewed Nazi anti-Semitism as at best a one-sided affair: 'In its Thursday edition of 3 November the *Völkischer Beobachter* could still write: "Who shall live? Jewish bankers or the people?" In reality, however, the Nazi leaders sit with Thyssen and his Jewish bankers in order to destroy working-class organizations.'[45]

The KPD, on the other hand, went one step further. As numerous articles in the *Neue Zeitung* suggest, the Communist Party was not in the least interested in confronting the *problem* of anti-Semitism as it existed for the Jewish community in Nuremberg. Rather, it identified Nazi Jew-baiting with tactical manoeuvring, with attempts, in other words, to hide secret contacts between the NSDAP and prominent capitalists who also happened to be Jewish. At times Communist analyses proved humorous, but more often than not they passed the bounds of good taste and de-scended to calumny. For example, Alfred Rosenberg's racist ideology was proclaimed outdated since the Old Testament had already developed a theory 'whereby on the basis of racial theory the Jewish people was promoted to the "chosen" people, to the "racially higher". . .'.[46] Or, because the 'Jew' Goldschmidt supposedly financed Nazi activities, Hitler and Goebbels had decided to omit the obligatory 'Jew perish! [*Juda verrecke*!]' from party speeches.[47] As if that were not enough, the *Neue Zeitung* insinuated a relationship betweeen rabbis and Nazi members of parliament:

Now, the following took place in the Thuringian parliament: the MPs were to vote on the 3.2 million designated to the Church by the government. Also included in this sum was the salary of the two rabbis in Eisenach and Meiningen. The Nazis

[44] StAN C7/IX SRP 478, 29.7.1932 'Hitler in Judas' Händen'.

[45] Ibid., 3.11.1932 'Hitler und Jakob Goldschmidt'.

[46] *Neue Zeitung*, 18.8.1930 'Hitlers Rassensozialismus'.

[47] Ibid., speech by Hermann Remmele in Nuremberg: 'Kommunismus oder Faschismus?' See also 22.7.1932 'Jud und Nazi': 'the Nazi leadership can no longer deny such facts given that it itself ordered that the rallying cry "Judah perish" be discontinued. In its stead the Nazis are organizing a nasty murder campaign against the workers. Well, Nazi proletarian, what do you say to that?' Remmele was a long-standing member of the Commu-nist Central Office or *Zentrale*. For an anti-Semitic speech of his in 1923, see C. Fischer, *The German Communists and the Rise of Nazism* (London, 1991), 60.

were alerted to this fact. Lo and behold: to a man all Nazi MPs voted in favour of the rabbis' salary.[48]

While the KPD focused mainly on 'Jewish aid' to the *völkisch* movement,[49] it also reminded its followers that Communism was much less 'tainted' with Jewish influence than the NSDAP. To be sure, the 'Marxist-inspired working class opposed all forms of reactionary anti-Semitism', but this did not prevent the party from maintaining that National Socialism was only superficially racialist:

For Hitler and his cronies every Marxist and Communist is a Jew. However, this no longer pertains to Germany. The National Socialists . . . must live with the fact that within the NSDAP more names (Rosenberg) and more mugs point to a greater number of Jews [*Judengesichter*] than within the revolutionary working-class movement.[50]

Only once, in late September 1932, was there a somewhat more critical appraisal of Jew-hatred. Taking the general view that anti-Semitism was a method whereby reactionaries hoped to corrupt the class consciousness of the proletariat, the *Neue Zeitung* indirectly conceded that the KPD had failed to immunize its supporters against this dangerous '*Volksverhetzung*'—for the article ended with a note of concern that not all Communists 'had been able to free themselves' of the anti-Semitic bacillus.[51] Again, if we consider earlier reports that the far Left and the far Right had worked together (and as late as 1930 a memorandum referred to isolated instances of cooperation between the two)[52] we can understand better why the KPD resorted to anti-Jewish imagery in its campaign material.

We must be careful, however, not to overestimate the above findings. In particular, left-wing anti-Semitism was never a mere response to Nazi successes but constituted a part of Nuremberg's political culture in the Weimar years. From the outset, both socialist parties (as well as the USPD) stooped to popular pressure, thereby vindicating, albeit unintentionally, Marx's principle that man is both a product and an agent of history. Looking at the 1932 election results, for example, we should note that in the modern working-class district of Gartenstadt, whose population consisted mainly of skilled workers and foremen, the NSDAP vote never exceeded 8 per cent. By contrast, the factory workers of Gibitzenhof

---

[48] Ibid., 1.7.1932 'Rabbiner unter Hakenkreuzschutz'.

[49] See, for example, 20.7.1932 'Glosse vom Tage'; 22.7.1932 'Jüdische Kapitalisten liefern die Notverordnungsjacken'; 23.10.1932 'Nazi-Trustkönig Thyssen und seine Bankjuden'; 5.11.1932 'Adolf Hitler und David Schnur'.

[50] Ibid., 26.7.1932 'Hitlers "Sozialismus der dummen Kerls".'

[51] Ibid., 24.9.1932 'Die Juden sind an allem Schuld!'   [52] Reiche, *Development*, 137.

most definitely contributed to the strong showing (24.5 per cent) of the Nazi Party in their district.[53] Still, the combined total of the Left remained fairly stable, declining by only 3 per cent over the years, and thus qualifying accounts about possible connections between the Left and the far Right.

More likely, the above approach to the 'Jewish question' exposed the Left's inability to overcome widespread prejudices at a time when Nuremberg's populace was far from receptive to reasoning and the politics of moderation. Both socialist parties reacted to, but also sustained, an atmosphere of distrust which transcended ideological barriers. In short, Marxism failed to provide an antidote to deeper feelings of anxiety and ill will, just as liberalism failed to hold an electorate that on the whole felt cheated and left out by traditional forms of politics.

DÜSSELDORF

If unemployment meant suffering and disillusionment in Nuremberg, its effects were hardly less disruptive in the Rhenish city. Düsseldorf's volatile job market offered little encouragement for those without work, as unemployment figures rose steadily to an all-time high of 64,129 (27.3 per cent of the workforce) in early 1933. Although the unskilled suffered most, all occupational sectors eventually faced lay-offs, including those in the civil service, where job security was now a thing of the past.[54]

We need to remember, however, that unemployment itself was only one, if a very important, factor in determining Düsseldorf's political future. Prior to the September 1930 Reichstag elections, for example, which saw the NSDAP gain 13.6 per cent of the vote, the economic situation for many artisans and small shopkeepers remained fairly stable. According to Volker Franke, there was no reason to speak of a collapse or a catastrophe in these months, given that the overwhelming majority of the self-employed had been only marginally affected by the economic downturn by the time of the Reichstag elections, although many were disenchanted with the politics of the traditional parties.[55] This political estrangement was also visible among white-collar workers, whose disappointment with their perceived loss of social status was reflected early on in such organizations as the DHV, where former political allies such as the

[53] Reiche, *Development*, 98–100.

[54] P. Hüttenberger, *Düsseldorf. Geschichte von den Ursprüngen bis ins 20. Jahrhundert.* Band 3: *Die Industrie- und Verwaltungsstadt (20. Jahrhundert)* (Düsseldorf, 1989), 412–13. Nuremberg's all-time high was 27.2 per cent of the workforce in 1932.

[55] V. Franke, *Der Aufstieg der NSDAP in Düsseldorf. Die nationalsozialistische Basis in einer katholischen Großstadt* (Essen, 1987), 53.

DNVP came under heavy and sustained attack. The *Stahlhelm* leadership, moreover, indirectly encouraged its membership to support the NSDAP by asserting that all other parties had proved 'incapable of saving the German fatherland'.[56]

It was hardly surprising, therefore, that together the DVP and DNVP lost over 10,000 votes in September 1930, while the KPD (25 per cent) and NSDAP greatly improved their share of the ballot. (The *Wirtschaftsbund*, Centre Party, and SPD all gained votes, but because the voter turnout was so much higher than in 1928, their overall percentage declined.) None the less, Hitler's success in Düsseldorf owed less to brilliant propaganda campaigns or an efficient organization (before the elections the local chapter counted only 750 active members, a number that increased to 1425 following the party's victory at the polls) than to a general distrust of the traditional political system.[57] Two years later, this distrust resulted in an even greater defeat for the 'bourgeois middle', when National Socialism emerged as the strongest political force in the city in July 1932. The DVP, *Staatspartei*, and *Wirtschaftsbund*, whose combined share in 1930 had amounted to 16.1 per cent, now received only 2.9 per cent of the vote. Both the NSDAP (29.1 per cent) and DNVP (5.4 per cent) benefited from this poor performance of the moderate parties, while the Centre Party and the KPD gained mainly at the expense of the SPD.[58] However, in the November Reichstag elections, the National Socialists suffered a severe setback, declining to 23.3 per cent of the vote and leaving the KPD as the largest party in Düsseldorf (28.6 per cent). Contemporary accounts suggest that Nazi attacks on Chancellor Franz von Papen upset the 'middle-class' electorate, who favoured a tougher stance against the left-wing enemy in the city. This is also confirmed by various studies of the Nazi constituency: while the NSDAP clearly profited from the turmoil caused by the depression, its main support came from areas where rising unemployment was not quite as common as, say, in the working-class districts of Düsseldorf.[59]

[56] Ibid., 55–6.

[57] Hüttenberger, *Düsseldorf*, 428–9. The NSDAP benefited most from first-time voters and disaffected DNVP supporters. See also Franke, *NSDAP*, 60.

[58] Franke, *NSDAP*, 77–8; B. Brücher et al., *Dokumentation zur Geschichte der Stadt Düsseldorf. Düsseldorf während der Weimarer Republik 1919–1933. Quellensammlung* (Düsseldorf, 1985), 194.

[59] Franke, *NSDAP*, 81–2. Civil servants, independents, and members of the free professions were the most consistent supporters of the Nazi Party. See also Hamilton, *Hitler*, 184. These results appear to qualify more recent studies which stress that religion was the most important correlate of the Nazi vote, while 'neither the percentage of blue-collar workers . . . nor the percentage of self-employed nor the degree of urbanization nor any other of the variables displays a stronger statistical association with the NSDAP vote before

Anti-Semitism, on the other hand, seems to have had little impact on voting patterns in this period. An official report of September 1931, for example, conceded that Nazi Jew-baiting was a serious problem, but also revealed that anti-Semitism was deemed less of a menace in the Rhineland than in other parts of Germany: 'The incident proves that the anti-Semitic and Nazi press has *also* become a threat to public safety and order in the Rhine province.'[60] According to the *Jüdisches Gemeindeblatt*, moreover, the Jewish theatre group *Habimah* was welcomed in Düsseldorf, while directors in other cities, fearing Nazi reprisals, had asked the performers to seek engagements elsewhere; in fact, *Habimah* even occasioned respectful comments from the anti-Jewish press.[61] Likewise, a series of lectures in the synagogue attracted a wide and sympathetic audience, including prominent city officials like Mayor Lehr, and received positive coverage in the local press.[62] Finally, Düsseldorf's butcher's guild requested its members to attend the funeral of Isidor Winter, whose work over the years demanded 'always faithful remembrance'.[63] Thus, in spite of existing tensions, Jewish–Gentile relations in Düsseldorf were marked by apparent peace and respect.

'PROTESTANT BOURGEOISIE'

Unfortunately we have little material on the DDP/*Staatspartei* for this period. Only once do we come across an official response to anti-Semitism by a Democrat. In March 1930, the municipal council member, Elkan, condemned Nazi Jew-baiting and criticized the city for its leniency towards right-wing racism: 'If the city administration offers its halls [*Säle*] to such a party, then it must apply the same set of standards to the Communist Party.'[64] Other than that, however, we must rely on the *Lokalzeitung* to discover how left liberals responded to anti-Semitism. Two articles in particular indicate that sarcasm was often the preferred means of combating racial hatred. In September 1931, for instance, the

March 1933'. See J. W. Falter, 'The First German *Volkspartei*: The Social Foundations of the NSDAP', in: K. Rohe (ed.), *Elections, Parties and Political Traditions. Social Foundations of German Parties and Party Systems, 1867–1987* (New York, Oxford, Munich, 1990), 71.

[60] HStAD Reg. Düss. 30658a, Nr.158 Oberpräsident der Rheinprovinz; my emphasis.

[61] *Jüdisches Gemeindeblatt*, 14.11.1930 'Habimah in Düsseldorf' and 1.12.1930 'Habimah unter Polizeischutz'. The city's main theatre was headed by Louise Dumont and her Jewish husband, Albert Lindemann. Still, reactions in the press indicate that this had no influence on the decision to stage *Habimah*.

[62] *DN*, 6.3.1931 'Vorträge in der Synagoge'.

[63] Ibid., 19.7.1931 Ad section 'Fleischer-Innung Düsseldorf'.

[64] *Stenographische Verhandlungsberichte der Stadtverordnetenversammlung* (SVSt), 12.3.1930, 67.

paper accused the editor-in-chief of the Social Democratic *Volkszeitung*, Schulz, of anti-Semitic slander after the latter had voiced his doubts about the artistic capabilities of Sascha Horenstein, the 'Ukrainian' conductor of Düsseldorf's main orchestra: 'Ukrainian, therein lies no anti-Semitism of course, Schulz merely fed the lines to the *Volksparole* [a Nazi paper]. We even believe Mr Schulz when he claims that he is absolutely no anti-Semite. Only sometimes . . . does he seem to find small blows and insinuations useful.'[65] In the same vein, the paper dismissed National Socialist attacks on Bernhard Weiß, Vice-President of the Berlin police, as lacking even the slightest sense of honour or good taste: 'Should it require the cited "German conception of honour [*Ehrbegriff*]" to condone such methods . . . then one may congratulate Dr Weiß for not having one.'[66]

In short, the left liberal *Lokalzeitung* objected to both right- and left-wing anti-Semitism, and did so rudely, without doubt or hesitation. It seems likely, therefore, that the same circles who defended the Jews prior to 1930 also defended them in the last years of the Republic; only now they were reduced to complete insignificance in the political life of the Rhenish city.

The same could be said of the German People's Party. While the DVP managed to obtain 4 per cent of the vote in November 1932, it never really recovered from its poor showings of the past and the exodus of prominent party members in the summer of 1932.[67] Moreover, the party's attempts to form a 'bourgeois coalition' with the DNVP after October 1931 also failed,[68] so that the People's Party was unable to regain power or influence in its former stronghold of Düsseldorf.

On the subject of anti-Semitism, the DVP again steered an uneasy course, remaining largely aloof and refusing to take sides. For example, when a gang of Nazi youths assaulted two Jews on the busy Königsallee, the party organ spoke of a 'political confrontation', although it knew full well that the attack was intended to hit Jews and no one else.[69] Similarly,

---

[65] *LZ*, 17.9.1931 'Eine Bombe sollte platzen'. The paper continued: 'For he is the editor-in-chief of the Volkszeiting, a paper which has for years been calling the *Düsseldorfer Nachrichten* "Salomonsohn press", a pretty epithet which laymen cannot easily identify as socialism—not to mention the assaults on us.'

[66] Ibid., 16.7.1932 'Ritterlicher Kampf'.

[67] Among those who left the party and joined the DNVP were the former mayor and state secretary, Karl Schmid, Dr Kurt Poengsen, and Dr Wex. See G. J. Gemein, *Die deutschnationale Volkspartei in Düsseldorf 1918–1933*, unpublished Ph.D. thesis (Cologne, 1969), 83.

[68] H. Romeyk, 'Die Deutsche Volkspartei in Rheinland und Westfalen 1918–1933', in: *Rheinische Vierteljahresblätter*, 39 (1975), 210.

[69] *Stadt-Anzeiger*, 20.9.1931 'Durch Messerstiche schwer verletzt' and 21.9.1931 'Der Ueberfall auf der Königsallee'.

DVP leaflets and posters usually avoided the 'Jewish question' and only occasionally referred to 'overstating [*Überspannung*] the idea of race' or the difference between Christianity and 'materialistic belief in race'. Criticism of National Socialism rarely if ever mentioned Hitler's anti-Semitism.[70] The *Anzeiger's* article on the *Habimah* theatre group, furthermore, was a mixture of general approval and lingering prejudices: 'He [the director] exploits Gutzkow's theatricalism, but he sets the cultic world of the Talmud above it. One might say that this was regression. Yet the determination with which this Jewish world manages to pull through its cultic dynamism [*kultische Dynamik*] is an event . . . Even if it is also underpinned and coloured by oriental traditions.'[71] This approach was equally visible in a speech by the DVP's Schäfer, who responded to Nazi Jew-baiting in the municipal council by explaining that everyone was entitled to a specific position on the matter, but that the way in which this was articulated remained important. Yet he then went on to condemn the basis of National Socialist racism: 'We protest against one group of our population being attacked in such a way, for no reason . . . (Agreement among DVP members . . .).'[72] Thus the DVP in this period was more outspoken against anti-Semitism than ever before, and if anything, it was the Nazi threat which provoked this change of heart. Even the *Düsseldorfer Nachrichten*, which in the past had strongly opposed 'Jewish influence', now described the *Habimah* performance as a 'great artistic experience',[73] and greeted a lecture series on Judaism as a chance for all to sit down and reassess the terms of the debate:

If, at a time when the eternal struggle surrounding Judaism is threatening to become ever more dangerous, Düsseldorf's Jewish community [*Synagogengemeinde*] tries, in a series of public lectures, to explain the bases of the Jewish creed and to thereby emphasize what all faiths have in common, namely the eternally humane [*Ewig-Menschliche*], then this search for calm and reconciliation deserves unconditional support.[74]

While it would be wrong to describe the People's Party as an enemy of the *völkisch* creed,[75] it would also be wrong not to account for the shift within the DVP from 1918 to 1932. This shift did not mean that

---

[70] See StAD Plakatsammlung Mappe 18 leaflets 'Deutsche Kultur in Gefahr', 'Drei Fragen hinter der Tür', and, as an example of a critique of National Socialism, the *Niederrheinische Stimmen* of 27.8.1930.

[71] *Stadt-Anzeiger*, 3.11.1930. See also the DVP ad in the *Düsseldorfer Nachrichten* of 5.11.1932 (Abend): 'The election outbursts by the Nazis are an appeal to the lowest instincts.'

[72] *SVSt*, 18.3.1931, 115–16.

[73] *DN*, 3.11.1930 'Habima [*sic*] Gastspiel im Schauspielhaus'.

[74] Ibid., 25.2.1931 (Morgen) 'Der Gott der Rache'; 3.3.1931 'Auserwähltes Volk'.

[75] See, for example, *DN*, 13.10.1932 (Morgen) 'Gobineau und Richard Wagner'.

the party had become philo-Semitic; rather, it reflected the growing concern with National Socialism, which also involved a growing concern with the brutalization of politics. Finally, it appears that the 'Jewish question' in this period was considered unimportant, given the many other problems facing a practically defunct German People's Party.

Against this, the DNVP continued to espouse racist standpoints, though here too the tone was less vociferous. In fact, the DNVP was also preoccupied with matters unrelated to the 'Jewish question'. One such issue was the conflict between the supporters of Hugenberg and those members of the party who backed a more cautious political programme. The former group, led by the chairman of the local branch, Kossmann, and the Stahlhelm leader, Dr Otto Gisevius, wanted to 'revolutionize' and 'cleanse' the DNVP. The latter faction, comprising representatives of the Protestant unions, the Church, and a number of high-school teachers and officials, wished to defend Düsseldorf's mayor, Robert Lehr, against attacks from his critics within the party, who disapproved of the mayor's indifference toward the Schlageter memorial, as well as his refusal to sign the initiative for the dissolution of the Prussian state parliament. Although Lehr was able to assert himself in the long run, one of his staunchest supporters, Ellenbeck, lost influence in the course of the struggle.[76]

The other issue which absorbed the DNVP in these years was how to stem the tide of National Socialism. As the conservative party gradually lost votes to the extreme Right, falling to an all-time low of 3.6 per cent in April 1932, it soon became obvious that very little could be done to restore confidence in the old DNVP. Yet paradoxically, it was the old DNVP and not Hugenberg's 'new' creation that appealed to the electorate in Düsseldorf. Especially after July 1932, many voters felt drawn to the more respectable politics of conservative nationalism, which seemed to overcome parliamentary democracy in the form of Papen and von Hindenburg without degenerating into chaos and revolution. The Nazis, by contrast, who suddenly portrayed themselves as the guardians of the constitution, attacked von Papen and the DNVP as a 'pack of bourgeois bastards [*bürgerliche Schweinebande*]', who were manipulating the system to their own advantage.[77] None the less, Hugenberg's party improved its share of the vote from 5.4 per cent in July to 7.8 per cent in November 1932, thereby capitalizing on the NDSAP's difficulty in keeping up its momentum of growth and vigour.

[76] Gemein, *DNVP*, 68–71.   [77] Ibid., 81–5.

In the run-up to the Reichstag elections, the DNVP paper seldom touched on the 'Jewish question', but when it did, 'mild' anti-Semitism was almost always the order of the day. In September 1930, for example, most propaganda material dealt with the Young Plan, the politics of fulfilment, and Social Democracy. One article, however, used anti-Semitic slurs to ridicule the *Berliner Tageblatt*'s criticism of Jew-baiting in the Centre Party.[78] Two years later the DNVP organ complained about the immigration of Eastern Jews,[79] linked the Brüning cabinet to 'liberal and Jewish' elements, 'who . . . have more and more made their peace with the post-war Centre Party,'[80] and demanded that the new government rid the nation 'of all Jewish-liberal influence, which for us younger people has been the most agonizing experience of the past 13 years of socialist leadership'.[81] Finally, in October 1932 the *Führer* carried three articles claiming that the Centre Party and NSDAP received Jewish electoral support and that both parties put forward Jewish candidates.[82]

Compared to earlier periods, the Nationalist Party rarely emphasized the importance of the 'Jewish question', an issue which now seemed all but dominated by Nazi rhetoric and agitation. At the same time, other parties close to DNVP ideology distanced themselves from the extreme Right; this was especially true for the *Christlich-sozialer Volksdienst*, whose main objection to Nazi anti-Semitism was that it spread discord and hatred.[83] As a 'Christian' party, the *Volksdienst* rejected 'the belief in an Aryan blood of nobility [*Edelblut*] and the supremacy of the Aryan race'.[84] Nazi Jew-baiting in particular was unacceptable:

The Jews are being persecuted with the most bitter and venemous of hatreds. We too defend ourselves against Jews, and especially the degenerate, irreligious ones, wielding too great and disastrous an influence in public life, trade, and banking, in the arts and theatre. Nevertheless, we can never approve of National Socialism's hatred of the Jews, which excludes the latter from any form of ethics.[85]

This point of view, in which opposition to racial fanaticism existed side by side with the belief that 'Jewish influence' was harmful, largely resem-

---

[78] *Führer*, 13.9.1930 'Achtung! Hühneraugen! "Zentrumsantisemitismus".'
[79] Ibid., 2.7.1932 'Gegen die Ostjudenplage'.
[80] Ibid., 23.7.1932 'Die entscheidende Frage'.   [81] Ibid., 'Jugend an die Front!'
[82] Ibid., 7.10.1932 'Der Jude Saalfeldt und die NSDAP'; 22.10.1932 'Jüdische Zentrumswähler'; 29.10.1932 'Zentrum, Christentum und DNVP'.
[83] *DN*, 23.7.1932 (Abend) 'Wahlkundgebung des Christlich-Sozialen Volksdienstes': 'Slander, class and racial hatred in the end lead only to division [*Zersplitterung*] . . . In regard to National Socialism, whose good sides he would not wish to deny, he found the teaching of a positive Christianity reprehensible.'
[84] StAD Plakatsammlung Mappe 2 Leaflet 'Dennoch'.
[85] StAD Plakatsammlung Mappe 2 Leaflet 'Hakenkreuz oder Christentum'. See also 'Deutsches, evangelisches Volk wach auf!'

bled the attitude of the Protestant Church in Düsseldorf. Although the *Glaubensbewegung Deutscher Christen* was as yet weak and insignificant, the Church mainly responded to the racialism of this movement whenever it commented on the problem of anti-Semitism. Thus, 'German Christians' were blinded by 'the worship [*Vergötzung*] of race and the German people',[86] which had nothing in common with one's 'homeland [*Heimat*], the impact [*Zusammenhang*] of blood, or historical leadership'.[87] All this was rather tenuous, however, for the Church often felt obliged to soften or qualify its criticism of *völkisch* anti-Semitism. For example, the claim that marriages between 'Jews' and 'Germans' led to 'a blurring of races [*Rassenverschleierung*] and bastardization' was countered not with the dismissal of such an idea, but with the argument that couples who were denied a religious wedding could always turn to the local town hall, where civil marriage would take care of any attempt to keep the two 'races' apart.[88] Another response to attacks by the *Deutschchristen* distinguished between the Old Testament as an act of God and the Old Testament as a Jewish creation: 'We profess, together with the men of the Reformation, our belief in God's word found in both the Old and the New Testament. At the same time we distinguish between the Old Testament as it reflects God's revelation and the Old Testament as it stems from Jewish *völkisch* life or degeneration [*Entartung*].'[89] In other words, it remained difficult for many Protestants in Düsseldorf, whether organized in parties like the *Volksdienst* or not, to move beyond formal condemnations of racism to a recognition of the underlying dangers posed by 'milder' forms of anti-Semitism. In spite of differences with the NSDAP and the *Deutschchristen*, therefore, the Church played into the hands of its enemies by employing the language of exclusion and separation. Whether this was done consciously—in order to accommodate nationalist feeling, for example—or whether it reflected the widespread belief in *völkisch* values, hardly matters in the light of its consequences for the future of Jewish-Gentile relations.

CATHOLICISM

In his book on the DNVP, Gisbert Gemein states that anti-Semitism in the Catholic *Düsseldorfer Tageblatt* occurred more frequently after 1930.[90]

---

[86] *SB*, 30.8.1931 'Von den "Deutschgläubigen".'

[87] Ibid., 29.5.1932 'Kirche und Volkstum' Speech by *Generalsuperintendent* Zöllner. See also the speech by *Sozialpfarrer* Menn in 'Das Wesen der Kirche und die Stellung des evangelischen Glaubens zu Rasse, Volk und Staat', 17.7.1932 and 'Die Richtlinien der Deutschen Christen', 9.10.1932.

[88] Ibid., 16.10.1932 'Die Richtlinien der Deutschen Christen'.

[89] Ibid., 13.11.1932 'Gemeinde Nachrichten'.   [90] Gemein, *DNVP*, 152.

Although he cites few examples (and then only in passing), Gemein's assertion merits closer attention.

The Centre Party disowned racist anti-Semitism from 1925 to 1929, but retained a pronounced dislike of 'Jewish influence' in certain areas of German life. In the final years of the Republic, however, this changed. Now concern with 'Jewish influence' disappeared, giving way to anxiety over the fact that National Socialism was threatening Catholic dogma. To be sure, there were signs that the Centre Party too envisaged authoritarian solutions to Weimar's dilemmas; and there was also support in 1932 for the inclusion of the NSDAP in a coalition government. Yet opposition to Nazism continued throughout this period, even if many Catholics became disillusioned with traditional forms of politics.

In August 1930, for example, the *Tageblatt* praised the words of a *Staatspartei* politician who had defended the Republican colours and castigated *völkisch* racism.[91] In a series of articles leading up to the elections, moreover, the Centre organ contrasted Christian ethics with National Socialist perceptions of race, arguing that the latter resembled 'an infatuation [*Affenliebe*] with one's own race'.[92] The divide between the two positions was unbridgeable, according to the *Tageblatt*, for

political discussion is impossible with people who want to save the German *Volk* by sacrificing its minorities and their old and high culture, and calling this *völkisch* politics; who want to overcome the Jewish problem, which can only be approached via metaphysics, through the most superficial and idiotic of means, namely with knuckledusters and blackjacks.[93]

While the Centre Party neither explained the 'metaphysical' background of the 'Jewish question' nor further discussed its attitude towards recent immigrants or Jews who decided not to comply with 'German ways', its resistance to Nazi racism was certainly credible.

This was especially true early in 1931, when the party youth organized a 'Week of Struggle [Kampfwoche] against the Swastika and Soviet Star [*Sowjetstern*]'.[94] Although many of the speakers borrowed language from

[91] *DT*, 18.8.1930 'Es blühen die Rosen'.

[92] Ibid., 24.8.1930 'Wir haben nichts gemein!' See also 13.9.1930 'Blüten aus dem Nazireich', 'Düsseldorfer Wahlkampf', and the leaflet 'Kann ein Katholik National Sozialist sein?' in StAD XXI 28.

[93] *DT*, 10.9.1930 'Das Gesicht des "Dritten Reiches".' See also 7.9.1930 'Ein unvereinbarer Gegensatz': 'National Socialism's mistake is that it rejects every Jew, even the one whose family has been residing in Germany for centuries. This hatred of the Jews disguises the fact that we owe Jewry a great deal . . . It is therefore necessary to subsume the *völkisch* idea—however valuable it might be—under the Christian, God-given, idea of humanity.'

[94] For reports on the events, see StAD XXI 28 and StAD XXI 51.

the far Right (i.e. '*Lebensraum* for our people'),[95] the overall tenor of the meetings was summed up by the promise to protect the Weimar constitution.[96] In fact, one speaker maintained that the Marxist struggle was child's play against the racial hatred of National Socialism.[97]

Most participants, it seems, agreed with this assessment. The Centre council member Winkler, for instance, dissociated his party from 'the un-Christian hatred against the Jews',[98] while an internal paper of the *Junge Katholische Volksfront* denounced 'hypernationalism' and racism as 'stupid and pretty apolitical'.[99] Finally, in mid-February the *Tageblatt* challenged the view that Jews represented capital and high finance: 'If ruthless circles maintain that the Jews, of all people, are the representatives of capital, they ought to take a look in Düsseldorf's "Ghetto", and they will discover that the Jewish merchants and tradespeople have become just as proletarianized as wide sections of our population.'[100]

In subsequent months, however, the Centre took a more detached line, employing sarcasm rather than straightforward criticism in its treatment of anti-Semitism. Schulz's remarks about the 'Ukrainian' Horenstein, for example, were considered 'unusual' given the conductor's Jewish background, his previous engagements in workers' orchestras, and his preference for contemporary music. ('One should think that these facts made him anything but unpopular among the Left.') The article also displayed amusement over a meeting between the director of the theatre and a Nazi who presented his views on cultural affairs: 'The Nazis agree with everything. Only Offenbach is not to their liking, and then we have a very suspicious play called *The Girl from the Golden West* which gives them anxiety dreams [Herzbeklemmung].'[101] Moreover, when a group of Nazi hooligans rudely interrupted a lecture on Heinrich Heine, the *Tageblatt* ironically dubbed this behaviour the '*völkisch* idea of intellectual life'.[102]

Following National Socialist victories at the polls and the unexpected fall of Brüning's government in May 1932, the Centre Party in Düsseldorf faced two options: either it could support von Papen's new cabinet (regardless of its reactionary character), or it could advocate a tactical

---

[95] See W. Stump, *Geschichte und Organisation der Zentrumspartei in Düsseldorf 1917–1933* (Düsseldorf, 1971), 81 and Hüttenberger, *Düsseldorf*, 424–5.

[96] Stump, *Organisation*, 81–2.

[97] *DT*, 29.1.1931 Meeting of Centre youth in Gerresheim.

[98] Ibid., 22.1.1931 'Kampf Gegen Hakenkreuz und Sowjetstern'.

[99] StAD XXI 51. See also *DT*, 22.1.1931 'An die Deutsche Katholische Jugend'.

[100] *DT*, 18.2.1931 'Im "Ghetto" von Düsseldorf'.

[101] Ibid., 9.7.1931 'Theater um das Theater'.

[102] Ibid., 17.12.1931 'Nazis gegen Heinevortrag'.

alignment with the strongest party in parliament, the NSDAP. Although most Centre politicians knew of Hitler's distaste for democracy, they chose the latter option in the vain hope of taming the far Right, just as they believed they had tamed the Left after 1918.[103] This did not imply, however, that the party suddenly renounced its hostility towards the NSDAP. On the contrary, since a coalition with the Nazis never materialized, the Centre was able to pursue its propaganda efforts against National Socialism unabated.[104] At the same time, the Centre Party failed to reassess its ever-closer affinities to right-wing ideology; most leaflets distributed in 1932, for example, contained notions like Lebensraum, 'national concentration', or 'Christian people's state'.[105] A virtual obsession with Heinrich Brüning, moreover, disclosed the party's reservations about representative democracy:

What did we have under Brüning's chancellorship? . . . A system that had overcome the excesses of a misunderstood democracy and had put the party cliques in their place . . . What do we have under Schleicher, Hitler, Röhm, and Papen? . . . A government of pseudo-patriots [*Gänsefüßchen-Nationalen*] about whom the whole world can only shake its head.[106]

The 'Jewish question', on the other hand, rarely if ever surfaced in the remaining months of the Republic. One piece in the *Tageblatt*, for instance, derided Nazi complaints about Jews' renting offices from a Catholic press syndicate, as this meant Gentiles could follow right-wing advice and 'relieve Jewish pockets'. The Centre organ also commented on the discovery of swastikas adorning a Jewish burial site.[107] But on the whole, Centre propaganda concentrated on Brüning's importance for the creation of a true *Volksstaat*,[108] Hitler's threat to the Catholic Church,[109] and the danger emanating from 'political and social reaction'.[110] Only once do

---

[103] Stump, *Organisation*, 88.   [104] Ibid., 89.

[105] See, for example, StAD XXI 31.

[106] StAD Plakatsammlung Mappe 2 'Jetzt gilt es!' See also Stump, *Organisation*, 91: 'The call for order and authority was justified by claiming that "a return to the ways and methods that had been practised between 1919 and 1930 was neither domestically nor internationally viable."'

[107] *DT*, 6.7.1932 'Eines unserer Verlagshäuser'; 16.7.1932 'O Schreck!': 'But in order to invoke the deadly danger of ridicule we suggest the swastika be joined with the Jewish ritual knife in such a way as to compete successfully against the Soviet-Russian cross between hammer and sickle.'

[108] See the reports on Centre meetings in the *Düsseldorfer Tageblatt* of 24./25.7.1932.

[109] *DT*, 19.7.1932 'Die christliche Kultur ist bedroht!' 21.10.1932 'Der Nationalsozialismus und die katholische Kirche'; and StAD Plakatsammlung Mappe 2 Leaflet (November 1932) 'Keine Stimme für Hitler'.

[110] Stump, *Organisation*, 92. Against this, the Centre Party tried to appeal to nationalist feelings in an election advertisement of 29.7.1932: 'Even the German Nationals know that it was to the Centre's great credit to have always distinguished between un-German Communists and German Socialists.'

we come across an article which touched on the 'Jewish question' in greater detail, and which showed how opposition to anti-Semitism persisted alongside older forms of prejudice. In late October, a certain Professor Lauscher responded to press attacks wherein Centre politicians had supported a Nazi motion banning all 'alien elements' from German radio: '. . . the entire history of my party proves that we absolutely rejected, both for ideological and legal reasons, anti-Semitic opinions and tendencies, and refused to have anything to do with any form of discrimination against our Jewish fellow citizens. On the other hand, we also never wished to see the Jewish element favoured. We had the impression that this was presently the case in the state's support of the arts.'[111]

Between 1919 and 1933, the annual drop in Düsseldorf's Catholic population was 0.38 per cent, compared to a 3.8 per cent decline for the Centre Party.[112] Yet at the same time, the Centre's support remained fairly stable in the final years of the Republic, gaining 21.2, 22.6, and 22.5 per cent of the vote in the last three Reichstag elections. If, in other words, election results had an impact on the party's approach to the 'Jewish question', they mattered little from 1930 onward. Instead, the Centre Party confronted the problem of anti-Semitism from its own standpoint of resistance to *völkisch* racism, which focused primarily on Hitler's and Rosenberg's 'new paganism' and 'Wotan's cult'. At times, however, the Centre Party acknowleged its continued distaste for 'Jewish predominance', whether this predominance actually existed or not.

THE LEFT

The SPD, on the other hand, altered its position only slightly, even if this shift revealed the extent to which most parties borrowed from each other. In the case of Social Democracy, occasional remarks pointed to Communist origins, as the battle between the parties often disguised the very real differences which separated the two.

For example, in the run-up to the 1930 Reichstag elections, the SPD simultaneously warned against, scoffed at, and depreciated Nazi anti-Semitism. Thus Düsseldorf's Democrats were advised to leave the new *Staatspartei* on the grounds that Arthur Mahraun's *Jungdeutscher Orden* entailed 'the danger of anti-Semitic cells being formed [*antisemitischer*

---

[111] *DT*, 24.10.1932 'Zentrum und Antisemitismus'.
[112] A. Kussmann, *Das kommunale Parteiensystem in Düsseldorf beim Übergang vom Kaiserreich zur Republik. Ein Beitrag zum Kontinuitätsproblem*, unpublished MA thesis (Berlin, 1982), 149–50.

Zellenbildung]'.[113] Similarly, Hitler's racialism was depicted as both absurd and base: 'Astrological rubbish: Hitler wins under the sign of Cancer! Speculations and insanities of those who never get enough [*die nie alle werden*]! Back to the disgrace of medieval madness; let's get the Jews: Judah perish! This incitement of the lowest of passions . . . That is the nation's awakening!'[114]

By contrast, the SPD's *Volkszeitung* argued that whenever Nazis needed money, they called for 'Samuel', and that Goebbels's nose, as well as Rosenberg's name, betrayed National Socialist relations with the 'Semitic' race.[115] What is more, the *Anti-Faschist*, a special leaflet for the September elections, claimed that 'the wife of the Jewish corn merchant Newman paid 1000 Marks a month into the Nazi chest'.[116]

This ambivalence within the SPD was equally discernible in 1931 and 1932. While the party defended Heinrich Heine against right-wing attacks,[117] dismissed the 'fairy-tales' about secret Jewish laws,[118] and strongly denounced Nazi assaults on Jewish students in Berlin,[119] it accepted the widely held (leftist) view that wealthy Jews knew from recent history 'that while during riots and pogroms against Jews small crooks [*Schächer*] must suffer, a Rothschild, Oppenheimer or Bleichröder is never harmed'. It was likely, therefore, that Hitler too would seek peace with Jewish capital. On the other hand, the *Volkszeitung* reminded its readers that a majority of Jews belonged to the proletarianized middle classes, and concluded with a statement summing up its overall position on the 'Jewish question' in this period: 'The Social Democratic Party is neither philo-Semitic nor anti-Semitic. It doesn't court Jewish votes; but it declares that no one is to be denied his or her political and social rights because of a free-thinking or religious persuasion.'[120]

Although the Communist Party was probably of the same opinion, it never gave the impression that this was so. Rather, its attacks on anti-Semitism ignored the Jewish victims and insisted that the NSDAP really

---

[113] *VZ*, 5.9.1930 'Demokraten, wählt SPD!' Traumann, Halstenberg, Erkelenz, and Uth, all former DDP members, joined the SPD.

[114] StAD Microfilm Nos 188/189 Leaflet 'Intellektuelle, Lehrer und Lehrerinnen!'

[115] *VZ*, 12.9.1930 'Der Goldstrom fließt weiter'.

[116] HStAD Reg. Düss. 17078. See also 'Erwerblosentribüne': 'In spite of Hitler's retreat the Nazis shout "Racial aliens out" whenever they can . . . this does not keep their prominent leaders from employing Polish reapers—and causing German ones to become unemployed.'

[117] *VZ*, 24.12.1930 'Heine, die Nazis und der Mann mit dem Barte'; 17.2.1931 'Heine'.

[118] Ibid., 10.3.1931 'Was ist's mit den jüdischen Geheimgesetzen?'

[119] Ibid., 1.7.1932 'Nazi-Lausbubereien an der Berliner Universität'. This was the only article in the Düsseldorf press on the Berlin incidents.

[120] Ibid., 24.10.1932 'Judentum und Hugenbergparole'.

intended to destroy the proletariat, regardless of whether individual workers were Jewish or not. In addition, the KPD in Düsseldorf continued to accuse the Nazis of complicity with 'Jewish' high finance, and occasionally maintained that the relationship between Hitler and the Jews was amicable indeed.

Prior to the September 1930 Reichstag elections, for example, the KPD focused on the 'injustices' of the Dawes and Young plans, and on the Versailles Treaty, but also established intimate ties between individual Nazis and German Jewry. Thus Robert Ley's 'Semitic looks' caused him trouble in Koblenz, where he was assaulted by a gang of SA men: 'Ley too claims to be a racially pure Aryan and has—like Goebbels and Hitler—Jewish "friends and patrons".'[121] These friends and well-wishers, the KPD added, had only one objective in mind, namely the destruction of Soviet Communism: 'War against the Soviet Union the Jewish bloodsucking bankers [*Bankhyänen*], the directors of trusts and conglomerates cry, together with the Nazis.'[122] Furthermore, reports on anti-Semitic incidents almost always ended with the inference that Nazi racism was directed against the *working class*, not against the Jews.[123]

Throughout 1931 and 1932, Düsseldorf's Communists repeated the above charges. While Goebbels received a grand piano from the Jewish firm of Salinger,[124] Hitler was busy selling away Germany 'to the rapacious financiers'.[125] Jewish capitalists still figured as 'agitators of Nazism's murderous politics against starving workers',[126] while individual National Socialists still faced 'embarrassing' questions about their own background.[127] All this was compounded by various articles and leaflets emphasizing Jewish financial assistance to the Nazi cause.[128] Once the KPD

---

[121] *Freiheit*, 13.9.1930 'Juda verrecke'.

[122] StAD Plakatsammlung Mappe 13 Poster 'Wo ist die Rettung?' See also 'Eure Stimme gehört den Kommunisten!'

[123] See *Freiheit*, 20.8.1930 'Die braune Mordpest!' 20.12.1930 'Judenpogrom in der Altstadt'; 8.7.1931 'Pogromhetze auf dem Rheindampfer "Frauenlob"'; 17.9.1931 'Trauriges Ende eines Operettengastspiels'.

[124] Ibid., 28.2.1931 'Goebbels am jüdischen Flügel': 'Perhaps Nazi workers will think about what is being done to them.'

[125] Ibid., 17.7.1932. The term, of course, was *verschachern*.

[126] Ibid., 8.7.1932: 'The workers will show the circumcised and uncircumcised exploiters that they know how to defend themselves against the terror of the employers at the workplace and the murderous terror of the mercenary troops paid for by the industrialists.'

[127] See the reply to Nazi Jew-baiting by the Communist council member, Dunder: 'Schwarz (NSDAP), rummage through Hitler's family tree and you'll be in for a nasty shock when you discover that he's descended from Abraham!' *SVSt*, 18.3.1931, pp. 115–16.

[128] *Freiheit*, 16./17.11.1932 'Jüdische Faschisten in Nöten'; 24./25.10.1932 'Nazi-Trustkönig und seine Bankjuden'; StAD Plakatsammlung Mappe 13 'Für Brot und Freiheit' and 'Wähler! Ein letztes Wort'; StAD Microfilm Nos. 188/189 'Werktätige Jugend Deutschlands höre!'

assumed power, however, capitalists of all shades would find themselves deprived of the privileges they had once enjoyed: 'Then the likes of Thyssen, Klöckner, and Goldschmitt [*sic*], the blond and dark-haired captains of industry and bloodsucking bankers will be expropriated, and their factories, businesses, and offices will be given to those who will manage them in the interest of all workers.'[129]

There remained, then, a distinct difference between the way in which the SPD treated the 'Jewish question' from the way it was discussed among Communists. Whereas the former tended to combine criticism with innuendo, the latter avoided criticism and submitted to innuendo; whereas Social Democrats expressed their displeasure with anti-Semitism but reproved Jewish capitalists, Communists reproved Jewish capitalists but were indifferent to the *problem* of anti-Semitism. What separated the two parties, therefore, was not so much the content of their respective positions, though that too was important, but rather their willingness to subordinate content to style. For the KPD it became increasingly difficult to keep the two apart; its Social Democratic counterpart, on the other hand, managed to preserve a sense of priority, however tenuous this may have been.

SUMMARY

Generally, it appears that Jew-baiting was much less of an electoral asset between 1929 and 1933 than in earlier periods; from 1925 to 1929, for example, anti-Semitism was marginal because 'stability' was pervasive; now, however, at a time of renewed political conflict, National Socialism monopolized the 'Jewish question'. Concurrently, other parties and groups were forced to take sides, and it is here that we encounter similarities and dissimilarities between the two cities.

The similarities were such that the 'Protestant bourgeoisie' (with the exception of the DDP/*Staatspartei*) remained firmly in the *völkisch* camp, although this was possibly more the case in Nuremberg than in Düsseldorf. Both the *Volksdienst* and the Protestant Church, for example, stressed the uniqueness of the German *Volk*, though both also criticized extreme anti-Semitism. The *Wirtschaftspartei* in Nuremberg, moreover, as well as the DVP in Düsseldorf, dispensed with Jew-baiting, at a time when consensus on the importance of *völkisch* 'awareness' had been reached and Hitler could hardly be outdone. Finally, the Communists in

---

[129] *Freiheit*, 1./2.11.1932 'Kommunisten ans Ruder!'

both cities employed anti-Semitic imagery whenever it advanced their cause.

The main difference, of course, lay in Jewish–Gentile relations for, while *völkisch* sentiments existed in both towns, they had a much greater impact on Nuremberg's Jews. Two of Hitler's most outspoken enemies, for instance, the left-wing SPD and the Catholic Centre Party (in Bavaria the BVP), behaved differently in Nuremberg and in Düsseldorf. In the former city the SPD had never really confronted the problem of anti-Semitism, while its Rhenish counterpart only now used language uncritical of Nazi Jew-baiting. The Centre Party, meanwhile, was more pronounced in its opposition to *völkisch* racism than Nuremberg's BVP, even though both continued to distinguish between 'religious' and 'subversive' Jews. On the whole, then, the political climate in Düsseldorf provided the Jewish community with a greater semblance of peace and order than in Nuremberg.

Conclusion

Plato thought that the way to get people to be nicer to each other was to point out what they all had in common: rationality. But it does little good to point out . . . that many Muslims and women are good at mathematics or engineering or jurisprudence. Resentful young Nazi toughs were quite aware that many Jews were clever and learned, but this only added to the pleasure they took in beating such Jews. Nor does it do much good to get such people to read Kant and agree that one should not treat rational agents simply as means. For everything turns on who counts as a fellow human being, as a rational agent in the only relevant sense—the sense in which rational agency is synonymous with membership in *our* moral community.

Richard Rorty in Stephen Shute and Susan Henley (eds.),
On Human Rights: The Oxford Amnesty Lectures (1993)

If we look at the period 1910–33 in both Düsseldorf and Nuremberg, it is difficult to agree with Ian Kershaw's verdict that the 'relative indifference of most Germans towards the "Jewish Question" before 1933 meant that the Nazis had a job on their hands after the takeover of power to persuade them of the need for active discrimination and persecution of the Jews'.[1] Indeed, even though most Gentiles were only occasionally preoccupied with the 'Jewish question', it is hard not to be surprised at such an assessment in the light of widespread support for anti-Semitic parties like the DNVP and NSDAP during the Weimar Republic. While many followers of the Right were not necessarily attracted to both parties because of their anti-Semitic platforms, they usually held views on issues concerning the *Volk* and fatherland which made it possible to accept Nazi racism after 1933.

---

[1] I. Kershaw, 'The Persecution of the Jews and German Popular Opinion in the Third Reich', in: *LBIY* (1981), 264. See also p. 272, where he mentions that by September 1935 Nazi propaganda 'was leaving its traces: people were losing their impartiality about the Jews and were beginning to say the Nazis were right in their struggle'. A few months later a Sopade report pointed out that 'the feeling that the Jews are another race is today a general one' (p. 274). It is doubtful whether Nazi agitation alone was responsible for these sentiments. See also Hans Mommsen and Susanne Willems (eds), *Herrschaftsalltag im Dritten Reich. Studien und Texte* (Düsseldorf, 1988), 377.

In this context we also need to qualify statements regarding Hitler's supposed lack of interest in the 'Jewish question' towards the end of the Republic.[2] Not only do such arguments overlook what happened at local and regional levels, where National Socialists continued their campaign against the Jews, they also ignore the fact that 'saturation' can set in fairly early for an electorate to believe in the contents of a given piece of propaganda.[3] In other words, if prominent Nazis decided to emphasize other aspects of their ideology in 1931 or 1932, they did so not only because they wanted to appear respectable but also because they could rely on the effects of previous efforts to isolate the Jews. Throughout the Weimar years *völkisch* values had become part of the political culture, and it was fairly easy for Hitler to play down anti-Semitism at a point when members of the élite and not so much the average citizen would decide the fate of his party.

What follows is an attempt to recapitulate some of the developments which led to this confidence on Hitler's part. It is divided into four sections, the first giving an account of the more general attitudes towards the 'Jewish question' in both cities, the second discussing possible explanations for differences in approach, the third assessing the extent to which both cities were representative of Germany at large, and the fourth offering concluding remarks on the implications of the above study.

The meaning given to the 'Jewish question' between 1910 and 1918 was marked by what was then a 'progressive/reactionary' divide. While liberals and socialists saw themselves as defenders of enlightened views, the Centre Party and Conservatives rejected most of these notions as anathema to the German nation. Even National Liberals in Nuremberg, who spoke of Jewry's corrosive influence, opposed the Right's 'reactionary' rhetoric as un-modern and backward. Racism was absent from *mainstream* political life at this time, when the debate still centred on 'traditional' responses to the problem of anti-Semitism, most of which were embedded in the context of moderation.

---

[2] See, for example, R. Zitelmann, *Hitler. Selbstverständnis eines Revolutionärs* (Darmstadt, 1989), 36. We should also remember that Hitler did make discreet references to 'international financial capital' in his speeches which all listeners would have understood as being aimed at the Jews, and that in Nazi propaganda material Marxists, Bolsheviks, and Jews were given more or less identical treatment.

[3] It is precisely for this reason that I have refrained from comparing the NSDAP in both towns. The abundance of anti-Semitism found in Nazi material, as well as Streicher's unique stance on the issue, made it seem rather futile to ask where anti-Semitism was more pronounced. A brief glance at the sources shows that there was plenty of it, so that any doubts in this matter must derive from an undue emphasis on the speeches and texts of certain Nazi bigwigs.

This changed after the end of the war (and possibly did so during the war itself). Now there was a quantitative and qualitative shift in perception of the 'Jewish question': if before 1918 there existed language which defined the subject along the lines of inherent differences between 'Germans' and 'Jews', it belonged largely to the inventory of ideologues whose influence was limited. After the war, however, racism emerged as a widespread phenomenon, entering the common parlance of the so-called 'respectable bourgeoisie'. This did not mean that older forms of Jew-baiting vanished. Rather, it implied that the racist element of what we ideal-typically called 'anti-Semitism' assimilated the available normative language (which had hitherto comprised religious, economic, and cultural prejudices) to press ahead with the exclusion and separation of the Jewish community from the rest of society. On the quantitative side this was accomplished by infiltrating newspapers and political parties which prior to the war had shown no signs of sympathy for the anti-Semitic cause. Thus, whereas before 1918 moderation meant that Jew-hatred was considered antiquated, after the war the idea of moderation was transformed to the extent that Jew-hatred was now accepted as long as it did not entail violence and extremism.

The so-called 'golden twenties' witnessed the gradual acceptance of *völkisch* thinking. To be sure, not everyone was affected, but even those who remained immune to exclusionist ideology paid tribute to its impact by trying to avoid the issue. By 1933, wide sections of the 'Protestant bourgeoisie' welcomed the contribution *völkisch* values had made to the spiritual 'reawakening' of the German people, even if many rejected certain forms of anti-Semitism which appeared too radical or violent. It was the style and tactics rather than the actual content of right-wing thought, therefore, which occasionally gave rise to concern, and in this sense the reactions to the *Reichskristallnacht* of 1938 were distinctly prefigured. This also accounts for the refusal of many Germans to accept responsibility for the crimes of Hitler after the Second World War. For a majority it was the fanatics and extremists in the party, those who had actively participated in the genocide, who were to blame. Again, Jew-hatred as such was not the main concern, but rather the choice of methods of putting it into effect.[4]

Finally, while it is true that some parties, such as the *Wirtschaftspartei* in Nuremberg and the DVP in Düsseldorf, refrained from Jew-baiting in the final years of the Republic, we need to remember that this was related to two crucial developments: first, a general tendency *not* to defend Jewish

[4] See J. Friedrich, *Die kalte Amnestie. NS-Täter in der Bundesrepublik* (Munich, 1994), 143–4.

rights and to choose silence over solidarity; and second, a general recognition that National Socialism was monopolizing the 'Jewish question' to such a degree that little could be added except the odd comment denouncing Hitler's extreme methods. It was often the absence of condemnation that underlined the effects of post-war anti-Semitism.

We were able to observe above that considerable differences existed between Düsseldorf and Nuremberg regarding the 'Jewish question'. We also noted that these had little to do with economic performances and that, although religion was an important factor, it alone could not explain why Düsseldorf was less hostile to the Jews than Nuremberg. Catholic politicians in the Franconian city, for example, were seldom sympathetic to the Jews, while Düsseldorf's Protestant Church was more aggressive in this respect than its Nuremberg counterpart. This might suggest that the Catholic minority in the latter city was either anti-Semitic from the start or became so as a result of appropriating the dominant Protestant culture; equally, it might suggest that the Protestant minority in the Rhenish town was reacting to the sudden collapse of an era which had guaranteed political and social hegemony.

Other explanations could be offered too. Perhaps Nuremberg's Centre Party (and later BVP), which never gained more than 9 per cent of the vote in spite of a substantially higher Catholic population, exploited the 'Jewish question' out of a sense of impotence and desperation. By contrast, Düsseldorf's Catholics could fight from a position of relative strength, wielding influence in *both* the city council and Prussian state parliament. Similarly, the Revolution of 1918/19 abruptly altered the Bavarian situation, and at least until 1920, when the SPD was ousted from power, many Catholics believed that 'their' state was in the hands of 'alien' elements. It is therefore possible that the BVP in Nuremberg felt equally estranged from the new situation, seeking to explain events in terms of Jewish proclivities to subversion and radicalism. Finally, established wisdom has it that the Centre in Düsseldorf and the Rhineland was more open, more liberal, and more tolerant than Catholic parties elsewhere. Compared to Bavaria or Austria, for example, both of which were heavily Catholic, Düsseldorf's population was less traditional, and consequently less inclined to retain anti-Jewish prejudices. Against this Nuremberg's Catholics, who mostly hailed from Upper Bavaria, may have been influenced by vocal anti-Semites in the Centre Party and BVP, such as Georg Heim and Johann Baptist Sigl.

However, we must be careful not to mistake trends for actual causes. To describe the Rhenish Centre Party as liberal, for instance, is hardly accurate. In Düsseldorf the party had cooperated with Stöcker's Christian

Socials in the first half of the twentieth century, and during the war Centre notables joined Conservatives and National Liberals to found the local chapter of the *Vaterlandspartei*. The *Düsseldorfer Tageblatt*, moreover, sharply criticized Erzberger's policies towards peace and electoral reform in the Reichstag. It was only after the war that a group representing the Catholic unions became more vocal in the party, and even this did not prevent the Centre from supporting the DNVP-led city government. It is also not clear whether the situation in Nuremberg was comparable to the situation in Bavaria as a whole. Nuremberg was not Munich. The former had no Schwabing, no bohemian radicals, no Soviet Republics. Catholics in Nuremberg may have been alienated by the events of November 1918, they may also have been upset about the rise of Social Democracy in the state, but in their own town the transition to democracy was smooth and the SPD a familiar sight. Finally, we must remember that Catholicism, though largely immune to National Socialism, was not always immune to anti-Semitism. The two should be kept apart for, as the example of the BVP in Nuremberg suggests, one could be both politically (and ideologically) opposed to Nazism and still accept anti-Semitic stereotypes.

There are some grounds for believing that individual actors played an important role *vis-à-vis* the 'Jewish question'. Streicher's massive and constant flow of propaganda, for example, was instrumental in spreading an atmosphere of fear and intimidation in Nuremberg and Franconia. His uncompromising style intensified the polarization between those who accepted the Republic and those who wanted a different form of government. It also destroyed popular confidence in the capacity of state authorities to maintain law and order. Likewise, Nuremberg's police force under Heinrich Gareis seriously damaged any prospects for a swift and thorough treatment of Nazi actions against Jews and Democrats. Instead, both groups confronted a hostile public whose principal representatives shared some of Streicher's views but refused to endorse most of his methods. We must remember, however, that Streicher and Gareis gained notoriety in the early 1920s, whereas anti-Semitism was strongest in the immediate post-war era. Streicher's achievement thus lay in channelling and intensifying existing prejudices, not so much in creating new ones.

In Düsseldorf the situation was very different. Here French officials prevented the NSDAP from effectively mobilizing the electorate, and here a Social Democratic provincial governor opposed all forms of racial incitement. Above all, Düsseldorf had nobody like Streicher with the fanaticism to help the Nazi cause in the Rhineland. What is more,

Düsseldorf's mayor, Robert Lehr, was less of a threat to conservatives and nationalists than his left liberal counterpart Hermann Luppe, who faced a deeply suspicious populace. In other words, while Luppe only enjoyed the full support of his own, rapidly dwindling party and that of the SPD, Lehr was able to point to Centre Party assistance, as well as to the fact that many liberals found his pragmatic approach to politics acceptable. Finally, the differences between the Prussian and Bavarian state governments also accounted for distinct reactions to anti-Semitism in the Weimar period. While the former was constantly on guard against the right-wing danger (at least until July 1932), the latter was more concerned with the Left, as well as with the maintenance of law and order. Thus, if Gareis was able to ignore anti-Semitic excesses in his district, it was also because Munich welcomed or condoned the policies followed in Middle Franconia.

Liberalism: National Liberalism in Düsseldorf showed no signs of anti-Semitism before 1918. A considerable number of Jews held important positions in the city's *Liberale Vereinigung*, which not only reflected the need of the party to secure Jewish votes, but also indicated a certain measure of tolerance. National Liberalism in Nuremberg, on the other hand, occasionally coquetted with anti-Semitism, and in this was probably more representative of Germany as a whole. After the war, however, these differences vanished. Especially in the period 1918–25, both Bavarian National Liberals and the DVP employed anti-Jewish stereotypes in their propaganda material and only rarely dissociated themselves from the *völkisch* movement. It is therefore fair to say that whatever Stresemann's approach on the matter, and however much racism disappeared towards the end of the Republic, conservative liberals rarely resisted anti-Semitism, and often contributed to a general dislike of the Jewish minority in the years 1918 to 1933.

By contrast, left liberalism was not only much more favourable to the Jewish cause, but also consistently opposed to all forms of anti-Semitism. Both the Progressives and the DDP put up Jewish candidates in Düsseldorf and Nuremberg, and both refrained from appeals to the 'national community' or the 'German *Volk*'. Both refused to cooperate with the far Right, and both avoided utterances of the sort found among the more cynical parties of the Left. Even the creation of the State Party in 1930 did not lead to a shift in perception, though it disclosed how easily Jewish fears could be overridden in the struggle for political survival (and it was the latter reason rather than growing anti-Semitism which caused many Jews to desert the *Staatspartei* for the Centre and the SPD). Finally, we need to recall that all this did not prevent left liberal politicians from voicing their prejudice in private, as the examples of Luppe and Gessler so clearly revealed.

Conservatism: On the whole, it seems accurate to describe most 'conservatives' after 1918 as followers of a 'radical-nationalist counter-utopia' which combined resentment of the Revolution with a sense of how Germany was to change in order to avoid future defeats.[5]

One element in this picture was anti-Semitism, which no longer focused on 'Jewish influence' or 'Jewish radicalism' but included exclusionist thinking on a grander scale. Both the DNVP in Düsseldorf and the *Mittelpartei* in Nuremberg supported a separation of 'Jews' and 'Germans', and although the Nazis promoted this message far more aggressively, conservative nationalists expressed few doubts as to the truth of such views. Even the *Christlich-sozialer Volksdienst*, which shied away from committing itself to a 'Germanic ideology', agreed that Hitler's programme contained valuable elements which had to be given serious consideration. Again, if we can still speak of conservatism in this period, it was largely because the men and women who belonged to this creed feared the consequences of their own beliefs; and if conservative propaganda made less of the 'Jewish question' towards the end of the Republic, it was largely because no one could outdo Hitler and the Nazis in this respect.

Protestantism: Before 1918 the Protestant Church in Nuremberg was largely indifferent to the 'Jewish question'. In fact, there is no evidence to support the view that Lutheranism was responsible for unfriendly treatment of the Jews at the time. After the collapse of the monarchy, however, the Protestant Church joined the ever-growing chorus of Jew-baiters who demanded a separation of things 'Jewish' from things 'German'. This was also true in Düsseldorf, where the Church had already been critical of certain Jews between 1910 and 1918. Following the Revolution, racist language crept into its coverage of the 'Jewish question', and later *völkisch* thought was proclaimed valuable and necessary. In both towns the Protestant Church displayed a sense of concern about the implications of racist ideology (which in many ways was a theologically motivated distaste for right-wing extremism) and a predilection for *völkisch* doctrines. To square the two remained an impossible task, and we are left with the impression that here, as in the country at large, Protestants opposed the extreme Right on grounds of style rather than content.

[5] G. Eley, *Reshaping the German Right. Radical Nationalism and Political Change after Bismarck* (London, 1980), 358.

Catholicism: Since we discussed the impact of religion on political behaviour above, we need to focus briefly on two further factors in our analysis of Catholicism and the 'Jewish question'. First, the Catholic Church in Nuremberg was often intent on finding differences between 'Germans' and 'Jews', so that racism was less of a problem here than elsewhere in Germany. In this respect Nuremberg was unusual, for even if racist tenets were not absent from Centre Party language, they were seldom part of a conscious attempt to propagate the *völkisch* cause. In Düsseldorf, for example, which was probably more representative of Germany as a whole, Catholic politicians were more fearful that Nazi Jew-baiting could lead to the persecution of Christians.

Second, and related to this, was the fact that the Centre Party supplied its constituency with answers to most problems facing Germans at the time, which enabled them to reject Nazism for a number of reasons, anti-Semitism not being one of the most pressing ones. Like many socialists and Communists, therefore, Catholics were able to retain certain prejudices without feeling that this compromised their overall stance on the issue.

Socialism: Socialists often exhibited conflicting views on the 'Jewish question'. When the SPD did flirt with anti-Semitism, however, it often held on to older beliefs that people were marked out by their relationship to the means of production. Jews, according to this interpretation, figured as the supporters of the extreme Right because both represented the interests of capitalism in its struggle against socialism. Again, it seems that Düsseldorf's SPD was very similar to party organizations elsewhere in Germany, while its Nuremberg counterpart was a rather exceptional case. Not only was the latter opportunistic in its approach to the problem of anti-Semitism, it also appropriated *völkisch* language and submitted to anti-Jewish feelings among the electorate. What is more, Social Democrats in Nuremberg rarely if ever condemned racist propaganda, whereas the SPD in Düsseldorf, for all its cynicism towards the end of the Republic, repeatedly castigated all forms of right-wing anti-Semitism. The difference between both parties, in other words, lay not so much in the need to secure votes and thus to appeal to popular instincts, but in the refusal of Nuremberg's Social Democrats to confront the *danger* inherent in the *völkisch* movement.

The KPD, on the other hand, was thoroughly cynical in both cities, though again in Nuremberg they seem to have moved beyond purely tactical considerations. Lastly it was this response to anti-Semitism by the most radical adversary of National Socialism that indicated how far Jew-baiting was taken for granted in the Weimar Republic. If at first this reflected power-political interests, it soon became so ingrained that Hitler could feel fairly confident of Communist 'complicity' in his effort to isolate the Jews after 1933.[6]

A number of concluding remarks seem appropriate. First, Weimar in many ways resembled the Nazi period more closely than has previously been assumed. At least as far as the 'Jewish question' was concerned, the years 1918–33 saw a change in both the content and style of German anti-Semitism, which was to prove momentous once the Nazis came to power. While some scholars have shown how this shift occurred among publish-ers and the intellectual élite, local studies may prove helpful in further underlining how 'the German notion of *Volk* underwent a postwar inflation no less dramatic and no less portentous than that of the German currency'.[7]

Second, it is at best inaccurate to speak of popular indifference towards the 'Jewish question' after 1933.[8] Lack of interest usually implies neutral-ity, but judging from the above details many Germans were indeed con-cerned with and hardly indifferent to the subject of anti-Semitism before 1933. We must therefore distinguish between those for whom anti-Semitism was a way of life and those for whom the 'Jewish question' took on added significance at certain moments in their lives. Furthermore, *not* acting, that is, not *defending* the Jews was in many ways just as much of a statement on the 'Jewish question' as destroying synagogues or desecrat-ing cemeteries. Here we must mention again how *völkisch beliefs* rather than Nazi *tactics* had influenced a large number of Germans in the Weimar Republic. It is therefore misleading to suggest that abstract anti-Semitism had had no impact on the German public.[9] On the contrary, the image of

---

[6] For KPD 'indifference' to the Jewish fate after 1933 see, for example, D. Peukert, *Die KPD im Widerstand. Verfolgung und Untergrundarbeit an Rhein und Ruhr 1933 bis 1945* (Wuppertal, 1980), 301 and E. Silberner, *Kommunisten zur Judenfrage. Zur Geschichte von Theorie und Praxis des Kommunismus* (Opladen, 1983), 287 ff.

[7] G. D. Stark, *Entrepreneurs of Ideology. Neoconservative Publishers in Germany, 1890–1933* (Chapel Hill, 1981), 186. See also 141, 208–9, where he notes how the publisher Eugen Diederichs changed his mind on the 'Jewish question' after the war by accepting racial differences between Germans and Jews. For the conservative-nationalist élite, see K. Sontheimer, *Antidemokratisches Denken in der Weimarer Republik. Die politischen Ideen des deutschen Nationalismus zwischen 1918 und 1933* (Munich, 1978), 244 ff.; for members of the clerical élite, see J. R. C. Wright, *'Above Parties': The Political Attitudes of the German Protestant Church Leadership 1918–1933* (London, 1979), 54 ff.

[8] See note 1 above.

[9] See William Sheridan Allen's comment in his *The Nazi Seizure of Power. The Experience of a Single German Town 1922–1945* (New York, 1984), 84: 'Many who voted Nazi simply

the conceptual Jew contributed to a hardening of attitudes towards the 'flesh and blood' Jews and to their plight after 1933.

Finally, even if we concede that regional differences existed and that certain areas proved less hospitable to the implementation of anti-Jewish policies after 1933,[10] it does not follow that these differences resulted in any active resistance to anti-Semitism under the Nazis. Because 'locality' became less important in the early twentieth century, and because the 'Jewish question' had in many ways become an 'abstract' issue as a result of the wide circulation of anti-Semitic texts (and later the impact of radio broadcasts), it was not very surprising that Hitler could capitalize on earlier developments in making regional and religious affiliations even less important after 1933. This was especially the case during the war, when social background played a far less important role in deciding young people's positions toward the regime than 'we would expect from patterns of support to [sic] the Nazi party before the "seizure of power"'.[11] In a distressing sense, then, our comparison of Nuremberg and Düsseldorf has left us with the conclusion that differences between German cities and states in the Weimar period were of little if any importance some ten years later, when the Nazi state built on and exploited further the more common images of the Jew:

I found no document, not even a private, handwritten note, in which any German officer or NCO ever expressed the slightest sympathy with Italian behaviour to the Jews. In the entire enormous file of the German armies in the Balkans, I only saw one German document in which the word 'ethical' appears. Italian documents use such vocabulary all the time.[12]

The Jews had long since disappeared from the German moral community.

ignored or rationalized the anti-Semitism of the party, just as they ignored other unpleasant aspects of the Nazi movement.' What they ignored was not anti-Semitism but its violent manifestations.

[10] This is argued in the following works: Mommsen and Willems, *Herrschaftsalltag*, 380; R. Gellately, *The Gestapo and German Society. Enforcing Racial Policy 1933–1945* (Oxford, 1990), 103 ff.; K. Düwell, *Die Rheingebiete in der Judenpolitik des Nationalsozialismus vor 1942. Beitrag zu einer vergleichenden zeitgeschichtlichen Landeskunde* (Bonn, 1968), 79 ff.

[11] O. Bartov, *Hitler's Army. Soldiers, Nazis, and War in the Third Reich* (Oxford and New York, 1991), 110–11.

[12] J. Steinberg, *All or Nothing. The Axis and the Holocaust 1941–43* (London, 1991), 8. For further depressing material, see also W. Manoschek (ed.), *'Es gibt nur eins für das Judentum: Vernichtung'. Das Judenbild in deutschen Soldatenbriefen 1939–1944* (Hamburg, 1995).

APPENDIX I

Reichstag election results in Düsseldorf (percentages)

	KPD	USPD	SPD	DDP (StP)	DVP	DNVP	WB	Centre	NS
19.1.1919[1]	—	24.9	14.4	12	—	9.5	—	38.9	—
6.6.1920	1.3	36.1	7	3.6	11.8	9.5	—	30.2	—
4.5.1924	24	1.7	9	4.5	10.8	16	—	28.2	—
7.12.1924	22.6	0.8	11.9	4.1	10.9	14	—	29.1	—
20.5.1928	23	—	16.6	3.5	10.5	11.4	6.8	23.1	1.6
14.9.1930	25	—	14.7	2.2	7.3	4.7	6.6	21.2	13.6
31.7.1932	25.9	—	12.7	0.2	1.6	5.4	1.1	22.6	29.1
6.11.1932	28.6	—	11.4	0.3	4	7.8	0.6	22.5	23.3

Source: Bodo Brücher et al., *Dokumentation zur Geschichte der Stadt Düsseldorf. Düsseldorf während der Weimarer Republik. 1919–1933. Quellensammlung* (Düsseldorf 1985), p. 194.
[1] National Assembly Elections
Stp *Staatspartei*
WB *Wirtschaftsbund*
NS *Nationalsozialistische Arbeiterpartei Deutschlands*

APPENDIX II

Reichstag election results in Nuremberg (percentages)

	KPD	USPD	SPD	DDP (StP)	DVP	DNVP[1]	WP	BVP	NS
19.1.1919 6.6.1920	—	7.5	51.7	28.7[2]	—	3	—	9.1	—
4.5.1924	13	—	34	3.5	—	7	6	6	26
7.12.1924	7.2	—	41	6.6	1.2	16.1	6.4	7.5	10.6
20.5.1928	6.7	—	42.7	5.2	2.8	11.6	6.3	8.6	10.6
14.9.1930	8.1	—	38.5			2.4		8.3	24
31.7.1932	12.6	—	33.5			2.9		8.4	37.8
6.11.1932	15.2	—	31.1			6.4		8.3	32.8

Source: Eric C. Reiche, *The development of the SA in Nürnberg, 1922–1934* (Cambridge, 1986), pp. 9, 84, 94–5.

[1] In Bavaria *Mittelpartei*
[2] *Deutsche Volkspartei in Bayern* (National Assembly Elections)
StP *Staatspartei*
NS *Nationalsozialistische Arbeiterpartei Deutschlands*

BIBLIOGRAPHY

PRIMARY SOURCES

Düsseldorf

Stadtarchiv (StAD):
  III: 6096, 6319, 7798
  XXI: 11, 14, 18–31, 44–5, 48–9, 51, 94–106, 108, 120–24, 137, 150, 173, 194, 199, 225–26, 228, 230–1, 238–39, 246, 251, 304–09, 311, 313–17, 318b, 320, 339, 393
  XXIII: 8, 87, 1230
  XXIV: 901, 991, 1060, 1094, 1116–17, 1282
  Nachlass Lehr: 7, 13
  Microfilm Nos. 188–89
  Plakatsammlung: 1–2, 4, 8, 10–13, 16–18
  Stenographische Verhandlungsberichte der
  Stadtverordnetenversammlung, 1910–1933 (SVSt)

Nordrheinwestfälisches Hauptstaatsarchiv (HStAD):
  Regierung Düsseldorf: 8884, 8892, 8933, 8993, 9084, 15045, 15450, 15523, 15592, 15606, 15609, 15624, 15654, 15667, 15674, 15813, 15828, 15835, 15854, 15869, 15871, 15959, 15974–75, 15981, 15985, 16012–13, 16047, 16749, 16765, 16778, 16793, 16800, 16804, 16808–09, 16825, 16870, 16893–94, 17054, 17077–78, 17202, 30272, 30658–59a, 30666–68, 41719

Nuremberg

Stadtarchiv (StAN):
  C7/I GR: 101–20, 2806, 2847, 2850, 2884–85, 2915, 2946, 2958–60, 2963, 2968–70, 2978–80, 2982
  C7/V VP: 141, 749, 841, 1183, 1295, 1452, 1820, 2431, 2436, 2631, 2703, 2787, 2996, 3049, 3301, 3331, 3621, 3713, 3992, 4152, 4316, 4429, 4510, 4568, 4592, 4763, 5109, 5142, 5278, 5345, 5382, 5413, 5545, 5677, 5688, 5728, 5750, 5818, 6022, 6040, 6068, 6115, 6121, 6151, 6233, 6270, 6297, 6400a
  C7/IX Stadtratsprotokolle (SRP): 277–530
  E9 NW 33: 1041, 1088, 1351, 1355, 1565–68, 1673, 1680, 1694
  F5 QND: 404a, 405, 494
  Stadtchronik, 1910–1933

Bayerisches Staatsarchiv Nürnberg (BStAN):
Rep. 218/1 IV: 6, 211, 216, 294, 330–39, 433, 443, 516, 524–29, 531–32, 538, 542–43, 549–50, 552, 554, 559–60, 564–67, 571, 574, 579, 581, 587–88, 592, 599, 696, 784, 789–803, 806–08, 812–15, 817–18, 820–23, 830, 838–9, 841, 846, 848, 851, 854–57, 861, 863, 867, 869, 873, 880, 889, 893, 898–9, 917–18, 922, 937–28, 933, 935
Rep. 270 IV: Ic 31, 38–40; II 189, 229, 235, 321, 673–74, 698, 702, 705, 714; XVII 159, 163
Rep. 270 IV Judensachen: 4, 18–19
Rep. 503 Sammlung Streicher: 61–65, 74, 132–35

Stadtbibliothek Nürnberg: Nor. 547 20, 881 20, 2258 20
Protokollbuch der Jüdischen Kultusgemeinde Nürnberg, 1910–1933

Universitätsbibliothek Erlangen: Korrespondenz(blätter) der bayerischen Mittelpartei, 40 Hist. 525; Die Wacht. Wochenschrift für nationale und liberale Politik, 40 Hist. 121 yf

Bayerisches Hauptstaatsarchiv München (BHStA):
Abt. I: MA 73725, 97667–68, 100116, 10043, 100445
       MK 19288–90
       MInn 80439
Abt. IV: MKr. 13346, 13352, 13359
        Kriegsamtstelle Nürnberg Bd. 9/I
Abt. V: FlSlg 58, 65, 992

Staatsbibliothek München: 20 H. Un. App. 28n, 40 Bavar. 3157 v8
NSDAP Hauptarchiv, St. Antony's College, Oxford: Reels 3a, 17a, 24–5, 32a, 53, 58, 64, 67, 76, 80–5, 91, 97–8

Newspapers

Aufwärts
Bayerische Israelitische Gemeindezeitung
Bayerischer Volksfreund
Bergischer Türmer
CV-Zeitung. Blätter für Deutschtum und Judentum
Der Christliche Volksdienst
Düsseldorfer Beobachter
Düsseldorfer Freie Presse
Düsseldorfer Lokal-Zeitung (LZ)
Düsseldorfer Nachrichten (DN)
Düsseldorfer Sonntagsblatt. Kirchlicher Anzeiger der evangelischen Gemeinden zu Düsseldorf (SB)

Düsseldorfer Stadt-Anzeiger
Düsseldorfer Tageblatt (DT)
Düsseldorfer Volkszeitung (VZ)
Düsseldorfer Zeitung (DZ)
Echo
Evangelisches Gemeindeblatt Nürnberg (EvN)
Fränkische Mittelstandzeitung (Süddeutsche Mittelstandszei-tung)
Fränkischer Kurier (FK)
Fränkische Tagespost (FT)
Freiheit
Der Führer
Im deutschen Reich. Zeitschrift des Centralvereins deutscher
Staatsbürger jüdischen Glaubens
Jüdisches Gemeindeblatt und Mitteilungsblatt für die israelitischen Gemeinden
   Düsseldorf und Krefeld
Jüdische Zeitung. Düsseldorfer Jüdisches Wochenblatt
Mittag
Mitteilungen aus dem Verein zur Abwehr des Antisemitismus (Abwehrblätter)
Nordbayerische Volkszeitung (Neue Zeitung)
Nürnberger Anzeiger (NAZ)
Nürnberger Bürgerzeitung
Nürnberger Israelitisches Gemeindeblatt (NIG)
Nürnberger Volkszeitung (Bayerische Volkszeitung) (BV)
Nürnberg-Fürther Morgenpresse (NFM)
Rheinische Tageszeitung
Sozialdemokrat
Die Wacht (am Niederrhein)
Die Wacht. Wochenschrift für nationale und liberale Politik
Westdeutsche Mittelstands-Zeitung

SECONDARY SOURCES

Abraham, David, *The Collapse of the Weimar Republic. Political Economy and Crisis*
   (New York, 1986)
Adler-Rudel, S., *Ostjuden in Deutschland 1880–1940. Zugleich eine Geschichte der
   Organisationen, die sie betreuten* (Tübingen, 1959)
Adorno, Theodor W., *Studien zum autoritären Charakter* (Frankfurt, 1973)
Altmann, Wolfgang, *Die Judenfrage in evangelischen und katholischen Zeitschriften
   zwischen 1918 und 1933* (Munich, 1971)
Anderson, Margaret L., *Windhorst. A Political Biography* (Oxford, 1981)
Andratschke, Gabriele, *Nationalsozialismus und Antisemitismus in der Zen-
   trumspresse Münsters*, Staatsarbeit (Bonn, 1985)

Angress, Werner T., 'Juden im politischen Leben der Revolutionszeit', in: Werner Mosse and Arnold Paucker (eds), *Deutsches Judentum in Krieg und Revolution 1916–1923* (Tübingen, 1971)

—— 'The German Army's "Judenzählung" of 1916. Genesis—Consequences—Significance', in: *LBIY* (1978), 117–37

—— 'The Impact of the "Judenwahlen" of 1912 on the Jewish Question. A Synthesis', in: *LBIY* (1983), 367–410

Aschheim, Steven E., *Brothers and Strangers. The East European Jew in German and German Jewish Consciousness, 1800–1923* (Madison, Wis., 1982)

Ay, Karl-Ludwig, *Die Entstehung einer Revolution. Die Volksstimmung in Bayern während des Ersten Weltkrieges* (Berlin, 1968)

Baier, Helmut, *Die Deutschen Christen Bayerns im Rahmen des bayerischen Kirchenkampfes* (Nuremberg, 1968)

—— 'Die Anfälligkeit des fränkischen Protestantismus gegenüber dem Nationalsozialismus', in: *Der Nationalsozialismus in Franken. Ein Land unter der Last seiner Geschichte*, Tutzinger Studien 2 (1979)

Bartov, Omer, *Hitler's Army. Soldiers, Nazis, and War in the Third Reich* (Oxford and New York, 1991)

Bein, Alex, 'The Jewish Parasite—Notes on the Semantics of the Jewish Problem, with special reference to Germany', in: *LBIY* (1964), 3–40

Bering, Dietz, *Der Name als Stigma. Antisemitismus im deutschen Alltag 1812–1933* (Stuttgart, 1987)

Bessel, Richard, 'Why did the Weimar Republic Collapse?' in: Ian Kershaw (ed.), *Weimar: Why did German Democracy Fail?* (London, 1990), 120–52

Blackbourn, David, 'The *Mittelstand* in German Society and Politics, 1871–1914', in: *Social History*, 4 (1977), 409–33

—— *Class, Religion and Local Politics in Wilhelmine Germany. The Centre Party in Württemberg before 1914* (New Haven and London, 1980)

—— 'Roman Catholics, Anti-Semitism and the Centre Party in Imperial Germany', in: Paul Kennedy and Anthony Nicholls (eds), *Nationalist and Racialist Movements in Britain and Germany before 1914* (London, 1981), 106–29

—— 'The Politics of Demagogy in Imperial Germany', in: *Past and Present*, 113 (1986), 152–84

Blaschke, Olaf, 'Wider die "Herrschaft des modern-jüdischen Geistes": Der Katholizismus zwischen traditionellem Antijudaismus und modernen Antisemitismus', in: Wilfried Loth (ed.), *Deutscher Katholizismus im Umbruch zur Moderne* (Stuttgart, Berlin, Cologne, 1991), 236–65

Boehlich, Walter (ed.), *Der Berliner Antisemitismusstreit* (Frankfurt, 1965)

Brücher, Bodo (ed.), *Dokumentation zur Geschichte der Stadt Düsseldorf. Düsseldorf während der Weimarer Republik 1919–1933. Quellensammlung* (Düsseldorf, 1985)

Carlebach, Julius, *Karl Marx and the Radical Critique of Judaism* (London, 1978)

Chickering, Roger, *We Men Who Feel Most German. A Cultural Study of the Pan-German League 1886–1914* (London, 1984)

Childers, Thomas, 'Inflation, Stabilization, and Political Realignment in Germany 1919–1928,' in: Gerhard Feldmann et al., *Die Deutsche Inflation. Eine Zwischenbilanz* (Berlin and New York, 1982), 409–31

—— *The Nazi Voter. The Social Foundations of Fascism in Germany, 1919–1933* (Chapel Hill, NC, 1983)

—— 'Languages of Liberalism. Liberal Political Discourse in the Weimar Republic', in: Konrad Jarausch and Larry E. Jones (eds), *In Search of a Liberal Germany. Studies in the History of German Liberalism from 1789 to the Present* (Oxford, 1990), 323–59

—— 'The Social Language of Politics in Germany: The Sociology of Political Discourse in the Weimar Republic', in: *American Historical Review*, April (1990), 331–58

Dilthey, Wilhelm, *Selected Writings*. Volume 1. *Introduction to the Human Sciences* (Princeton, 1989)

Dittrich, Christina, *Pressegeschichtliche Aspekte zum Aufstieg der NSDAP in Franken, aufgezeigt am Beispiel Nürnberger Zeitungen*, unpublished Ph.D. thesis (Erlangen-Nuremberg, 1983)

Düwell, Kurt, *Die Rheingebiete in der Judenpolitik des Nationalsozialismus vor 1942. Beitrag zu einer vergleichenden zeitgeschichtlichen Landeskunde* (Bonn, 1968)

Eksteins, Modris, *The Limits of Reason. The German Democratic Press and the Collapse of Weimar Democracy* (London, 1975)

Ehlers, Carol Jean, *Nuremberg, Julius Streicher and the Bourgeois Transition to Nazism, 1918–1924*, unpublished Ph.D. thesis (Colorado, 1975)

Eissenhauer, Michael, 'Die Nürnberger Synagoge von 1874. Zwischen Emanzipation und Assimilation', in: Manfred Treml and Josef Kirmeier, *Geschichte und Kultur der Juden in Bayern. Aufsätze* (Munich, 1988)

Eley, Geoff, *Reshaping the German Right. Radical Nationalism and Political Change after Bismarck* (London, 1980)

Elias, Norbert, *Studien über die Deutschen. Machtkämpfe und Habitusentwicklung im 19. und 20. Jahrhundert* (Frankfurt, 1989)

Epstein, Klaus, *Matthias Erzberger and the Dilemma of German Democracy* (Princeton, 1959)

Eschelbacher, Max, *Festschrift zur Feier des 25 jährigen Bestehens der Synagoge* (Düsseldorf, 1929)

Evans, Richard, *Kneipengespräche im Kaiserreich. Stimmungsberichte der Hamburger Politischen Polizei 1892–1914* (Hamburg, 1989)

Eyck, Erich, *A History of the Weimar Republic*. Volume I. *From the Collapse of the Empire to Hindenburg's Election* (Cambridge, Mass., 1962)

—— *A History of the Weimar Republic*. Volume II. *From the Locarno Conference to Hitler's Seizure of Power* (Cambridge, Mass., 1963)

Feldmann, Gerald D., *Army, Industry, and Labor in Germany. 1914–1918* (Oxford, 1992)

—— *The Great Disorder: Politics, Economics, and Society in the German Inflation, 1914–1924* (New York and Oxford, 1993)

Fenske, Hans, *Konservatismus und Rechtsradikalismus in Bayern nach 1918* (Bad Homburg, 1969)

Fischer, Conan, *The German Communists and the Rise of Nazism* (London, 1991)

Flechtheim, Ossip K., *Die KPD in der Weimarer Republik* (Frankfurt, 1969)

Först, Walter, *Robert Lehr als Oberbürgermeister. Ein Kapitel deutscher Kommunalpolitik* (Düsseldorf, 1962)

Franke, Volker, *Der Aufstieg der NSDAP in Düsseldorf. Die nationalsozialistische Basis in einer katholischen Großstadt* (Essen, 1987)

Franze, Manfred, *Die Erlanger Studentenschaft 1918–1945* (Würzburg, 1972)

Freudenthal, Max, *Die israelitische Kultusgemeinde Nürnberg 1874–1924* (Nuremberg, 1925)

Fritzsche, Peter, *Rehearsals for Fascism. Populism and Political Mobilization in Weimar Germany* (Oxford, 1990)

Frye, Bruce, 'The German Democratic Party and the "Jewish Problem" in the Weimar Republic', in: *LBIY* (1976), 143–72.

Fussell, Paul, *The Great War and Modern Memory* (London, 1975)

Gay, Peter, *Freud For Historians* (Oxford and New York, 1985)

Gellately, Robert, *The Politics of Economic Despair: Shopkeepers and German Politics 1890–1914* (London, 1974)

—— *The Gestapo and German Society. Enforcing Racial Policy 1933–1945* (Oxford, 1990)

Gemein, Giesbert Jörg, *Die DNVP in Düsseldorf 1918–1933*, unpublished Ph.D. thesis (Cologne, 1969)

Gessler, Otto, *Reichswehrpolitik in der Weimarer Republik* (Stuttgart, 1958)

Gömmel, Rainer, *Wachstum und Konjunktur der Nürnberger Wirtschaft (1815–1914)* (Nuremberg, 1978)

Gordon, Sarah Ann, *German Opposition to Nazi Anti-Semitic Measures Between 1933 and 1945, With Particular Reference to the Rhine-Ruhr Area*, unpublished Ph.D. thesis (SUNY, Buffalo, 1979)

Greiffenhagen, Martin, *Das Dilemma des Konservatismus in Deutschland* (Frankfurt, 1986)

Greive, Hermann, *Theologie und Ideologie. Katholizismus und Judentum in Deutschland und Österreich 1918–1935* (Heidelberg, 1969)

—— *Geschichte des modernen Antisemitismus in Deutschland* (Darmstadt, 1983)

Groß, Armin, *Glück und Elend des 'Fränkischen Kuriers'* (Nuremberg, 1967)

Haase, Armin, *Katholische Presse und die Judenfrage* (Munich, 1975)

Hambrecht, Rainer, *Der Aufstieg der NSDAP in Mittel- und Oberfranken (1925–1933)* (Nuremberg, 1976)

Hamel, Iris, *Völkischer Verband und nationale Gewerkschaft: Der Deutschnationale Handlungsgehilfen-Verband* (Frankfurt, 1967)

Hannot, Walter, *Die Judenfrage in der Katholischen Tagespresse Deutschlands und Österreichs 1923–1933* (Mainz, 1990)

Hanschel, Hermann, *Oberbürgermeister Hermann Luppe. Nürnberger Kommunalpolitik in der Weimarer Republik* (Nuremberg, 1977)

Harris, James F., 'Public Opinion and the Proposed Emancipation of the Jews in Bavaria in 1849–1850', in: *LBIY* (1989), 67–79

Hartenstein, Wolfgang, *Die Anfänge der Deutschen Volkspartei 1918–1920* (Düsseldorf, 1962)

Hennecke, Klaus-Peter, *Die Vereinigung der Mittelparteien und die Liberale Vereinigung in Düsseldorf 1900–1919*, Hausarbeit (Düsseldorf, 1987)

Henning, Friedrich-Wilhelm, *Düsseldorf und seine Wirtschaft. Zur Geschichte einer Region*. Band 2: *Von 1860 bis zur Gegenwart* (Düsseldorf, 1981)

Hertzmann, Lewis, *DNVP. Right-Wing Opposition in the Weimar Republic, 1918–1933* (Lincoln, Nebr., 1963)

Herzig, Arno, 'The Role of Antisemitism in the Early Years of the German Workers' Movement', in: *LBIY* (1981)

Hirschmann, Gerhard, 'Die evangelische Kirche seit 1800', in: Max Spindler (ed.), *Handbuch der Bayerischen Geschichte*. Vierter Band. *Das Neue Bayern 1800–1970* (Munich, 1975), 883–913

Hobsbawm, Eric J., *Nations and nationalism since 1870. Programme, Myth, Reality* (Cambridge, 1990)

Hofmann, Hanns H., 'Ländliches Judentum in Franken', in: *Tribüne—Zeitschrift zum Verständnis des Judentums*, 7 (1968)

Hsia, R. Po-chia, *The Myth of Ritual Murder. Jews and Magic in Reformation Germany* (New Haven, 1988)

Hübner, Thomas, *Nürnberg im Kommunikationszentrum der Zeit des Nationalsozialismus unter besonderer Berücksichtigung der Tagespresse*, Diplomarbeit (Nuremberg, 1991)

Hüttenberger, Peter, *Düsseldorf. Geschichte von den Ursprüngen bis ins 20. Jahrhundert*. Band 3: *Die Industrie- und Verwaltungsstadt (20. Jahrhundert)* (Düsseldorf, 1989)

Jochmann, Werner, *Gesellschaftskrise und Judenfeindschaft in Deutschland 1870–1945* (Hamburg, 1988)

Jones, Larry Eugene, 'The Crisis of White Collar Interest Politics: Deutschnationaler Handlungsgehilfen-Verband und Deutsche Volkspartei in the World Economic Crisis', in: Hans Mommsen et al., *Industrielles Sytem und Politische Entwicklung in der Weimarer Republik* (Düsseldorf, 1974), 811–23

—— *German Liberalism and the Dissolution of the Weimar Party System, 1918–1933* (Chapel Hill, NC, 1988)

Kampe, Norbert, *Studenten und 'Judenfrage' im Deutschen Reich. Die Entstehung einer akademischen Trägerschicht des Antisemitismus* (Göttingen, 1988)

Katz, Jacob, *Vom Vorurteil bis zur Vernichtung. Der Antisemitismus 1700–1933* (Munich, 1989)

Kershaw, Ian, 'The Persecution of the Jews and German Popular Opinion in the Third Reich', in: *LBIY* (1981)

—— *Popular Opinion and Political Dissent in the Third Reich. Bavaria 1933–1945* (New York, 1983)

Klemperer, Victor, *LTI. Die Sprache des Dritten Reiches. Notizbuch eines Philologen* (Leipzig, 1991)

Knütter, Hans-Helmut, *Die Juden und die deutsche Linke in der Weimarer Republik 1918–1933* (Düsseldorf, 1971)

Kocka, Jürgen, *Klassengesellschaft im Krieg. Deutsche Sozialgeschichte 1914–1918* (Frankfurt, 1988)

Kolakowski, Leszek, *Modernity on Endless Trial* (Chicago, 1990)

Köllmann, Wolfgang, *Bevölkerung in der industriellen Revolution. Studien zur Bevölkerungsgeschichte Deutschlands* (Göttingen, 1974)

Koshar, Rudy, *Social Life, Local Politics, and Nazism. Marburg, 1880–1935* (Chapel Hill, NC, 1986)

Koszyk, Kurt, *Deutsche Presse 1914–1945. Geschichte der deutschen Presse.* Teil III (Berlin, 1972)

—— *Gustav Stresemann. Der kaisertreue Demokrat. Eine Biographie* (Cologne, 1989)

Kraus, Hans-Joachim, 'Die Evangelische Kirche', in: Werner Mosse and Arnold Paucker (eds), *Entscheidungsjahr 1932. Zur Judenfrage in der Endphase der Weimarer Republik. Ein Sammelband* (Tübingen, 1965), 249–69

Krohn, Helga, *Die Juden in Hamburg. Die Politische, Soziale und Kulturelle Entwicklung einer Grossstadtgemeinde nach der Emanzipation 1848–1918* (Hamburg, 1974)

Kussmann, Andreas, *Das kommunale Parteiensystem in Düsseldorf beim Übergang vom Kaiserreich zur Republik. Ein Beitrag zum Kontinuitätsproblem*, unpublished MA thesis (Berlin, 1982)

Lamberti, Marjorie, 'Liberals, Socialists and the Defence against Antisemitism in the Wilhelminian Period', in: *LBIY* (1980), 147–62

Lamm, Hans, *Von Juden in München. Ein Gedenkbuch* (Munich, 1958)

Langewiesche, Dieter, *Liberalismus in Deutschland* (Frankfurt, 1988)

Lenman, Robin, *Julius Streicher and the Origins of National Socialism in Nuremberg 1918–1923*, unpublished B.Phil. thesis (Oxford, 1968)

Leuschen-Seppel, Rosemarie, *Sozialdemokratie und Antisemitismus im Kaiserreich* (Bonn, 1978)

Levy, Richard, *The Downfall of the Anti-Semitic Parties in Imperial Germany* (New Haven and London, 1975)

Lichtblau, Albert, *Antisemitismus und soziale Spannung in Berlin und Wien 1867–1914* (Berlin, 1994)

Liebe, Werner, *Die Deutschnationale Volkspartei 1918–1924* (Düsseldorf, 1956)

Lindemann, Albert S., *The Jew Accused. Three Anti-Semitic Affairs (Dreyfus, Beilis, Frank 1894–1914)* (Cambridge, 1991)

Lispki, Stephan, *Der Arbeiter- und Soldatenrat in Düsseldorf (Zwischen den Novemberereignissen und dem Zweiten Rätekongreß, November 1918 bis April 1919). Vom politischen Organ zur wirtschaftlichen Interessenvertretung*, unpublished Ph.D. thesis (Düsseldorf, 1978)

—— *Dokumentation zur Geschichte der Stadt Düsseldorf. Düsseldorf während der*

Revolution 1918–1919 (November 1918 bis März 1919). Quellensammlung (Düsseldorf, no date)

Lohalm, Uwe, *Völkischer Radikalismus. Die Geschichte des Deutschvölkischen Schutz- und Trutz-Bundes 1919–1923* (Hamburg, 1970)

Luppe, Hermann, *Mein Leben* (Nuremberg, 1977)

McCullagh, C. Behan, *Justifying Historical Descriptions* (Cambridge, 1984)

Mayer, Paul, *Bruno Schoenlank 1859–1901. Reformer der sozialistischen Tagespresse* (Hanover, 1971)

Massing, Paul W., *Vorgeschichte des politischen Antisemitismus* (Frankfurt, 1986)

Matull, Wilhelm, *Der Freiheit eine Gasse. Geschichte der Düsseldorfer Arbeiterbewegung* (Bonn, 1980)

Maurer, Trude, *Ostjuden in Deutschland 1918–1933* (Hamburg, 1986)

Mazura, Uwe, *Zentrumspartei und Judenfrage 1870/71–1933. Verfassungsstaat und Minderheitenschutz* (Mainz, 1994)

Mehringer, Hartmut, 'Die KPD in Bayern 1919–1945. Vorgeschichte, Verfolgung und Widerstand', in: Martin Broszat and Hartmut Mehringer (eds), *Bayern in der NS-Zeit. Die Parteien KPD, SPD, BVP in Verfolgung und Widerstand* (Munich, 1983), 1–286

Meier, Kurt, *Der Evangelische Kirchenkampf.* Band 1. *Der Kampf um die 'Reichskirche'* (Göttingen, 1976)

Mielke, Siegfried, *Der Hansa-Bund für Gewerbe, Handel und Industrie 1909–1914 Der gescheiterte Versuch einer antifeudalen Sammlungspolitik* (Göttingen, 1976)

Mitchell, Allan, *Revolution in Bavaria 1918–1919. The Eisner Regime and the Soviet Republic* (Princeton, 1965)

Moeller, Robert, *German Peasants and Agrarian Politics, 1914–1924. The Rhineland and Westphalia* (Chapel Hill, NC, 1986)

Mommsen, Wolfgang, *Der autoritäre Nationalstaat. Verfassung, Gesellschaft und Kultur im deutschen Kaiserreich* (Frankfurt, 1990)

Moore-Ziegler, Martha, *The Socio-Economic and Demographic Bases of Political Behavior in Nuremberg during the Weimar Republic, 1919–1933*, unpublished Ph.D. thesis (Virginia, 1976)

Morsey, Rudolf, *Die Deutsche Zentrumspartei 1917–1923* (Düsseldorf, 1966)

Mosse, George L., 'German Socialists and the Jewish Question in the Weimar Republic', in: *LBIY* (1971), 123–51

—— *Germans and Jews. The Right, the Left and the Search for a 'Third Force' in Pre-Nazi Germany* (Detroit, 1983)

—— *Fallen Soldiers. Reshaping the Memory of the World Wars* (Oxford, 1990)

Mosse, Werner, *The German-Jewish Economic Elite 1820–1935. A Socio-cultural Profile* (Oxford, 1989)

Müller, Arnd, *Geschichte der Juden in Nürnberg 1146–1945* (Nuremberg, 1968)

Müller, Petrus, *Liberalismus in Nürnberg 1800 bis 1871: Eine Fallstudie zur Ideen- und Sozialgeschichte des Liberalismus in Deutschland im 19. Jahrhundert* (Nuremberg, 1990)

Neuhäußer-Wespy, Ulrich, *Die KPD in Nordbayern 1919–1933* (Nuremberg, 1981)

Nicholls, Anthony, 'Hitler and the Bavarian Background to National Socialism', in: Erich Matthias and Anthony Nicholls (eds), *German Democracy and the Triumph of Hitler. Essays in Recent German History* (London, 1971), 99–128

Niewyk, Donald L., *Socialist, Anti-Semite, and Jew: German Social Democracy Confronts the Problem of Anti-Semitism, 1918–1933* (Baton Rouge, La., 1971)

—— *The Jews in Weimar Germany* (Manchester, 1980)

—— 'Das Selbstverständnis der Juden und ihre Beteiligung am politischen Leben des Kaiserreichs und der Weimarer Republik', in: Manfred Treml and Josef Kirmeier, *Juden in Bayern* (Munich, 1988)

Nipperdey, Thomas, *Deutsche Geschichte 1800–1866. Bürgerwelt und starker Staat* (Munich, 1983)

Nitzl, Gerhard, *Modernisierung in den liberalen Parteien des deutschen Kaiserreichs, 1871–1914. Eine Untersuchung am Beispiel der Stadt Nürnberg, unter besonderer Berücksichtigung der Fortschrittspartei*, Magisterarbeit (Erlangen-Nuremberg, 1988)

Nolan, Mary, *Social Democracy and society. Working-class radicalism in Düsseldorf, 1890–1920* (Cambridge, 1981)

Ophir, Baruch Z., and Wiesemann, Falk, *Die Jüdischen Gemeinden in Bayern 1918–1945. Geschichte und Zerstörung* (Munich, 1979)

Opitz, Günther, *Der Christlich-soziale Volksdienst. Versuch einer protestantischen Partei in der Weimarer Republik* (Düsseldorf, 1969)

Paret, Peter, *The Berlin Secession. Modernism and its Enemies in Imperial Germany* (Cambridge, Mass., 1980)

Paucker, Arnold, *Der jüdische Abwehrkampf gegen Antisemitismus und Nationalsozialismus in den letzten Jahren der Weimarer Republik* (Hamburg, 1969)

Paul, Gerhard, *Aufstand der Bilder. Die NS-Propaganda vor 1933* (Bonn, 1990)

Peukert, Detlev, *Die KPD im Widerstand. Verfolgung und Untergrundarbeit an Rhein und Ruhr 1933 bis 1945* (Wuppertal, 1980)

Pfeiffer, Gerhard (ed.), *Nürnberg. Geschichte einer europäischen Stadt* (Munich, 1971)

Preiß, Heinz, *Die Anfänge der Völkischen Bewegung in Franken* (Nuremberg, 1937)

Pridham, Geoffrey, *Hitler's Rise to Power. The Nazi Movement in Bavaria, 1923–1933* (London, 1973)

Puhle, Hans Jürgen, *Agrarische Interessenpolitik und Preussischer Konservatismus im Wilhelminischen Reich. Ein Beitrag zur Analyse des Nationalismus in Deutschland am Beispiel des Bundes der Landwirte und der Deutsch-Konservativen Partei* (Hanover, 1966)

Pulzer, Peter, *The Rise of Political Anti-Semitism in Germany and Austria* (London, 1988)

—— *Jews and the German State. The Political History of a Minority, 1848–1933* (Oxford, 1992)

Reiche, Eric C., *The Development of the SA in Nürnberg, 1922–1934* (Cambridge, 1986)

Retallak, James, *Notables of the Right. The Conservative Party and Political Mobilization in Germany, 1876–1918* (London, 1988)

Richarz, Monika, 'Emancipation and Continuity. German Jews in the Rural Economy', in: Werner Mosse et al., *Revolution and Evolution. 1848 in German-Jewish History* (Tübingen, 1981), 95–115

Ritter, Gerhard, and Tenfelde, Klaus, *Arbeiter im Deutschen Kaiserreich 1871 bis 1914* (Bonn, 1992)

Rohrbacher, Stefan, 'Ritualmord-Beschuldigungen am Niederrhein. Christlicher Aberglaube und antijüdische Agitation im 19. Jahrhundert', in: *Menora. Jahrbuch für deutsch-jüdische Geschichte* (1990)

Rohrbacher, Stefan, and Schmidt, Michael, *Judenbilder. Kulturgeschichte antijüdischer Mythen und antisemitischer Vorurteile* (Hamburg, 1991)

Romeyk, Horst, 'Die Deutsche Volkspartei in Rheinland und Westfalen 1918–1933', in: *Rheinische Vierteljahresblätter* (1975)

Rorty, Richard, *Contingency, Irony, and Solidarity* (Cambridge, 1989)

Rossmeissl, Dieter, *Arbeiterschaft und Sozialdemokratie in Nürnberg 1890–1914* (Nuremberg, 1977)

Rückel, Gert, *Die Fränkische Tagespost. Geschichte einer Parteizeitung* (Nuremberg, 1964)

Rürup, Reinhard, 'Emanzipation und Krise—Zur Geschichte der "Judenfrage" in Deutschland vor 1890', in: Werner Mosse and Arnold Paucker, *Juden im Wilhelminischen Deutschland 1890–1914* (Tübingen, 1976), 1–56

Schade, Franz, *Kurt Eisner und die bayerische Sozialdemokratie* (Hanover, 1961)

Schmidt, Jürgen, *Martin Niemöller im Kirchenkampf* (Hamburg, 1971)

Scholder, Klaus, *Die Kirchen und das Dritte Reich.* Band 1. *Vorgeschichte und Zeit der Illusionen 1918–1934* (Frankfurt, Berlin, Vienna, 1977)

—— 'Nürnberg und das 20. Jahrhundert', in: *Der Nationalsozialismus in Franken. Ein Landen unter der Last seiner Geschichte*, Tutzinger Studien 2 (1979)

Schönhoven, Klaus, *Die Bayerische Volkspartei 1924–1932* (Düsseldorf, 1972)

Schultheiß, Werner, *Kleine Geschichte Nürnbergs* (Nuremberg, 1966)

Schumacher, Martin, *Mittelstandsfront und Republik. Die Wirtschaftspartei—Reichspartei des deutschen Mittelstandes 1919–1933* (Düsseldorf, 1972)

Schwarz, Klaus-Dieter, *Weltkrieg und Revolution in Nürnberg. Ein Beitrag zur Geschichte der deutschen Arbeiterbewegung* (Stuttgart, 1971)

Schwarz, Stefan, *Die Juden in Bayern im Wandel der Zeiten* (Munich and Vienna, 1963)

Showalter, Dennis, *Little man, what now? Der Stürmer in the Weimar Republic* (Hamden, 1982)

Siegle-Wenschkewitz, Leonore, *Nationalsozialismus und Kirchen. Religionspolitik von Partei und Staat bis 1935* (Düsseldorf, 1974)

Silbergleit, Heinrich, *Die Bevölkerungs- und Berufsverhältnisse der Juden im Deutschen Reich. I Freistaat Preussen* (Berlin, 1930)

Silberner, Edmund, *Sozialisten zur Judenfrage* (Berlin, 1962)

—— *Kommunisten zur Judenfrage. Zur Geschichte von Theorie und Praxis des Kommunismus* (Opladen, 1983)

Sontheimer, Kurt, *Antidemokratisches Denken in der Weimarer Republik* (Munich, 1978)

Stark, Gary D., *Entrepreneurs of Ideology. Neoconservative Publishers in Germany, 1890–1933* (Chapel Hill, NC, 1981)

Stegmann, Dirk, *Die Erben Bismarcks. Parteien und Verbände in der Spätphase des Wilhelminischen Deutschlands. Sammlungspolitik 1897–1918* (Cologne and Berlin, 1970)

—— 'Vom Neokonservatismus zum Proto-Faschismus: Konservative Partei, Vereine und Verbände 1893–1920', in: Dirk Stegmann et al., *Deutscher Konservatismus im 19. und 20. Jahrhundert* (Bonn, 1983), 199–230

Sterling, Eleonore, *Judenhaß. Die Anfänge des politischen Antisemitismus in Deutschland (1815–1850)* (Frankfurt, 1969)

Stump, Wolfgang, *Geschichte und Organisation der Zentrumspartei in Düsseldorf, 1917–1933* (Düsseldorf, 1971)

Suchy, Barbara, 'The Verein zur Abwehr des Antisemitismus (I). From its Beginning to the First World War', in: *LBIY* (1983), 205–39

—— 'Antisemitismus in den Jahren vor dem Ersten Weltkrieg', in: Jutta Bohnke Kollwitz et al., *Köln und das rheinische Judentum. Festschrift Germania Judaica 1959–1984* (Cologne, 1984)

Tal, Uriel, *Christians and Jews in Germany. Religion, Politics, and Ideology in the Second Reich, 1870–1914* (Ithaca, 1975)

Thieme, Karl, 'Deutsche Katholiken', in: Werner E. Mosse and Arnold Paucker, *Entscheidungsjahr* (1965), 271–87

Tiedemann, Eva-Maria, 'Erscheinungsformen des Antisemitismus in Bayern am Beispiel der Bayerischen Antisemitischen Volkspartei und ihrer Nachfolgeorganisationen', in: Manfred Treml and Josef Kirmeier, *Juden in Bayern* (Munich, 1988)

Tully, James (ed.), *Meaning and Context. Quentin Skinner and his Critics* (Cambridge and Oxford, 1988)

Varga, William, *Julius Streicher: A Political Biography, 1885–1933*, unpublished Ph.D. thesis (Ohio State University, 1974)

Verein für Socialpolitik, *Der Wucher auf dem Lande. Berichte und Gutachten* (Leipzig, 1887)

Voigt, Angelika, *Nationalsozialistische Judenverfolgung in Düsseldorf 1930–1942*, Hausarbeit (Düsseldorf, 1981)

Volkov, Schulamit, 'Kontinuität und Diskontinuität im deutschen Antisemitismus', in: *VfZ* 2 (1985), 221–43

Wassermann, Henry, 'The Fliegende Blätter as a Source for the Social History of German Jewry', in: *LBIY* (1983), 93–138

—— 'Jews in Judendstil. The Simplicissimus, 1896–1914', in: *LBIY* (1986), 71–104

—— 'Jews and Judaism in the Gartenlaube', in: *LBIY* (1978), 47–60

Weidenhaupt, Hugo (ed.), *Düsseldorf. Geschichte von den Ursprüngen bis ins 20. Jahrhundert.* Band 2: *Von der Residenzstadt zur Beamtenstadt (1614–1900)* (Düsseldorf, 1988)

Wertheimer, Jack, *Unwelcome Strangers. East European Jews in Imperial Germany* (Oxford, 1987)

White, Dan S., *The Splintered Party. National Liberalism in Hessen and the Reich 1867–1918* (Cambridge, Mass., and London, 1976)

Winkler, Heinrich August, *Von der Revolution zur Stabilisierung. Arbeiter und Arbeiterbewegung in der Weimarer Republik 1918 bis 1924* (Bonn and Berlin, 1984)

Wiener, P.B., 'Die Parteien der Mitte', in: Werner Mosse and Arnold Paucker, *Entscheidungsjahr* (Tübingen, 1965), 289–321

Wiesemann, Falk, 'Kurt Eisner. Studie zu seiner politischen Biographie', in: Karl Bosl (ed.), *Bayern im Umbruch. Die Revolution von 1918. Ihre Vorraussetzungen, ihr Verlauf und ihre Folgen* (Munich, 1969), 387–426

—— *Die Vorgeschichte der nationalsozialistischen Machtübernahme in Bayern 1932/ 1933* (Berlin, 1975)

Winch, Peter, *The Idea of a Social Science and its Relation to Philosophy* (London, 1990)

Wistrich, Robert S., *Socialism and the Jews. The Dilemmas of Assimilation in Germany and Austria-Hungary* (East Brunswick and London, 1982)

Wright, J.R.C., *'Above Parties': The Political Attitudes of the German Protestant Church Leadership 1918–1933* (London, 1974)

Zechlin, Egmont, *Die deutsche Politik und die Juden im Ersten Weltkrieg* (Göttingen, 1969)

Zitelmann, Rainer, *Hitler. Selbstverständnis eines Revolutionärs* (Darmstadt, 1989)

INDEX